1001
TO IMPROVE YO
AND S

Thousands have come to depend on Herbert Prochnow's "Public Speaker's Treasure Chest" as a key to speech eloquence. What the "Treasure Chest" has done to improve platform performance, this sequel will do for anyone who aspires to become a versatile conversationalist as well as a competent speaker.

Here are all the tools and techniques that offer unlimited possibilities for study and self-improvement. Here in one volume are thousands of apt phrases, 'bon mots', figures of speech and quotations that transform commonplace talk into lively, forceful conversation.

At the outset the author provides clear and helpful instructions on how to develop your day-to-day speaking ability. He describes systematic methods of building a vocabulary, points out common errors and pitfalls, and illustrates numerous ways of adding vitality to what you want to say.

In the pages that follow the reader will find a rich abundance of the raw materials that make the fabric of interesting and witty conversation: choice selections from the great thinkers and writers of history; jests and humorous anecdotes for every occasion; inspirational stories that will provide new ideas and fresh points of view; plus a detailed list of suggestions for a lifetime of reading for self-development.

1001 WAYS TO IMPROVE YOUR CONVERSATION & SPEECHES

HERBERT V. PROCHNOW

JAICO PUBLISHING HOUSE
Mumbai • Delhi • Bangalore
Kolkata • Hyderabad • Chennai

© 1952, by Harper & Brothers

No part of this book may be reproduced or utilized in any form or by any means, electronic or mechanical including photocopying, recording or by any information storage and retrieval system, without permission in writing from the publishers.

Complete & Unabridged
Published in India by arrangement with
Harper & Row, Publisher
49 East, 33rd Street,
New York 16. N.Y.

1001 WAYS TO IMPROVE YOUR CONVERSATION
AND SPEECHES
ISBN 81-7224-330-8

First Jaico Impression : 1987
Twelfth Jaico Impression : 1997
Thirteenth Jaico Impression : 1999
Fourteenth Jaico Impression : 2001

Published by :
Ashwin J. Shah
Jaico Publishing House
121, Mahatma Gandhi Road
Mumbai – 400 023.

Printed by:
Pramod Bhogate
Snehesh Printers
320-A, Shah & Nahar Ind. Est. – A-1,
Lower Parel, Mumbai – 400 013.

CONTENTS

	Preface	vii
I	What It Means to You to Speak Well	1
II	The Essentials of Good Conversation	8
III	Ways to Gain Effective Conversation and Speech	26
IV	From Effective Conversation to Effective Speeches	37
V	One Hundred Common Errors in English	45
VI	Building Your Vocabulary	59
VII	Figures of Speech and Other Speech Tools	76
VIII	Two Hundred Similes	87
IX	Two Hundred and Fifty Hackneyed Expressions	96
X	Four Hundred Epigrams	100
XI	Two Hundred Humorous Stories	122
XII	Sixteen Hundred Quotations from Literature	161
XIII	Six Hundred Biblical Quotations	276
XIV	Facts, Fiction, and Fables	314
XV	Improving Conversation and Speeches by Reading	348

PREFACE

This book aims to give practical help to those who wish to talk effectively and to present their ideas clearly and forcefully in public speeches.

Conversation plays a major role in indicating the extent of our mental alertness, our intellectual capacity, and our understanding of problems. Hundreds of words without an idea; frequent exaggerated comments; ideas expressed without organization, coherence, or logic; repeated interruptions of others; wholly irrelevant questions; lengthy remarks on details without a recognition of major points—how much such conversation reveals. How important, then, it becomes that we perfect this tool of conversation to our greatest possible advantage and good. To talk better is to speak better in public, and to write better. These are assets of inestimable value.

Many of the same principles that result in effective discussion in small audiences will enable one to address large audiences with far more assurance. These principles are discussed at length in this book. In addition, there are included a number of chapters with several thousand helpful items that will give practical assistance to the person who wishes to converse well and to deliver a good speech. These items include hundreds of epigrams, witticisms, and humorous stories, over two thousand quotations, lists of scores of great books to read to broaden one's knowledge, a hundred common English errors to avoid, numerous hackneyed phrases it is best to eliminate from one's conversation, systematic ways to build a vocabulary, and discussions with illustrations of many types of speech tools, such as similes, metaphors, alliteration, and hyperboles. Here is material that constitutes a source book for repeated use over many years. The book is planned to be so comprehensive that it will offer even the accomplished conversationalist and public speaker almost unlimited possibilities for study and self improvement.

The determination to become an effective conversationalist and speaker almost inevitably leads to a serious study of various ways of personal improvement. When one fully realizes the significant fact that his speech reflects his mind, he will seek constructive ways to develop his mind and the art of conversation through which he expresses his thoughts.

A few minutes each day devoted to a systematic and thoughtful effort to improve one's conversation and speeches should be richly rewarding in one's profession or business, and in social relationships. Such study may be instructive, interesting, and even entertaining.

HERBERT V. PROCHNOW

Evanston, Illinois
September 1, 1951

Chapter 1

WHAT IT MEANS TO YOU TO SPEAK WELL

GEORGE BERNARD SHAW once said, "I often quote myself; it adds spice to my conversation." Most of us are not quite so certain as Shaw about our ability to enliven conversation. We have more in common with the remark of Frank McKinney (Kin) Hubbard, American humorist and creator of "Abe Martin," when he commented, "Don't knock the weather; nine-tenths of the people couldn't start a conversation if it didn't change once in a while."

The ability to talk effectively and speak well in public is an asset of immeasurable value, whether one uses this ability to converse across a table to one person or to address an audience of five hundred people. We ordinarily think of conversation simply as talking with one person or at most a small group. But public speaking is similar except that audiences may be composed of ten or ten thousand persons. If one learns to talk clearly and intelligently in small groups, bringing all his talents into play, he should also be able to speak well in public.

Emerson has rightly said, "Conversation is an art in which a man has all mankind for his competitors." Such competition is difficult. Anyone who does not strive for the ability to talk with the greatest possible effectiveness he can command is not using his latent ability to best advantage. He may have ideas in his business or profession, but he is not presenting them convincingly. He may have interesting experiences, but he is not conveying them to his friends at social events in an entertaining manner. Whether a person is applying for a job, selling goods or services to his prospects, playing golf with a friend, or having luncheon with his associates, he engages in conversation. Hundreds of words, yes, thousands, are spoken every day by each of us—words that help or hinder us, make friends or enemies, lead us to failure or success. How important it is, then, that we do everything possible to use conversation to our greatest advantage.

INSPIRES CONFIDENCE

Let us now examine specifically what it means for you to speak well. In the first place, if you know that you can express your ideas clearly and effectively, you will inspire confidence in your listener and in yourself. Others are going to say when you talk that you make sense. Your ideas are logical. Your comments are clear. When you know that you talk in this manner, you acquire a confidence that gives you inner strength and outward composure in serious conversations that may have an important bearing on your entire life. You will handle yourself well in any such discussion. You will not leave meetings of importance saying, "I wish I had the confidence and assurance to express my ideas." You will have it. Milton declared that "Confidence imparts a wondrous inspiration to its possessor."

BUILDS RESPECT IN BUSINESS AND SOCIAL LIFE

The ability to speak well will build respect for you in business and in your social life. No person speaks well who has a disorganized mind. Mental laziness and confused thinking are not the parents of clear, concise and intelligent conversation. Two thousand years ago Publilius Syrus wisely commented that "Conversation is the image of the mind. As the man is, so is his talk." Intelligent conversation makes others respect the speaker. It makes others listen to his views and often change their opinions so that the speaker's views prevail. They listen attentively because he has something to say and he says it well

When you determine to develop your ability to talk well, you will also simultaneously do everything possible to improve your mind by reading and study. Good conversation flows from good minds. An English novelist, Anthony Hope, once asserted, "Your ignorance cramps my conversation." However, one's ignorance is no less a factor in cramping his own conversation than it is that of others. The incentive to speak effectively will be an important factor in persuading you to improve yourself in various ways.

In business, one is greatly handicapped who possesses good ideas but is unable to present them clearly, forcefully, and with confidence. By the same token, men in business listen to those who have the ability to convey worth-while ideas with clarity and assurance. In business conversation men also exchange viewpoints, find the weak points in their own reasoning, and so strengthen their ideas and plans.

In social life, men and women welcome a companion whose conversational ability is somewhat broader than a mere "Is that so?" at convenient intervals. As will be pointed out later, social conversation, as well as business conversation, is not simply a problem of finding something to say continuously. In a discussion group, silence is at times the greatest contribution one can make.

George Ade, American humorist, once observed that "For parlor use the vague generality is a life saver." George Ade was speaking humorously. A vague generality may be a lifesaver when one has nothing worthwhile to contribute to a social conversation, but it reminds one of what George Bryan, an English poet, once called "society"—that "polished horde, formed of two mighty tribes, the Bores and Bored." In social conversation, and in business, one builds respect for himself through discussion that is interesting, informative, or entertaining and that others feel is well worth their time. The best conversation is important. As Ordway Tead has said, "Conversation is the fine art of mutual consideration and communication about matters of common interest that basically have some human importance."

Conversation and Speeches Help Make Friends

Conversation may also be the means of adding to one's friends. In Chapter II some ways of alienating people by conversation are carefully described. But conversation is a good method of making friends. Obviously, businessmen wish to talk with others from whom they gain by interchanging views. Intelligent and progressive business leaders welcome being "sold" an idea in a discussion if the idea is clearly presented and valuable. Men who can present ideas of this kind in this manner are welcomed as friends.

Public speaking may likewise be a major means of increasing the circle of one's friends. One thoughtfully prepared speech to one hundred persons who find the speech helpful makes one hundred friends in twenty or thirty minutes. The preparation for the speech may, however, have taken twenty or thirty hours. A good speech, well given, is one of the best methods of adding rapidly to one's acquaintances and friends. In business, or in the professions, a speech which shows an unusual grasp of some aspect of a subject will often help greatly to build a favorable reputation. There is no acceptable excuse for a speech for which the speaker has failed to make careful preparation. It is an inexcusable imposition upon an audience.

Develop a Distinct Personality

The ability to talk well and the ability to make public speeches effectively enable one to develop a distinct personality. They help to lift one out of the crowd which is pressing constantly for recognition. As George Ade also remarked, "Anyone can win, unless there happens to be a second entry." In life there is ordinarily not only a second entry, but there are hundreds of entries—hundreds of persons with whom we compete for position and advancement. How important it is, then, to be able to express ourselves well, to state our ideas in clear, forceful language. Through your conversation and speeches you can become known as a person who organizes his thoughts well, sticks to the subject and does not wander in his thinking, cuts through to the heart of a subject in a discussion, analyzes a problem critically and constructively, and conveys an air of assurance and conviction.

One may thus develop for himself a distinct personality with which others will welcome association.

Reveal Your Ability to Others

Through your speech you have opportunities many times each day to reveal your ability in your work, your insight into problems, and the facility with which you handle people. Your conversation will indicate the readiness with which you meet and solve a problem and the depth of your thinking on a subject. Countless times each week, and often many times each day, you may be given the chance to show by conversation with business and professional associates the extent of your competence. The failure to use these opportunities fruitfully may greatly handicap a person and retard seriously his development in his chosen work. Similar opportunities present themselves many times socially. Even a small improvement in your ability to talk effectively, spread over a life-time, can make an immense difference in your life.

The ability to talk well can be a major factor in indicating to others your real worth. It is unfortunate that so many of us neglect the art of conversation, for it affords the means of vastly increasing our powers and our possibilities of growth. Conversational ability is potential personal power. It enables one to persuade others to embrace his viewpoints. It induces others to accept his leadership. It wins respect in business and the professions, and it builds valuable friendships.

Views of Great Thinkers on Conversation

Conversation teaches more than meditation. *H. G. Bohn*

The tone of good conversation is brilliant and natural. It is neither tedious nor frivolous. It is instructive without pedantry; gay, without tumultuousness; polished, without affectation; gallant, without insipidity; waggish, without equivocation. *Rousseau*

The free conversation of a friend is what I would prefer to any entertainment. *David Hume*

Speak not but what may benefit others or yourself; avoid trifling conversation. *Benjamin Franklin*

Conversation is a traffic. If you enter into it without some stock of knowledge to balance the account perpetually betwixt you and another, the trade drops at once. *Sterne*

Conversation should be pleasant without scurrility, witty without affectation, free without indecency, learned without conceitedness, novel without falsehood. *Shakespeare*

He who sedulously attends, pointedly asks, calmly speaks, coolly answers, and ceases when he has no more to say, is in possession of some of the best requisites of conversation. *Lavater*

If the minds of men were laid open, we should see but little difference between that of the wise man and that of the fool. The great difference is that the first knows how to pick and cull his thoughts for conversation, by suppressing some and communicating others; whereas the other lets them all indifferently fly out in words. *Joseph Addison*

The most necessary talent in a man of conversation is good judgment. He that hath this in perfection is master of his companion without letting him see it. He has the same advantage over men of any other qualifications, as one that can see would have over a blind man of ten times his strength. *Steele*

The secret of tiring is, to say everything that can be said on a subject. *Voltaire*

The extreme pleasure we take in talking of ourselves should make us fear that we give very little to those that hear us. *Rochefoucauld*

It is when you come close to a man in conversation that you discover what his real abilities are. *Johnson*

Conversation opens our views, and gives our faculties a more vigorous play; it puts us upon turning our notions on every side, and holds them up to a light that discovers those latent flaws which would probably have lain concealed in the gloom of unagitated abstraction. *Melmoth*

The pith of conversation does not consist in exhibiting your own superior knowledge on matters of small importance, but in enlarging, improving, and correcting the information you possess, by the authority of others. *Walter Scott*

It is not necessary to be garrulous in order to be entertaining. To be a judicious and sympathetic listener will go far toward making you an agreeable companion, self-forgetful, self-possessed, but not selfish enough to monopolize the conversation. *A. L. Jack*

Conversation warms the mind, enlivens the imagination, and is continually starting fresh game that is immediately pursued and taken, which would never have occurred in the duller intercourse of epistolary correspondence. *Franklin*

A man is seldom better than his conversation. *German proverb*

It is good to vary, and mix speech of the present occasion with arguments, tales with reasons, asking of questions with telling of opinions, and jest with earnest. *Francis Bacon*

Ten Ways to Lose Friends in Conversation

1. Do you freely volunteer information in conversation or speeches when you are uninformed?
2. Do you tend to monopolize every conversation?
3. Do you repeatedly interrupt others in the middle of their conversation?
4. Do you find a secret satisfaction in contradicting the speaker or showing him where he is wrong?
5. Do you ask a question and then interrupt to ask another before the first question is answered?
6. Do you talk continually about yourself, your family, your achievements, and your interests?
7. Do you have a tendency to exaggerate?
8. Do you fail to show consideration for the sincere opinions of others on controversial matters?
9. Do you converse at great length about details and sometimes about nothing?
10. Do you often gossip about others?

Chapter II

THE ESSENTIALS OF GOOD CONVERSATION

"A GOOD listener is not only popular everywhere," Wilson Mizner, American dramatist, once observed, "but after a while he knows something." That is an understatement. Having the good sense to listen intelligently to the comments of others is perhaps the single most important essential of good conversation.

Edgar Howe asserted, we may assume with a bit of cynicism, that "No man would listen to you talk if he didn't know it was his turn next." The next time you talk with anyone at some length watch carefully to see whether you are doing your share of listening. Are you giving him a full opportunity to express his views? Or are you monopolizing the conversation, interrupting when he pauses for a moment, and allowing him merely an occasional brief yes or perhaps only a nod as you proceed?

An intelligent conversationalist never makes the mistake of thinking he is the only person with ideas worthy of discussion. He may even be correct in believing that what he has to discuss is more important, but he gives the other person an opportunity to express his ideas. He listens patiently to the comments and questions of the one to whom he is speaking.

Spontaneity in Conversation

Achieving spontaneity along with the more conventional attributes of conversation requires thoughtful effort and constant practice. By reading good books, becoming informed on important subjects of local, national, and international significance, or understanding thoroughly some profession, business, or industry, a person acquires the background to become an interesting and stimulating conversationalist. Individuals with such knowledge are less inclined to engage in random talk and gossip because their minds are occupied with more important matters. They talk with spontaneity and complete naturalness about subjects worth discussing. Their minds are filled with such ideas. It is minds which are barren that produce barren conversation. Bruce Barton said, "My observation is that, generally speaking, poverty of speech is the outward evidence of poverty of mind."

Discussion is apt to be at a low ebb among persons who have little knowledge and information or who care little about the important problems of life. If one has little to discuss beyond baseball scores, betting odds or horse races, and championship prize fights, the conversation is certainly not likely to be of a high order. Something more may be expected of men and women who are engaged in great struggles for real achievement, who desire to make the most of the opportunity to live, and who are aware that life at its best results in mental and spiritual growth. In that growth, intelligent conversation plays a great part.

Conversation Between Two Persons

Conversation between two people requires a good listener. But a good listener is seldom one who is completely silent. Listening is imperative if one is to talk understandingly with another person. One listens sympathetically to the other individual's remarks in order to comment intelligently regarding them, to find points of agreement, to discover ways of amplifying a subject, to uncover common or unusual experiences, and to learn something. It is not easy to listen. It takes effort to listen to the comments of someone else, to evaluate them, and to carry on the discussion intelligently.

A person who monopolizes every conversation has no opportunity to learn anything. An intelligent listener follows another person's comments by facial expressions of interest, surprise, or pleasure. We may readily grant that a person whose mind is filled with a great deal of interesting and unusual information regarding a subject which is being discussed will be tempted constantly to interrupt another person. The temptation to interrupt the speaker increases with one's knowledge of a subject. However, it is advisable to guard against such interruptions. Be courteous and give the other person an opportunity to speak. He likes a good listener as well as you do!

Interruptions are sometimes permissible when there is a major mistake on an important matter. Correction of the mistake holds the conversation in the proper channels.

However, little interruptions on minor points in a conversation are annoying, particularly when one member of a family repeatedly interrupts another on details. Unfortunately, interruptions of this kind frequently occur in families. Most persons would hesitate to interrupt those they knew less well to call attention to insignificant matters. Interruptions of this character may turn a conversation to entirely unrelated subjects. In those relatively rare instances when one comes across an interminable bore in conversation who talks on forever, talks on details, or just gossips, it is permissible to interrupt carefully and attempt to bring the conversation to a higher level. It may be possible also to end the conversation and be about other business.

The person who is always looking for an opportunity to interrupt and argue about details not material to the main discussion is an annoyance. He will quibble about your pronunciation of a word, an error in grammar, or some other detail in your remarks. You may express appreciation for his suggestions, but it is never advisable to be led by such a quibbler into a discussion of irrelevant and trivial matters. On the other hand, when you and I are tempted to quibble, we ought also to remember how worthless and annoying quibbling is when others do it.

Group Conversation

When conversation takes place in a group, it is often held together successfully by someone who is well informed on the subject being discussed. As different subjects or different phases of a subject are discussed, leadership in the discussion may pass from one person to another. However, the person leading the conversation on any subject must be certain that interruptions

THE ESSENTIALS OF GOOD CONVERSATION 11

and an expansion of the conversation on details does not lead to a breaking up of a large group into small groups. When conversation among four people, for example, breaks into two discussion groups of two each, it ordinarily will lose much of its value.

In a group the discussion will frequently begin with "small talk" about what the members of the group have being doing, their day-to-day problems. This procedure has some advantage as it enables everyone to participate and to become acquainted. Gradually, after these minor subjects have been exhausted, the conversation will turn to closely related and more serious problems of life. There may be talk about a new automatic dish-washer one of the members of the group has purchased. Other members tell about the time saved by certain electric appliances, and gradually the discussion may turn to the broader subject of the use of time saved, how some people use their spare time to read good books, to hear lectures, and to engage in recreational activities with their children. The great question of how best to use the opportunity to live may then be discussed. When the discussion reaches this stage, one must be very careful to hold it on this high plane and not introduce small talk again about trivial matters.

Listening carefully to a group discussion in an office conference will often clarify one's views on a problem. You may think you know the problem being discussed better than anyone else. However, in any group of three or four persons, you will generally be agreeably surprised by the ideas presented if discussion is encouraged. As you listen attentively and with anticipation, the person speaking will see you are interested and he will be apt to give you his very best thinking. You may get an idea of unusual value in a business discussion when you listen sympathetically and encourage others to speak. When you repeatedly interrupt others who are discussing a business problem, and talk long and often yourself, those who hold views different from yours may be inclined more than ever to believe their ideas are correct. They may feel you are reluctant to hear them because you fear their ideas are better than yours. Instead of squelching a person who disagrees with you or out-talking him in a group, it is better policy to let him talk himself out. He will feel that he had a fair chance to tell his story. Certain weaknesses in his ideas will be exposed. Later, if the comments of members of the group reveal the disadvantages in his ideas, you will finally hear your ideas approved. But if the other person is right, his views will sooner or later prevail anyway, and you will wish to be on the side with the correct views. Therefore, listen.

Participate in the Discussion

Persons who are exceptionally retiring or modest will sometimes hold back or be hesitant about taking part in a group discussion, especially if the subject is one with which they are not familiar, or if those participating are principally strangers. In the first place, you can be an interested listener who gives close attention to the words of each speaker. Your interest will be noticed. You will be a real part of the group even while you are listening. Sooner than you anticipate, a small part in the conversation will be open to you. A question will be directed to you. A phase of the subject you know will be touched upon. You elaborate it, and you begin to take an active part in the conversation.

On the other hand, if you are an active participant in a conversation but notice someone in the group who is not sharing in the discussion, make every effort to draw in the listener. You may ask his opinion on the topic, or switch the conversation to subjects which may draw him into the discussion.

What Good Conversation Does

If you can leave a person with whom you talk pleased because he visited with you, the conversation was good. If your talk helps to inform someone who was pleased to receive the information, the conversation was good. The best conversation helps us to know our friends better, broadens our acquaintanceships, increase our knowl-

THE ESSENTIALS OF GOOD CONVERSATION 13

edge, and makes us live fuller, more significant lives. The best conversation is constructive and not destructive. It does not injure others in ways in which we would not wish to be injured.

ORGANISE YOUR THOUGHTS

Few things reveal the quality of a person's mind more than his conversation. Is his conversation thoughtful? Are his ideas presented logically? Can you follow easily the trend of his thinking as he speaks? These are earmarks of an orderly mind. "Order" may be, as Alexander Pope said in *An Essay on Man*, "Heaven's first law." Undoubtedly, orderly thinking is an essential of good conversation and of good speeches.

To have one thought follow another in logical sequence, to arrange our ideas so they march out in the most effective order for the point we are trying to make clear, for the objective we wish to attain, is the mark of a good mind. This is fundamental to the best conversation. When a person gives evidence in his speech that his thoughts are systematically marshalled, it is rightly assumed that the speaker has a disciplined mind.

Organizing your thinking does not mean an overemphasis on details. It does not mean you insist on presenting one after the other in order, and at length, a great many points your listeners already know. That indicates order but not intelligence. One need not ordinarily in conversation "distinguish and divide a hair 'twixt south and south-west side," as Samuel Butler once asserted a certain critic and analytic thinker could do. But it is a pleasure to talk with someone, or to hear a public address, in which ideas are expressed clearly and in their proper order. Orderly conversation and speeches come from orderly minds.

A good conversationalist plays down little ideas that are subordinate to the main subject. He tries to hold the discussion to major ideas, but he does not talk in general terms. He does not simply say, "You can have a good vacation in the West." He takes this general idea and makes specific comments about the fishing streams in Colorado, the drive over the Continental Divide, Old Faithful, or other items of definite vacation interest. Good conversation is filled with specific illustrations, word pictures, and reasons.

In successful conversation one does not ordinarily seek topics that lead to strong disagreement. Even in those instances where several people are exploring a subject and are debating the merits of a philosophy, it is best first to find points of agreement and later proceed to talk about those aspects of the subject where there is disagreement.

GIVING CONVERSATION AND SPEECHES COLOR

Color is an essential of good conversation. By color we mean vividness and picturesqueness in conversation and speeches. We may use descriptive words, stimulating and living verbs, similes, humorous stories, quotations, and sharp epigrams to give color when we speak. Chapters containing hundreds of humorous stories, quotations, similes, and epigrams are found later in the book and should be helpful to anyone who wishes to improve his conversation and speeches.

Instead of speaking in vague generalities, words can express size, shape, action, and position and in these ways give color to conversation.

When Fred Allen, American radio comedian, declared, "If a circus is half as good as it smells, it's a great show," his description of a circus had color. Compare his sentence with "A circus is a great show." You may say, "He is meek." Pope used a simile and said, "He is meek as a saint." One may observe that "President Coolidge was reticent in conversation," but this had been said more colorfully in the sentence: "His lips are thin, horizontal, disciplined against idle speech."

One may say, "It is necessary to work hard to become a master of some field." Newell Dwight Hillis, distinguished American preacher, said it more picturesquely: "A thousand days of study lie back of the poet's vision, the surgeon's skill, the orator's enchantment. A thousand sleepless nights lie back of the inventor's tool and the statesman's law." Noel Coward, actor and playwright, said, "Alfred Lunt [noted actor] has his head in the clouds and his feet in the box office," which was an unusual way of describing Lunt's extraordinary talents. How many of us are in agreement, in an election year especially, with the observation of Clare Boothe Luce that "The politicians were talking themselves red, white, and blue in the face."

Humorous stories, humorous comments, humorous personal experiences and illustrations of all kinds, are often the easiest conversational tools for most of us to use to give color to our remarks. Anyone who has studied even superficially the life of Lincoln has noted his effective use of humor and homely illustrations. Wide reading will be helpful also in giving one a large number of valuable ideas that will make conversation colorful and enlightening. Chapter XV presents a list of excellent books by which one can plan a program of systematic reading. Chapter XIV also gives illustrative material of a type that is helpful in making conversation and speeches colorful.

Cliches

One method by which conversation is certain to be made dull and uninteresting is the repeated use of cliches, or worn-out and hackneyed phrases. Chapter IX contains a number of such expressions which one should avoid. We hear many of these expressions frequently, and they creep into our talk and speeches. They show a lack of originality in our thinking and the careless acceptance of overworked expressions. They also indicate our failure to increase our vocabularies. Study carefully the list of hackneyed phrases in Chapter IX and make lists of expressions of this kind which you use but should avoid.

Pet Expressions

Many of us also have pet expressions we use repeatedly in our conversation. One very successful businessman begins many of his sentences with the word "look." For example, "Look, how do you handle this problem?"

"Look, how do I make an application for a city automobile license?" A certain professional man starts perhaps a third of his sentences with, "Uh-h-h." Other persons overuse such words as funny, sweet, lovely, awful, and O.K. Listen to yourself and see whether you are guilty of the overuse of some expression.

Closely related to the use of pet expressions is the use of expletives, oaths, or exclamations. Examples of these expressions are such words as jiminy crickets, gosh, drat, lawdy-mercy, begorrah, mercy sakes, darn, dang, gee-whiskers, and dad-blasted. Refined speech eliminates all such expressions.

Sense of Humor

Washington Irving believed that "Honest good humor is the oil and wine of a merry meeting, and there is no jovial companionship equal to that where the jokes are small and the laughter abundant." To have a sense of humor does not mean that a person must try to say something humorous every few minutes. It makes no demand that a man be a perpetual clown or jester. It means that he must have an agreeable, pleasant frame of mind which will make others enjoy his presence and his conversation. He does not go around each day with a look on his face as if he smelled something burning on the kitchen stove, as one author, perhaps in good humor, described a well-known American. He is ready to laugh at his own frailties and foibles. He is not pompous and conceited, nor does he take himself too seriously.

If one has a sense of humor, he places first things first, and he does not let insignificant irritations make him "boil" inside. He has an appreciation of the proper relationship of the values of life, and when the values of life are placed far out of their proper proportion, he sees the humor of the situation. To him an anthill is an anthill and not Pike's Peak. He knows how ridiculous he looks if he ever comes seriously to believe that most of the world's problems are on his shoulders. He is not wrapped up in himself. If he finds himself in a heated discussion, he realizes that a humorous observation on some phase of the problem often relieves the tension and leads to a calm analysis of the problem. To him a conversation isn't a battle, but a pleasant and welcome experience. He disagrees if necessary to make his position on an important matter unquestionably clear and positive, but he does not do it in a spirit of antagonism or bitterness. And he wins respect and good will.

The person who has a sense of humor never assumes that in his little circle of friends he is the teacher and his friends are the students. He does not talk because he is impressed with his own wisdom. When he is wrong, he admits it. He never talks big. He is earthy, real, human.

THE VALUE OF BREVITY

Benjamin Franklin's comment that "His conversation does not show the minute hand, but he strikes the hour very correctly" describes how all of us have felt at various times with long-winded friends. One reason that so many conversations, speeches, and business letters are too long is that it takes thought to make a concise statement. Thinking is difficult. As even the great philosopher and mathematician Pascal once noted, "I have made this a rather long letter because I haven't had time to make it shorter.". Henry Thoreau, American author, also said it, "Not that the story need be long, but it will take a long while to make it short."

No one wishes to be a windbag. It is one thing to have interesting and worth-while ideas about which to talk to others. It is another matter to express the ideas concisely. All of us know people who talk too much. Frequently it is due to enthusiasm, and we can excuse it if the enthusiasm is over something of sufficient value to warrant the expenditure of so many words. Sometimes wordiness and talkativeness are due to conceit. These persons feel they have many things of importance to discuss, and that what they have to say is much more worth-while than what others may have to contribute. Not infrequently they are show-offs. They like to monopolize the conversation, to be in the center of it, to have all attention directed to them.

One sometimes finds in business offices a form of talkativeness which is called "visiting." A personnel manager of a business with two hundred employees asked an officer of that business if Miss Jones in the officer's department was a competent employee. The officer felt that she was valuable and that the department could not get along without her help. The personnel manager replied, "You are getting along without her each day for a considerable period. We have observed for some time that Miss Jones visits at the desks of other girls an average of forty-five minutes every day, beginning early in the morning. In addition, the telephone operator reports that she receives a half dozen or more calls each day which take telephones out of service for the thirty minutes she uses them." Both the officer and personnel manager were right. Miss Jones was a competent employee when she worked, but she was injuring her opportunities for advancement by wasting her time and that of other employees by excessive visiting and telephone calls.

Persons who love to reminisce—and all of us do as we grow older—may often find themselves talking too much. Our experiences seem so interesting to us: "Jim, I must tell you what happened to me one time," or "When the children were young, we took them to a circus and . . ." "Dorothy, did I ever tell you about the number of fraternity dances I went to in college?"

It is easy to fall into the habit of talking too much on too many subjects too often. One then becomes a babbler who is always willing to exhibit his ignorance on any subject and on many subjects in the course of a half hour or even an entire evening. The best conversation on any subject ends and does not go on, like Tennyson's brook, forever. Some conversation ends even before the talking ceases, because everything worth saying has been said.

Changing Topics

If a group has been called together to discuss a single topic, the discussion should be held to that topic until some satisfactory disposition has been made of it. However, when a group of people are simply visiting for an evening, for example, the discussion should be shifted during the course of the evening from topic to topic. More people will have a chance to participate in the discussion on subjects about which they are informed. But no change in subjects should be made abruptly and before everyone has had an opportunity to speak.

Sincerity

Sincerity is a major essential of good conversation. It means that the speaker is earnest. He has convictions and he expresses his views truthfully. When he says, "John, you prepared a good report," you know he means it. If he makes a suggestion, it does not mean he is deliberately trying to be critical. He is trying to be helpful and constructive. You can rely on him, for he gives you his considered and best judgment.

Sincerity obviously must be combined with intelligence to be effective. A combination of ignorance, sincerity and enthusiasm may be disastrous in human relationships

In salesmanship a knowledge of the good points of a product and of exactly what it will do gives the salesman confidence and assurance. Confidence creates enthusiasm because the salesman knows he has a product which will be satisfactory. He knows what his product will do. His sales talk then is intelligent, enthusiastic, and sincere.

Praising Oneself

"I don't like to say this, but no one in the office is as efficient as I am." You may think so, but the chances are you and I are *slightly* prejudiced in our own favor. Even if we are more efficient than anyone else in the office, self-praise wins no good will, and it reflects qualities none of us likes in others. Patting oneself on the back is a difficult physical feat, and no one does it gracefully or well.

Commending ourselves for our high ethical, moral, and spiritual qualities is one of the most distasteful forms of self-praise. "My husband and I may not go to church regularly, but we do few things that are wrong, and we live much better than many who go to church." "John and I don't spend everything we have the way our neighbors do." One is reminded of the Pharisee who thanked God he was not like the sinner who stood near him. Such self-praise makes poor conversation.

THE ABILITY TO COMMEND

The ability to commend means having the intelligence, alertness, and power of observation to see the good points in the ideas of other persons, and in their work, criticisms, plans, and accomplishments, and then to commend them. This ability is so simple to acquire, and is so effective. If we could only shift our thinking a little of the time from ourselves and sincerely commend the good things we see in others—even those we may unfortunately not like—we would acquire one of the most valuable essentials of good conversation.

Henry's health is much improved, John did a good job bringing a business through a sharp decline in sales, Sam delivered a splendid speech to the Chamber of Commerce, George wrote a thoughtful article for a magazine, Bill was elected president of the state druggists' association—*but did we commend them?* Hundreds of opportunities to build and strengthen friendships and win good will in professions, in business, and socially are lost because of the failure to commend others.

When one meets an old friend after an absence, there is frequently an opportunity to open the discussion with a favorable comment. Generally this starts a conversation off well. You remark how well he looks, or how you have missed your former visits with him. You tell him the good things you have heard about his progress in his new work, or how well he handled his affairs before he left the community. Any favorable comment which you can make is desirable. Any expression of your esteem or good will for him and any sympathetic understanding you may show of his problems will help the conversation to move along the best channels. If an old friend comes to confide in you regarding a problem that is worrying him, listen as he explains it and do your best to help him. Above all, keep his confidence. Pass along any complimentary remarks you may have heard regarding him. These may even help him with his problem. By the same token, never greet an old friend with some uncomplimentary remark you may have heard about him. Nothing chills a conversation faster.

Closely related to the willingness to commend is the matter of avoiding any unfavorable comment regarding another person's physical shortcomings. One may joke about being too nearsighted to see the eye chart in the doctor's office, as millions of us wear glasses. It is, however, another matter to make fun of or to call attention critically to someone's stammering, the loss of a limb, blindness, or any other serious physical problem that causes embarrassment.

Composure—Anger—Tolerance—Snobbery—Teasing—Questioning

Righteous anger in the face of wrongdoing is not to be condemned. Nor has tolerance a place when one is confronted with unfair activities, violations of the rights and property of people, and invitations to gossip and injure the character of others.

Calmness and composure, together with tolerance for the sincere convictions of one's friends and associates, are, however, essentials in developing conversational ability. Jonathan Swift, English poet and satirist, was probably correct in saying that "Argument is the worst sort of conversation." When we become angry, we so often say things we do not mean. Then we must either retract them and admit our comments were foolish or let the remarks stand and weaken the respect others may have for us.

Uncontrolled anger, when the speaker loses his judgment, is to be condemned. But there are degrees of anger that are a natural part of conversation on many occasions. Strong convictions on important questions may lead to exciting discussions and a sort of fighting anger which is permissible. Great national issues often lead to debate in which men express their viewpoints with a spirited anger that reveals the depth of their convictions.

If we lack tolerance, our opinions and our judgment will not be sought by our associates. Most problems of business and social and family life have at least something to be said on both sides. The person who comes to be known as fair and tolerant in hearing all sides becomes the individual to whom others come for advice and assistance.

Tolerance in conversation also means that if we are in a group whose interests are different from ours, we will do our best to participate in discussing the subjects that are of major interest to the group. Consideration for the happiness and pleasure of those with whom we talk is a sure method of becoming a welcome conversationalist in any group.

Webster's Collegiate Dictionary defines a snob as "One who blatantly imitates, fawningly admires, or vulgarly seeks association with those whom he regards as his superiors." He "repels the advances of those whom he regards as his inferiors." Snobbery is bigotry by insignificant people in intellectual and social matters. It is a combination consisting of equal parts of ignorance and egotism.

Severe razzing, teasing, and "nosy" questioning easily leads one into conversational trouble.

You razz someone about his old automobile, when it is the best he can afford, and you may lose a friend. You tease a young married woman about the cake she has done her best to bake for you, and you have used poor judgment, to say the least.

You ask nosy questions about personal matters that are none of your business, and your questions should be ignored or half answered; if they are fully answered, you may be certain the speaker inwardly resents such thoughtless inquiries. "What did your husband's folks give you for your wedding anniversary?" "Where did you go to college? Harvard?" (Maybe he did not go to college.) "How much did the dress you have on cost?" "How much did you give to the community fund?" "How do you get along with your brother-in-law?" Such questions as these are, frankly, none of the questioner's business.

TACTLESSNESS

Tactlessness is probably the single greatest cause of conversational offenses. Our talk is filled with tactless remarks. Mr. Jones says, "I have completed vacation plans to go fishing in Lake Orton," and Mr. Smith replies, "I understand fishing is much better in Lake Elton now than it is in Lake Orton." Mrs. Johnson comments, "John and I have saved enough money to have our home carpeted. We've chosen mulberry-colored carpet." Mrs. Olson observes, "A friend of mine told me last week that gray is now the color most highly recommended by interior decorators for carpeting." Mr. Brown states, "I've just agreed to have our house painted by the Ogden brothers," and his neighbor answers, "Well, I had them paint our place four years ago, and it was the worst job of painting we ever had." Someone reports, "Harry has just had the good luck to be made a vice-president of his company," and another person adds, "I hear the company is handing out vice-presidencies freely now to everyone who travels for the company, and they have vice-presidents all over the place." How thoughtless these remarks are. If they are intentional, they are malicious. If they are unintentional, they show a great lack of consideration for others.

VOICE—ENUNCIATION

The voice is the medium through which we express ourselves. In many instances a pleasant voice is perhaps a gift of Providence. But it is also true that a poor voice is not infrequently evidence of inexcusable carelessness in speech. The enunciation is slovenly, with syllables slurred, and no effort is made to do anything but speak in a dead monotone.

The least one can do is to speak clearly and loudly enough so the listener can hear, enunciating syllables carefully and having a flexibility of tone that expresses one's feelings and convictions. To cultivate the voice in this manner requires constant alertness, until having a good speaking voice becomes natural. Listen carefully to those who speak well and try to acquire the best qualities of their voices. It is not necessary to talk in a high-pitched, excited manner continually, nor is it necessary to whine each time one converses.

Some flexibility of tone can be developed by most of us with practice. Calmness, enthusiasm, strong convictions, and humor can all reflect themselves in our tone of voice. Disraeli thought there was "no index of character so sure as the voice." It may be too broad a generalization, but one may generally cultivate his voice so that it is the most effective instrument possible for conveying his ideas and helps to mark him as a person of culture.

Silence

We need to stress again and again the importance of listening. There are many times when, as Thomas Carlyle said, "Silence is more eloquent than words." We must not only know when to talk, but also when to keep quiet. Silence may be used to reprimand or rebuke. Several persons with you may start malicious gossip about a member of the group who is not present. You may remain silent and clearly refuse to participate in the discussion. If you follow a practice of not gossiping, you will win respect. Someone tells a questionable story in the presence of children. Your response can be one of complete silence with a rebuke implied.

However, as we have already stated, silence has more frequent uses in other ways. By questions you lead your listener to talk while you remain silent. By your silence and your manner you indicate a sympathetic interest in the other person's ideas which he will undoubtedly appreciate. He will like to talk with you. You are understanding. You break your silence only to draw him out further. You will learn more by listening as well as talking. There is profound philosophy in Robert Benchley's comment, "Drawing on my fine command of language, I said nothing." And to paraphrase Sir Thomas Browne in *Christian Morals*, written perhaps two hundred and fifty years ago, do not think silence is the wisdom of fools. If rightly timed, it is the expression of

THE ESSENTIALS OF GOOD CONVERSATION

wise men who have not the weakness but the virtue of silence.

When you are silent, you can be attentive, and at the same time you can be framing well your next comment. Always be as certain as you can that what you are about to say in conversation and in speeches is really worth taking the time of your listeners.

SOME OBSERVATIONS ON SILENCE

Silence is one great art of conversation. *William Hazlitt*

If you don't say anything, you won't be called on to repeat it. *Coolidge*

Silence is one of the hardest arguments to refute. *Josh Billings*

That man's silence is wonderful to listen to. *Thomas Hardy*

If a man keeps his trap shut, the world will beat a path to his door. *Franklin P. Adams*

Blessed are they who have nothing to say, and who can be persuaded to say it. *James Russell Lowell*

The only way to entertain some folks is to listen to them. *Frank McKinney Hubbard*

Silence is the perfectest herald of joy: I were but little happy if I could say how much. *Shakespeare*

He knew the precise psychological moment when to say nothing. *Oscar Wilde*

Silence is the unbearable repartee. *Gilbert K. Chesterton*

He missed an invaluable opportunity to hold his tongue. *Andrew Lang*

QUESTIONS TO AVOID ASKING IN CONVERSATION

1. Avoid asking tactless questions, such as, "How much did you pay for your suit?"

2. Avoid asking embarrassing questions, such as, "Why hasn't the company given you a promotion?" or "Did you go to college?"

3. Avoid asking questions which may reveal another person's lack of knowledge, such as, "How many books have you read this year?"

4. Avoid asking questions which compel a person to answer Yes, such as, "Did you find the gift we sent you useful?"

5. Avoid asking questions that are none of your business such as, "Do your sisters get along well with your stepmother?"

Chapter III

WAYS TO GAIN EFFECTIVE CONVERSATION AND SPEECH

In the chapters which follow, you will find several thousand quotations, epigrams, humorous stories, words to add to your vocabulary, hackneyed phrases you should avoid, a list of common errors in English, names of good books to read to improve your ability to converse, and illustrations of many conversation tools and figures of speech. Chapter III will be devoted to a discussion of some of the conversation and speech materials in these chapters and how to use them to your advantage.

Grammar and the Use of Good English

A command of good English is an asset of inestimable value in your social, professional, and business affairs. It helps you to speak with confidence whether you are addressing one person or a thousand. It assists you in presenting your thoughts clearly. If your ideas are good, you know they are assured of being expressed in the most acceptable manner.

Victor Hugo once said, "Everything bows to success, even grammar." Although there is some truth to this observation, many persons who are known as successful, but who know little of grammar, would undoubtedly give a great deal to know grammar well. The language and the grammar you use in conveying an idea is, however,

WAYS TO GAIN EFFECTIVE CONVERSATION AND SPEECH

only the means or the medium by which you transmit the idea to someone else. It is the idea which is important. In a choice between good ideas and poor grammar on one hand and poor ideas and good grammar on the other, the good ideas with poor grammar will win. There is something worth considering in Oscar Wilde's statement that "George Moore wrote brilliant English until he discovered grammar." The command of language should be so well developed that the language and the grammar are in a sense incidental and do not hamper the clear and effective presentation of the idea. One should not have to be concerned about his use of good English. It should be a part of his conversational equipment.

Chapter V contains one hundred common errors in English. A careful study of this list should help to eliminate from your speech any of these errors which you may now be committing. If you feel that you need a thorough review in grammar, it is suggested that you ask your local public library or a teacher of English in the high school in your community to recommend a book. Just a little study each day for a few weeks will help to give you the confidence in the use of English which you need to speak well.

Vocabulary

You may have a good knowledge of the use of language and of English grammar, but you may still lack the vocabulary necessary to give your speech color, precision, and strength. With an adequate vocabulary you will have at your command the right word to express your idea. One does not require a vocabulary consisting solely of long and seldom-used words. Live, descriptive, active words are needed, words that enable you to express yourself colorfully in the shop, office, and home, on social occasions, and in whatever situation you may find yourself. An excellent vocabulary helps to mark you as a person of culture. You will need a good command of words in your particular work whether it is medicine, the ministry, banking, education, law, business, agriculture, government, or some other activity. The vocabulary you may acquire beyond your own field is almost unlimited. For example, if you are a businessman, you may well acquire a knowledge of the meaning and use of a great many words in the arts, science, education, government, agriculture, and banking. You can give your life many interesting and worth-while facets if you gain command of new words. These new words indicate that your knowledge is increasing. Chapter VI presents a number of ways in which you may add to your vocabulary. All that is required is a small amount of your time given with some regularity. Mark Twain stated vividly how important it is to be able to use the right word when he said, "The difference between the right word and the almost right word, is the difference between lightning and the lightning bug."

SIMILES

Webster's Collegiate Dictionary describes a simile as "A figure of speech by which one thing, action, or relation is likened or explicitly compared, often with *as* or *like*, to something of different kind or quality." You may say, "He was as happy as a cat with a pan of fresh milk," and you will have a simile. You would also have a simile in the sentence, "The youngster was as restless as a Mexican jumping bean." Similes help to make speech colorful. Their effectiveness depends upon the ability to make unusual, unexpected, and interesting comparisons. It is a stimulating game to practice making similes. To use them too frequently in conversation is not advisable. Overworking any figure of speech tends to make conversation stilted and affected. Aristotle wisely said, "Similes should be sparingly used in prose, for they are at bottom poetical." Chapter VIII contains dozens of similes that will show you how colorful these expressions can be in speech and writing.

The metaphor is closely related to the simile and is described in Chapter VII. You will find also in Chapter VII descriptions of a number of figures of speech and tools of speech, such as the hyperbole, alliteration, and idioms.

HACKNEYED PHRASES

Many of us acquire, perhaps unconsciously, expressions that are overworked. These expressions are sometimes called cliches. They show a lack of thinking and a willingness to use repeatedly a phrase that is badly worn. Such phrases as "brave as a lion," "clear as crystal," "green as grass," "budding genius," "view with alarm," and "age before beauty" all fall in the category of hackneyed phrases. Chapter IX contains a list of such phrases which it would be desirable to avoid using if you wish your conversation to be original and to have freshness.

EPIGRAMS

An epigram is a witticism briefly and ingeniously expressed. Coleridge's definition of an epigram is the one perhaps most frequently heard:

> What is an epigram? A dwarfish whole,
> Its body brevity, and wit its soul.

Epigrams take the form of both prose and verse. The end of an epigram is often pointed, witty, and surprising. It is not always possible to tell humorous stories or give humorous illustrations in conversation or in a speech. A brief, witty comment of only one sentence may be exactly what is needed to emphasize a point in a discussion or speech. In this situation, an epigram is an excellent tool. However, it requires thought and some creative ability to originate epigrams. Perhaps most persons will find it helpful to memorize some of the best epigrams they find in their reading, and use them as the occasion permits. You may think this is difficult, but a little time spent in memorizing and repeating the best epigrams you read should make them a part of your conversational inventory not unlike new words you add to your vocabulary. Chapter X contains hundreds of epigrams for your use in conversation and speeches.

HUMOROUS STORIES

All of us have observed how effective humorous stories often are in helping to stress a point a speaker is trying to make, to lighten a conversation or speech which may otherwise be dry and heavy, and to bring calm analysis and fair consideration to a discussion in which the participants may have lost their tempers. Not everyone, however, can tell a humorous story well. To be able to use the humorous story for its greatest effectiveness in your conversation and speech it is well to keep in mind the following general rules:

1. You should not try to make the humorous story an effective tool in your conversation and speeches for the purpose of becoming known as a teller of humorous stories. You have little or nothing to gain by becoming known merely as a humorist unless you are expecting to enter such fields as radio or television in that capacity. A good sense of humor is invaluable, but telling humorous stories is hardly a full-time occupation for most persons. For our purposes the humorous story is a tool to improve conversation and speeches.

2. After a story is told, it should not be repeated to see if the listeners will continue their laughter. If a story produces little or no laughter, do not try to explain it. Go on to something else.

3. Do not tell your listeners, "This one is really funny. Get ready for a good one." Some of your listeners will be saying to themselves, "I don't believe it. I have probably heard it before." If it is as good as you say it is, they will know when you tell them.

4. Never use more words than necessary to tell your story. It is dangerous business to build up a long story for a little laugh. Any long story should have a big laugh at the end and should be interspersed, if possible, with little laughs along the way.

5. As a general rule, put the humorous point of the story exactly at the end of the story. No further narration should be necessary after you reach the humorous point.

6. Know the humorous story so well you can tell it casually and in your own language.

7. Do not lead the laughter for your own joke. It should not require that kind of support.

8. If the joke is on you, it will probably be even better received than if you tell it about someone else.

9. Tell your stories about subjects in which your listeners are interested; otherwise the stories will not be fully understood and will have a cold reception.

10. Generally avoid stories which make listeners laugh at the physical defects of others, such as stammering and the loss of limbs or eyes. There are too many good humorous stories which make it unnecessary to tell those that hurt people or lead others to laugh at serious physical problems and handicaps which our friends and neighbors may have.

Chapter XI contains two hundred humorous stories that may be used as they are on many occasions, or may be changed to adapt them for other situations. With a little practice, and with observance of the principles of storytelling given above, almost anyone can tell stories effectively. Gradually, also, with practice certain stories will become a part of your humorous-story inventory.

Quotations from Literature and the Bible

Chapter XII contains over 1,600 quotations from literature and Chapter XIII contains over 600 quotations from the Bible. To paraphrase Disraeli, in these quotations there is preserved the wisdom of the wise and the experience of the ages. In quotations you will find, as Coleridge did, a sentence, a story, or an illustration that does your heart good. They will help to make you a better conversationalist. Many of these quotations are the great thoughts of the great thinkers of all time. To browse in these quotations should give you new thoughts, new inspiration, and a new determination to improve your own ability to speak well.

Furthermore, you will find it possible to use quotations in your conversations and speeches. Obviously, one does not repeat quotations parrot-like every time he speaks. That would result in what might be called overornamentation of speech. But occasional quotations are effective and frequently enable one to emphasize a point or to summarize a long discussion in one concise sentence. A good quotation in speech is something like a sharp dressing in a salad. One naturally expects substance in the salad, but the sharp dressing accentuates the enjoyment of its substance.

INTERESTING STORIES AND FACTS

The most interesting part of a conversation or a speech often is a story or an unusual fact. We all like stories and illustrations, and we like facts if they are pertinent and well presented. The Founder of Christianity did effective teaching through parables. Men understood Him because He presented many of His ideas by means of stories and illustrations.

Chapter XIV illustrates the type of stories, illustrations, and facts that help to improve conversation and speeches. For example, the first story in that chapter is an unusual one, and almost any person who tells it on the proper occasion will find an interested listener or audience. You can also use material of this kind, which others have developed, by saying, "As Senator Jones stated in an address before the Springfield Forum . . ." Then you can quote the Senator. This enables you to use the story or illustration he gave, and it also makes your comments more interesting because you have brought a well-known person's name into your remarks. Current events and news events, as Chapter XIV indicates, may provide the material for stories and illustrations for conversation and speeches.

Dr. Robert A. Millikan uses facts in an effective manner in the short selection "Pure Science," which is quoted in Chapter XIV and is taken from one of his speeches. Anyone who makes an earnest effort to give listeners worth-while and instructive facts will find a good reception for his remarks. As Burke said, "Facts are to the mind what food is to the body." Too many persons will not even work really to master the facts in their own businesses or professions. Those persons who will make this effort will be rewarded in many ways, including the ability

WAYS TO GAIN EFFECTIVE CONVERSATION AND SPEECH 33

to converse intelligently and to make speeches others will wish to hear. They have something to give the listener.

GREAT BOOKS

It is hoped that there will be some readers of this book who will not only become able to use to their advantage the tools of conversation and speech which have so far been discussed, but who will take the additional step of planning a program of wide reading in the great books and on the great issues of life. Great books contain the great ideas of all time. They are worth discussing and they provide illustrations and stories that enliven discussion. All conversation and all speeches reflect the speaker's mind. To be widely read is to have lived in all ages and to be a contemporary of all men. To have read the great books of all literature is to have had the privilege of exchanging ideas with the great thinkers of all time. That experience is almost certain to enrich one's conversation and to mark one as a person of culture.

Chapter XV contains various lists of books which will be helpful in starting anyone on a systematic program of profitable and highly worth-while reading.

CONVERSATION OVER THE TELEPHONE

With an estimated 160,000,000 telephone conversations in the United States each day, it is apparent that this form of conversation is highly important. A great many business concerns now ask the telephone companies to help them improve their telephone conversation and manners so that they may render courteous and efficient service.

The author is indebted to the Illinois Bell Telephone Company for suggestions included here on ways of improving telephone conversation and, specifically, for "Practice Sentences" and "How to Make Friends by Telephone."

Your Voice is You

When you cannot see the person to whom you are speaking, there is a tendency to let your voice become monotonous and mechanical. Remember that over the telephone your voice is you. You can give your voice a pleasing tone and sparkle. Moreover, by an expression of interest and a helpful attitude you can have what the telephone company calls a personal interest tone. The following table of words shows the difference between a good telephone voice and a poor one.

The Voice Having Personal Interest Tone	*The Voice Lacking Personal Interest Tone*
+Pleasant	—Expressionless
+Friendly	—Mechanical
+Cordial	—Indifferent
+Cheerful	—Impatient
+Interested	—Inattentive
+Helpful	—Repelling
+Plus Personality	—Minus Personality

Clear Speech

Listen to your voice. Read or talk aloud in front of a mirror; see and hear whether your mouth action produces words clearly. Do you slide over syllables? Do you speak distinctly or do you mumble? Honestly, how do you sound?

The sentences which follow have a mixture of vowels and consonants. You will find it helpful to read these nine sentences aloud and to listen carefully to your own pronunciation. These sentences provide good exercises for your speech organs and at the same time present some practical speech suggestions. In addition to these nine practice sentences, tongue twisters all of us have tried, such as "Peter Piper picked a peck of pickled peppers" and "She sells sea shells," are useful in improving enunciation.

WAYS TO GAIN EFFECTIVE CONVERSATION AND SPEECH 35

Practice Sentences

1. For distinct enunciation, every word, every syllable, every sound, must be given its proper form and value.
2. Think of the mouth chamber as a mold, in which the correct form must be given to every sound.
3. Will you please move your lips more noticeably?
4. The teeth should never be kept closed in speech.
5. As your voice is the most direct expression of your inmost self, you should be careful, through it, to do yourself full justice.
6. You may know what you are saying, but others will not, unless you make it clear to them.
7. Through practice, we can learn to speak more rapidly, but still with perfect distinctness.
8. Good speech is within the reach of everyone, through conscientious practice.
9. The courtesy of face-to-face conversation, where the smile plays such an important part, can be expressed, over the telephone, only through the tone of voice and a careful choice of words.

How to Make Friends by Telephone

At one time the Illinois Bell Telephone Company prepared for its employees a number of simple suggestions on how to use the telephone properly. Some of these suggestions are summarized here to help one talk more effectively over the telephone.

1. When placing a call, be ready to talk when the called person answers. It is discourteous not to be ready to talk when the person you are calling answers the telephone. Stay on the line until your party answers or until you receive a report.
2. When telephoning, ask if it is convenient to talk. It is courteous to inquire of the person you call if it is convenient for him to talk. You would not break into a conference, and this same rule of etiquette applies over the telephone.
3. When telephoning, speak directly into the transmitter. Your lips should be half an inch from the mouthpiece and should be used freely to form your words.

4. When telephoning, it is unnecessary to shout. Shouting distorts your voice over the telephone. The instrument is tuned to a normal tone of voice and loud ones cause it to blur. A loud voice sounds gruff and unpleasant over the telephone. It is equally unpleasant to listen to someone who whispers or mumbles.

5. When telephoning, try to visualize the person. Speak to the person at the other end of the line, not to the telephone.

6. When telephoning, be attentive. The person to whom you are talking will appreciate your listening politely and attentively. You would not interrupt in a face-to-face conversation, and the same rules of etiquette apply in telephone conversations.

7. When telephoning, use the other person's name. There is no sweeter music to another person than the sound of his own name.

8. When telephoning, explain waits. The other person cannot see you or what you are doing. He has to depend on what he hears. Excessive waits are annoying. Offer to call back promptly if the information is not readily available. If you must leave the telephone, do not drop it on the desk.

9. When telephoning, apologize for mistakes. When you receive a wrong number, do you bang up the receiver or apologize to the other person for calling by mistake? It is equally courteous to be pleasant when someone calls you by mistake.

10. When receiving a call, greet the caller pleasantly. Remember, you do not know who is calling. It may be your best friend or one of your best customers. Greet him as pleasantly as you would if you were meeting face to face.

11. When receiving a call, it is well to identify yourself. Avoid such old-fashioned, time-wasting answers as "Hello" and "Yes." Identify yourself, your firm, or your department. Examples: "Mr. Brown" or "Mr. Brown speaking," "Roberts Company," "Bates Brothers, Mr. Jones speaking," "Shipping Department, Mr. O'Brien speaking."

12. When answering calls for others, ask questions tactfully. Ask only those questions that are necessary,

such as name and telephone number. You may want to use such phrases as "I'm sure Mr. Smith would like to know who is calling," or "when Mr. Smith returns, may I tell him who called?"

13. When through telephoning, who should end the call? Ordinarily, the person who originates the call ends the conversation. However, some business firms prefer to let the customer hang up first.

14. When through telephoning hang up gently. Slamming the receiver may cause an unpleasant noise in the receiver of the other telephone. It is as discourteous as slamming the door.

SOME DON'TS OF CONVERSATION

1. Don't get a reputation for exaggeration or overstatement.
2. Don't pretend you know more than you do.
3. Don't try to impress others with your importance.
4. Don't become known as a quibbler.
5. Don't be rude, noisy, or discourteous when others are speaking.
6. Don't go around looking for trouble.
7. Don't continue arguing after you know you are wrong.
8. Don't get the idea you can't learn anything from others.
9. Don't waste time on endless chatter about nothing.
10. Don't gossip—ever.

Chapter IV

FROM EFFECTIVE CONVERSATION TO EFFECTIVE SPEECHES

PUBLIC speaking is simply conversation magnified. Talking with a few friends and talking to an audience are essentially similar, except that with an audience we speak a little louder and more distinctly. Ordinarily, also, we have some advance notice of a speech so we can prepare our remarks.

Note how close effective conversation is to effective public speaking. Assume that you are talking with a half dozen friends in an assembly room. Your remarks are exceptionally interesting as you describe your experiences on a trip to Mexico. Some other friends drop by and join the group. Before you are aware of it the group has twenty persons. Someone suggests they sit down so all can hear you talk. Just when did your conversation become a speech? Was it when the group grew larger? Was it when the group sat down? You continued with your interesting remarks, and without your being aware of it your conversation became a speech. It's that simple to develop effective public speaking from effective conversation. It will help to make public speaking easier if you think of most public speaking as simply enlarged conversation.

Overcoming Fear

If you have some fear about making a public speech, it is well to begin with some preliminary steps. The next time you are a member of a group engaged in discussion or listening to a speech, ask a question if the opportunity presents itself. Do this whenever you find an occasion. After you have found how easy it is simply to ask a question, stand up in a group and make a brief remark about the subject being discussed. A few sentences will do. Asking questions and making remarks at small meetings will give you excellent experience. You will hear your own voice in public. You will stand in the presence of the group. If you know in advance the topic to be discussed, make some preparation so that you are informed. Your remarks will seem thoughtful to the group. You will gain confidence. Gradually you will be preparing for larger and more important assignments.

The Idea for Your Speech

There are certain fundamentals with which everyone who wishes to speak in public should be familiar. A knowledge of these essentials will save a great deal of time and will help materially one who desires to become an able speaker.

In the first place, a speech generally should have one major idea. The invitation you receive to make the speech may suggest the major idea or you may be permitted to choose the idea or subject for the discussion. For example, you may talk before the local chamber of commerce on the character of the growth of your community during the last ten years. That is your major idea. This idea may have several subheads, such as (1) growth in population, (2) industrial and business development, and (3) cultural and civic advancement. A carefully prepared major idea with subheads is imperative if one expects to make a good speech. This central idea needs to be divided into subheads so the audience can grasp it more easily and can follow the development of the idea logically to its conclusion. If the speaker has a fuzzy idea of his main subject and its subdivisions, how can he expect an audience to get a clear impression?

Organizing the Speech

For most speakers and for most subjects it is probably best to organize a speech into three parts, as follows: 1. the introduction; 2. the body of the speech, or the central idea, divided ordinarily into not more than three or four subheads; 3. the conclusion.

Every speech should be planned, even an "extemporaneous" address. A person may say he speaks extemporaneously without a plan or preparation. Obviously, however, one can hardly make intelligent comments when he is ignorant of a subject. If he has on some occasion given an effective speech on the spur of the moment, it was because he knew his subject from past experience, and mentally had gone over it previously. He had unconsciously organized his thinking.

Even when one has only a few minutes or hours to prepare a speech, it should be organized mentally, if not in writing, so the remarks are logical, consistent, and orderly. Dr. Harry Emerson Fosdick once advised the author that he spent a half hour in writing for each minute of a sermon. The late Senator Arthur H. Vandenberg also informed us that "Scrupulous and painstaking preparation is indispensable."

Any unorganized speech is in great danger of being a rambling effort with many unnecessary words. No speaker has the right to take the time of an audience while he rambles trying to collect his thoughts. That kind of public speaking is an imposition on an audience. The speaker's thoughts should be collected before he speaks, not after.

After a speech is planned with the three sections—the introduction, body, and conclusion—the speaker should stick to the plan. If he tries to insert in his carefully planned speech every idea that occurs to him after he starts speaking, he may wander a long way from his subject. He may never get back properly to it and he may exhaust the patience of his audience with his rambling. Consequently, it is essential that the speaker prepare the talk thoughtfully and stick to the plan.

THE INTRODUCTION

The introduction to a speech should always be short. The real substance of the speech should be in the body and not in the introduction. It is, therefore, never advisable to make long remarks preceding the presentation of the real substance of the address. There are a number of different types of introductions, of which the following are typical:

1. Refer to the occasion. If the occasion is a legal holiday, a centennial celebration, the dedication of a new building or some similar event, the speech may open with a reference to the occasion.

2. Announce the subject in the first sentence or paragraph. A speaker may say at the outset, "I should like to talk to you tonight on the subject of honesty in public office." Then he may go directly to the body of the speech.

3. Tell a humorous story which is closely related to the subject or the situation under which the speaker is appearing. A humorous story must never be told simply for the purpose of introducing humor. The story must definitely relate itself to the address. It is not only permissible but often is desirable if the speaker can tell a humorous story on himself relative to his appearance before the audience or the subject of the address.

4. Begin with an illustration or a story of human interest. For example, a speaker who talks about the conveniences of the modern American home might begin by describing the typical home of his youth with its lack of conveniences. He might even add humorous touches to his description.

5. Make a statement that challenges attention, arouses curiosity, surprises an audience, or gives unusual information. A speaker might say, "Remarkable as America's progress has been in the last century, I am here tonight to present a picture of America's future possibilities that will make our past achievements seem insignificant."

6. Ask a question. A thoughtful question may serve effectively to introduce an address. A speech on local government might begin with "How can you make your influence in local government count?"

7. Use a quotation. A talk on the subject of minding one's own business might begin with Oscar Wilde's observation in *Lady Windermere's Fan*, "My own business always bores me to death; I prefer other people's."

8. Make a statement that shows the importance of the subject to the audience. A speech on foreign trade in an industrial city might begin with these words, "One out of every four employees in heavy industry in this city works to produce machinery for export."

Although the introduction should be brief, it requires careful thought. Every effort must be made to secure the attention of the audience from the beginning of the speech.

THE BODY OF THE SPEECH

The body of the speech is the reason the audience comes to hear a speech. There is no acceptable excuse for poor preparation of the body of the talk. Every listener is entitled to receive something of value from a speech, whether it is entertainment, information, or inspiration. The following principles should be followed in preparing the body of a speech:

1. Keep clearly in mind the central idea of the speech. What major idea do you wish to leave with the audience?

2. Master the subject you discuss. By reading, by critical study, by questioning, and by discussion with others make yourself an authority on your subject. Poor preparation of the body of the speech and inadequate knowledge of the subject are inexcusable. Competent knowledge of your subject will give you enthusiasm and confidence.

3. Use illustrations freely. An audience understands illustrations more easily than abstract ideas and generalities. Have facts, illustrations, and even (if necessary to tell your story) some figures in various parts of the body of the speech.

4. Divide the body of the speech into two, three or four parts. If you were discussing American highways and the nation's growth, you might spend a short time on (a) early highways, then discuss (b) present highways, and finally give some ideas regarding (c) future highways and the development of the country. An audience will understand your major idea better if you subdivide it into smaller units. However, there is some danger in more than three or four subdivisions as the audience will not remember them and may become confused. Make your two, three, or four points completely clear. These points, or subdivisions, can be enumerated at the beginning of a speech, but it is generally best to give them one at a time with your explanation as the address proceeds.

5. Explain your central idea, but ordinarily do little arguing. The members of an audience will listen to an interesting and informative explanation of an idea, but few persons like to have the speaker argue with them. Give the audience information, facts, illustrations, and figures which tell your story, but do not give the impression that you are trying to argue with them.

6. Start the body of a speech as a rule with ideas on which there is agreement or which are understood. It is

EFFECTIVE CONVERSATION TO EFFECTIVE SPEECHES   43

then easier to discuss more debatable points or those less well understood.

The Conclusion

If the body of the speech has been competently prepared, the thought will become more and more intensified as the speaker comes to his conclusion. Building to a powerful climax at the end of a speech requires able analysis of the central idea so that each subdivision of the speech builds on the preceding point. A speech with a climax at the beginning or somewhere before the end leaves something to be desired. The introduction should get attention. Each succeeding point in the body of the speech should be better, if possible, than the last, and the climax should come at the end.

No speech should be given without a conclusion. The conclusion can take various forms, as follows:

1. Summarize briefly in outline form—one, two, three —the major points made in the speech.

2. Complete the speech with a quotation from literature or the Bible, or with a statement by some distinguished person.

3. Close with an encouraging statement, or compliment the audience. Assume you are to give an address on the problems of some industry or profession. You may conclude by an encouraging statement of what farsighted leadership in the industry or profession has already accomplished and express the conviction that this assures that present problems will be successfully met.

4. Tell the story of a great period or moment in history, in science, in business, or in the professions. There are hundreds of such instances which may be used to close an address. Lincoln's preparation for, and delivery of, the Gettysburg Address as told by Carl Sandburg in his important work on the life of Lincoln, and the story of Michael Pupin and his discovery of the means by which the long-distance telephone became a reality, are illustrations of the type of incident that can be used. Books in the field of biography are excellent sources of such stories. The incidents chosen should be definitely related to the

central idea of the speech and make a suitable climax for it.

5. Request the audience to take some action. Let us assume that you are to make a speech about problems facing your community. In the conclusion you might ask the audience to help solve these problems by (a) informing their neighbors about the problems, (b) electing city officials who were pledged to solve them, and (c) keeping after the city officials following their election.

6. Tell the audience a humorous story that illustrates clearly the central idea of the speech. The emphasis given the idea by a good humorous story will help the audience to remember the idea.

POLISHING THE SPEECH

When you have completed a written draft or rather complete outline of a speech, you will find it worth-while to revise it thoroughly, eliminating everything that does not help you to present strongly your major idea. This is the time also to add to the speech where you think your material is weak. Remember, anything less than your best effort is inadequate. Multiply the number of people who will hear your speech by the number of minutes you plan to speak and you have the total number of minutes of time you will take. Sixty people multiplied by twenty minutes would equal 1,200 minutes or twenty hours of combined time for the audience. You have no right to take that amount of their time with anything less than your best effort.

We shall assume now that the substance of your speech is ready. Go over it sentence by sentence to see if you can introduce an occasional phrase with alliteration, a pertinent, sharp epigram, a relevant humorous story at an appropriate point, figures that strengthen your central idea, an illustration or incident from a biography or play, or a suitable quotation. Your speech will begin then to have style and individuality.

Here and there intersperse an occasional very short sentence among longer sentences. This relieves monotony. The listener follows the speech more easily. The pace temporarily changes. Sometimes one finds it advantageous also to use a whole series of short sentences. These sentences will be brisk. They will be sharp. They will get attention.

Another method of keeping the attention of an audience is to ask a challenging question or a series of related questions. Questions serve to make an audience think with the speaker. They help to stress important points. Students of public speaking who would like to study further the subject of polishing a speech may find of value the chapter "How to Make Your Speech Sparkle" in the author's book, *The Public Speaker's Treasure Chest*.

Those who are interested in public speaking will find in other chapters of this book hundreds of items, such as epigrams, humorous stories, and quotations, which will assist them in the practical preparation of speeches and in giving them individuality and distinction.

Chapter V

ONE HUNDRED COMMON ERRORS IN ENGLISH

THE person who does not have a knowledge at least of the fundamentals of English grammar will find it difficult to converse or speak effectively. He will often lack confidence and assurance, and he will be fearful that he will betray his ignorance. But any public library or high school can recommend books which will familiarize him with the essentials of English grammar he needs to know. It is not an exceptionally difficult task to acquire this knowledge.

In this chapter there are presented a great many of the more common errors in English. A careful study of this list will help the reader to eliminate from his own conversation and speeches errors he has been making.

One Hundred Common Errors in English

1. Be certain that the subject of a sentence and the predicate are always in agreement. Always use a singular subject with a singular verb, a plural subject with a plural verb. Do not say, A period of ten months *were* required." Say "A period of ten months *was* required." "Period" is the subject, and it is singular.

2. Arrange the words in your sentences in correct order. Notice how the arrangement of the word *only* changes the meaning of the following sentences:

   A. Only John reported the accident to me.
   B. John only reported the accident to me.
   C. John reported only the accident to me.
   D. John reported the accident only to me.

3. Use only words you understand. Don't say, as one student did, "the *ibex* at the back of the book helps you to find things in the book." The correct word is "index." Don't say, "The matter is not *revelant*." The word is "relevant." Using words that the listener does not understand is the wrong way to try to impress him.

4. Make your thoughts follow logically in a sentence. Don't say, "The lecturer told of many unusual experiences while shooting game birds at the Business Women's luncheon." This is a good trick if the lecturer can do it. Better say, "At the Business Women's luncheon, the lecturer told of many unusual experiences while shooting game birds."

5. Avoid the use of "had" with "ought," as "You hadn't ought to do it." Say, "You ought not do it."

6. Either . . . or, neither . . . nor. "Or" is used with "either"; "nor" is used with "neither." Either red or blue; neither red nor blue.

7. "Don't" is the contraction of do not. It should never be used with he, she, or it. You do not say, "He don't believe me." You say, "He does not believe me," or "He doesn't believe me." However, "doesn't" is colloquial. At any rate, "don't" is never used as a contraction for doesn't.

8. "Due to" always modifies a noun and not a verb. Therefore, as a rule, no sentence should begin with "due

ONE HUNDRED COMMON ERRORS IN ENGLISH 47

to." Do not say, "He succeeded due to his intelligence." Say, "His success was due to his intelligence."

9. "All of" is often used in conversation where the "of" is not required. Do not say, "all of his books" or "She gave all of her antiques to the museum." Omit the "of." Say "*all* his books," and "She gave *all* her antiques to the museum."

10. "Among" is used in relation to more than two persons or objects. "Between" is used in relation to two persons or objects. For example, "The property was divided among six children" and "The property was divided between two children."

11. Avoid the use of "and" in place of "to." It is better to say, "Try to solve the problem" instead of "try and solve the problem."

12. You should be "angry at" a thing or situation, and "angry with" a person. For example, "John was angry at the delay resulting from the bad weather," and "John was angry with his associate.

13. Many persons mistakenly use "any" in place of "at all." Do not say, "Mary didn't sleep any at the hospital." Say, "Mary didn't sleep at all at the hospital."

14. "Ain't" just *ain't* good English. Do not use it.

15. Be careful not to use "like" for "as if." Say, "He looked as if he had lost his last friend," and not "like he had lost his last friend."

16. "As" is used when you compare things or persons of equal or about equal size or quality. "So" is used when you compare things or persons which are unequal. Say, "He weighs as much as his brother, but he does not weigh so much as his father."

17. Be careful also in not using "as" for "that." Do not say, "I don't know as I shall visit with him." Say, "I don't know that I shall visit with him."

18. "Very" is a greatly overworked adverb. It is better to use it less frequently than most of us do. Often "very" is used to modify a past participle, as "He was very disappointed" or "Mary was very pleased." Better say, "He was very much disappointed" or "Mary was very much pleased" or "very highly pleased."

19. "Anybody" and "everybody" are singular. Do not say, "If anybody leaves, will *they* please take *their*

coats," or "Everybody are asked to stay for the meeting." Substitute "one" for "body" and the meaning becomes clear "If anybody [one] leaves, will *he* please take *his* coat?" Everybody [one] is asked to stay for the meeting."

20. "Anxious" means you are worried. "Eager" means you are keenly desirous. Instead of saying, "I am anxious to meet John," you will say, "I am eager to meet John." A father may say, "I am anxious about the safety of my family."

21. You do not arrive "at about six o'clock." You arrive either "at six o'clock" or "about six o'clock."

22. We should remember that "awful" means "filled with awe or profoundly impressive." It isn't "an awfully good apple." It is a very good apple.

23. Many persons use the words "bad" and "badly" incorrectly. "Bad" means ill, sick, or in pain. For example, John feels "bad." Henry looks "bad." "Bad" is an adjective modifying John and Henry. "Badly" is an adverb. Therefore you do not say when you are sick, "I feel badly." To emphasize this point, let us repeat, "I feel bad."

24. "Balance" does not mean remainder or rest. You do not say "The balance of the apples are Jonathans." You say, "The remainder of the apples are Jonathans."

25. Be careful not to confuse the phrase "better part of" with "greater part of." "Better part of" refers to quality and not to quantity. Therefore you do not spend the "better part of" an hour in the library. An hour has no better part. You may say you spent "almost an hour" or the "greater part of" an hour in the library. The "better part of" a bushel of apples would mean the larger, riper apples.

26. Dangling phrases are phrases which either are related to no word or are related to the wrong word. For example, someone may say, "Carefully aiming his gun, a large duck fell to the ground." This means the duck carefully aimed his gun. (This duck belongs in a circus.) One might better say, "Carefully aiming the gun, I brought down a large duck." Another error would be to say, "While trying to sleep, a fly was buzzing around my room." This means "a fly while trying to sleep was

buzzing around my room." (An unusual fly.) Better say, "While I was trying to sleep, a fly was buzzing around my room."

27. It is better to use "that" in place of "but what." For example, do not say, "I have no doubt but what John will go to the station." Say, "I have no doubt that John will go to the station."

28. When using "cannot help" do not follow with the word "but." Do not say, "He cannot help but protest that the action was unwise." Say, "He cannot help protesting the action was unwise."

29. "Character" refers to moral excellence. "Reputation" means generally known qualities or the esteem in which one is held. Mr. Jones may have a reputation as a man of character. "Notorious" now is generally used to speak of some person unfavorably or to mean of ill repute.

30. In using the words "conditions" and "circumstances" one says "*under* these conditions" and "*in* these circumstances."

31. "Claim" should not be used to mean allege or maintain or assert. Claim means to demand what is due, or implies the right or title to something claimed. Do not say, "Harry claims the town is on Highway Sixteen." Say, "Harry insists [or maintains] the town is on Highway Sixteen." Do not say, "The doctor claims that the boy has enlarged tonsils." Say, "The doctor states [or says] that the boy has enlarged tonsils."

32. "Clever" is a greatly abused word. It means skillful, resourceful, or possessing quickness of intellect. It does not mean wise, educated, or attractive. A magician may perform a "clever" trick. Mary may be "clever" at embroidering.

33. In grammar there are only three sizes. Be careful in using the three degrees of comparison: (a) the positive, (b) the comparative, and (c) the superlative. The positive merely makes a statement about an object or describes it by itself; it does not compare it with another object. It has no relation to an increase or decrease in a quality or attribute of the object. For example, you say, "The peach is large; the Swiss watch is small; the oak tree is tall."

The comparative is generally formed by adding *er*. It is used to compare one object with another to show an increased or decreased degree of some quality, attribute, or amount. For example, you say, "This peach is the larger [not largest] of the two; the Swiss watch is the smaller [not smallest] of the two; the oak tree in the front yard is the taller [not tallest] of the two."

The superlative is generally formed by adding *est*, and it is used in comparing one object with two or more objects. It expresses the highest or the least degree of some quality, attribute, or amount. For example, you say, "This peach is the largest in the basket; this Swiss watch is the smallest in the jeweler's window; this oak tree is the tallest on Lincoln Street."

A few words of one or two syllables, and almost all words of three or more syllables, are compared by using *less, least, more,* and *most*. To illustrate:

Positive	*Comparative*	*Superlative*
Important	more, less, important	most, least, important
Beautiful	more, less, beautiful	most, least, beautiful

You would not say importanter, importantest, beautifuller, and beautifullest.

Avoid also the use of the double comparative and double superlative. Say, "The water is colder [not more colder] than it was yesterday." Say, "This watch is the costliest [not most costliest] in the jewelry store."

There are some words, such as "unique" and "perfect," which do not lend themselves to comparison. "Unique" means the only one of its kind; it permits no comparison. "Perfect" seems to express the superlative. If anything is perfect it can not be more perfect. However, if you wish, you may say "more nearly perfect" and "most nearly perfect." But the Founding Fathers said in the Constitution, "In order to make a more perfect Union."

A few words are wholly irregular in their comparison. To illustrate:

bad	worse	worst
good	better	best

You will find exceptions to these rules on comparisons in the writings of distinguished authors.

34. Unless you mean a group do not use "party" for "person." Do not say "The party that was in the library yesterday is working there again today." Say "person," "man," or "woman."

35. "Sure" is a word that carries too heavy a load in current conversation and speeches. "Sure" is an adjective. Do not use it in place of "surely" or "certainly." One should not say, "John sure was glad to return home from abroad." Say, "surely" or "certainly."

36. Watch out for the double negatives. Do not say, "He ain't no gentleman." Say, "He is no gentleman." It is wrong to say, "The company does not make no exceptions." Say, "The company does not make any exceptions," or "The company makes no exceptions."

37. Be careful not to use the expression "could of" for "could have." You say, "I could have [not *could of*] taken the boy to school."

38. "Couple" means two things which are linked together or are united. You may speak of "a married couple," but you do not say, "Give me a couple oranges." "Pair" applies to two things which belong or are used together. You speak of a "pair of gloves."

39. "Cute" is another word that is carrying too big a load and may die from overwork. It is sometimes used to mean clever, shrewd, and sharp-witted. *Webster's Collegiate Dictionary* defines "cute" as meaning "Attractive by reason of daintiness or picturesqueness, as a child." Too often we hear such expressions as "the cutest little roadster," "the cutest house," "the cutest boy friend," and "the cutest handbag." It would be a good idea to give "cute" a long rest.

40. "Data" is the plural of "datum." Say, "The data are presented in the appendix of the book."

41. Most authorities agree that "different" should be followed by "from" and not by "to" or "than." The red-brick house may be *larger than* the yellow-brick house. However, you say, "The red-brick house was *different from* the yellow-brick house."

42. You use "differ from" when you desire to show a contrast, or that one thing is unlike something else. It

is correct to say, "My suit differs from my brother's." You use "differ with" when someone disagrees with someone else. For example, one says, "They differ with you."

43. "Done" is often used incorrectly in the sense of finished," as "It will be an hour before I am done writing the lesson." It is better to say, "It will be an hour before I have finished writing the lesson." You should not say, "Are you done with your work?" Say, "Have you finished your work?" "Done" is the past participle of "do." It must have an auxiliary such as *have* or *had*. You do not say, "You have did it." You say, "You have done it."

44. When you use "doubt" or "doubtful," use *that* and not *whether*. For example, "I doubt that [or it is doubtful that] the stores will be open Monday evening." Avoid also the use of "but" with "doubt." To illustrate, "I do not doubt that he can do it." "But" is not needed in the sentence after the word "doubt."

45. "Drop" always refers to a liquid and "particle" to a solid. Say, "There was not a drop of milk in the bottle and not a particle of meat in the locker."

46. "Each other" refers to two only. "One another" refers to more than two. To illustrate, "The twins look after each other," and "The thirty members of the club help one another."

47. "Aggravate" means to make a condition or situation worse or more severe or more offensive. You do not use "aggravate" when you mean "to make angry." "Irritate" means to excite to momentary impatience or anger. "Annoy" means to disturb or irritate, especially by repeated acts. You would not say, "John aggravates me." "Irritates" and "annoys" are better words. You would say, "The soreness was aggravated by the negligence of the hospital attendants." A person may not be aggravated but a condition or situation may be. "Exasperate" means to arouse to keen or bitter vexation or to influence someone's anger. You may say, "Isn't it exasperating?"

48. "In connection with" is an overworked phrase. You may often substitute "on" or "about" for this phrase. It is better not to say, "Mr. Smith arranged an interview with Professor Jones in connection with John's grades." Substitute "about" for "in connection with."

49 In writing a business letter or in conversation in

ONE HUNDRED COMMON ERRORS IN ENGLISH 53

which you simply give information, it is better to avoid using "to advise," which means giving advice.

50. "Can" means the ability to do, whereas "may" means to have permission to. Many errors are made in using these two words. A young man does not say to his sweetheart (unless he is looking for trouble), "Can I take you home?" He says, "May I take you home?"

51. "Continuous" means to go on uninterrupted or without a break. "Continual" means to happen repeatedly at short intervals or to recur periodically. The rain may be continuous. One may receive continual reminders to take care of a matter.

52. Do not say, "equally as good." Eliminate the "as."

53. "Every now and then" is a colloquial expression. Omit the "every," as it serves no purpose. "Now and then" is an idiom which does not make much sense but is permissible because of its wide acceptance. One should also omit the "every" in "every once in a while." You may say, "John plays golf now and then [or occasionally]." You may also say, "Harry goes to Chicago [omit every] once in a while." "Regularly" or "frequently" may well be used for "once in a while."

54. When you try to analyze the phrase "every so often" it is difficult to explain what it means. This expression is used to mean "once in a while." It is better to say "occasionally," "often," or "frequently."

55. "Except" should not be used for "unless." "Except" means to omit or leave out. You do not say, "I shall not buy the automobile except you give me seat covers." Use "unless" in place of "except." You would say "I shall work every day except Sunday."

56. You "excuse" small faults or minor omissions. You "pardon" serious faults, crimes, or grave offenses. However, you may say, "Pardon me" as a form of courtesy. One "forgives" an offense done to oneself. You may say: "Please *excuse* my tardiness"; "The President *pardoned* the conscientious objector"; "The man *forgave* those who had criticized him in error."

57. When you look forward to some event, you "expect" it. You expect future events. You do not say, "I expect the man is a carpenter." You may say, "I suppose [or believe] the man is a carpenter." "Suspect"

means to have doubts or to imagine someone to be guilty. You do not say, "I suspect Robert is reading in the library." You may say, "I believe [or suppose] Robert is reading in the library." You may also say, "He suspected that the owner set fire to the building."

58. "Fascinate" and "fascination" are often used incorrectly. "Fascinate" means to bewitch, to hold spellbound, or to charm. You do not say, "I have a fascination for Mary Jones." That would mean you charm, bewitch, or hold Mary Jones spellbound. You should say, "I am attracted to Mary Jones." You may say, "Mary Jones fascinates me."

59. It is incorrect to say, "I have your *favor* of October 10." Use "letter," "report," "order," or some similar word.

60. "Faze," meaning to disconcert or worry, is colloquial in the United States. Its use should be avoided. Therefore, do not say, "Nothing fazes me."

61. When you "feel good," it means you feel happy, agreeable, or even virtuous. When you "feel well," it means you are in good health.

62. "To bring" means simply to come with something from a distant place or person to a nearer place or person. "To fetch" is to go to, get, and bring back. It implies a two-way trip. You say, "Bring me my umbrella," and "Fetch a loaf of bread when you go to the bakery." "To take" means to go away from the speaker or from some other person or place. You say, "Take this book to Mr. Jones."

63. "Few" applies to what you can count, and "little" applies to that which you can measure but not count. You say, "I have few study periods," and "I have little time for study."

64. "Fewer" is the comparative of "few," and "less" of "little." "Fewer" applies to numbers, persons, or articles that may be counted; "less" applies to degree, quality, or quantity. You may say, "Fewer meals were served," and "Less power would be desirable."

65. You do not say, "Henry is doing *finely* in college." You say, "Henry is doing well in college." Finely is the adverb of "fine." You may speak of *finely* ground coffee.

ONE HUNDRED COMMON ERRORS IN ENGLISH 55

66. "Fix" means to make firm, permanent, or fast. "Fix" is sometimes used colloquially to mean to repair, arrange, adjust, or tamper with, but such use is not recommended. You would not say, "Please fix my automobile." Say, "Please repair my automobile." You would say, "The shutters were fixed on the outside wall." Avoid also the use of "fix" as a noun in "You are in a bad fix." "Fix" in this latter case is slang. Say, "You are in a bad predicament."

67. Do not become confused in the use of the words "latest" and "last." "Latest" means most recent and "last" means final. An author does not say, "Have you read my last book?" unless he means this is his final book. He would say, "Have you read my latest book?"

68. You always say, "the first two" or "the last two" and not "the two first" or "the two last."

69. "Going to" is sometimes used colloquially to mean "just about." Instead of saying, "I was just going to mow the lawn," say "I was just about to mow the lawn."

70. You should say, "a half hour," not "half an hour."

71. You should not say, "It's an *actual fact* that gold was discovered." All facts are actualities. Omit "actual."

72. You should not say, "The two suits are identically the same." If they are identical, they are the same. Omit "identically" or say, "The two suits are identical."

73. Such words as "hate" and "love" should be used infrequently as they are too strong to use for normal emotions such as "like" and "dislike." How can you "love" the new draperies, the car, the cocker spaniel, and your husband?

74. "Healthy" means in a state of good health and "healthful" means serving to promote health. You say, "John is healthy because he eats healthful foods and lives in a healthful climate."

75. "Of the fact that" is another phrase that should generally be avoided. Do not say, "He was not aware of the fact that attendance was required." Say, "He was not aware that attendance was required."

76. Generally it is better to say "inside" in place of "inside of." You say, "The children had scarlet fever

and were kept inside [not inside of] the house." You also say, "Outside [not outside of] the house."

77. "Isn't but" is a common error. Do not say, "There isn't but one car in the garage." Say, "There is but one car in the garage."

78. It is better not to use "kind of" or "sort of" in place of "rather" or "somewhat" before adjectives. It is preferable to say, "He is rather [not sort of or kind of] tall," and "he is somewhat [not sort of or kind of] awkward." "Kind of" and "sort of" should not be used before verbs. Say, "I rather [not sort of or kind of] believe he will come on the next train." "Kind of" and "sort of" should not be followed by the article "a." Say, "I do not care for that kind of [not kind of a] suit."

79. The words "as to" are often used when they may be eliminated or a better preposition used. Say, "He never inquired about [not as to] his responsibilities."

80. "Line" is a greatly overused word. You hear, "William is in the furniture *line*." "Game" is even worse. "Business" is a better word than "line" or "game." You also hear such sentences as, "What's John's line?" "He sells maps, schoolbooks, school desks, and things along that line." Avoid the use of "line" and especially, "I have a line on him," in which "line" is slang.

81. "Listen" is followed by "to" and not by "at." Do not say, "Listen at him whistling at work." Say, "Listen *to his* whistling at work." Note also the correct use of the possessive pronoun "his" instead of "him." The incorrect use of the pronoun is common.

82. Avoid the use of "lots," "a lot," and "a whole lot" when you mean "much" or "a great deal." Say, "He expects to earn a great deal [not lots, a lot, or a whole lot] of money on his sale of farm products."

83. Be careful about using your adjectives in the proper place in sentences. Do not say, "Please give Mary a hot cup of chocolate." Say, "Please give Mary a cup of hot chocolate. Say, "John wishes to buy a pair of new shoes [not a new pair of shoes]."

84. Be careful not to add "of" or "from" to "off." Say: "He fell off [not off of] his horse." "Keep off

[not off of] the grass." "John took his hat off [not off of or off from] the shelf." The use of "off of" in place of "from" is to be avoided. Say, "We buy fruit from [not off of] a farmer."

85. You should use "plan to" and not "plan on." You say, "Mr. Brown planned to visit [not planned on visiting] his brother."

86. "Plenty" is a noun and is always followed by "of." Say, "We have plenty of food," not "plenty food." You also say, "They have plenty of room in the old house," not plenty room in the old house."

87. Avoid the use of "same" or "the same" to mean "he," "him," "them," or "it." Say, "If you have the large pencils available, please send them [not same] to me." This error is frequently made in business conversation and correspondence.

88. "Regards" means best wishes, greetings, compliments. Do not say in business conversation or correspondence, "In regards to your letter" Say, "In regard to your letter."

89. The third person singular, "says," should not be used with the first person singular pronoun, "I." You should not say, "*I says* to him, 'move your car to the curb,' *I says*. Then he says, 'Who says so?' and *I says*, 'I said so,' *I says*." Correct: "I said to him, 'Move your car to the curb.'"

90. "Rarely ever," "rarely or ever," "seldom ever," and "seldom or ever" are not acceptable. "Rarely if ever," "seldom if ever," and "seldom or never" are correct. Do not say, "He seldom ever goes to the city." Say, "He seldom [or hardly ever] goes to the city."

91. It is easy to confuse "some" and "somewhat." "Some" means an unspecified or indefinite number. "Somewhat" means in some degree or measure or a little. To illustrate, "John ate some green apples." "He was very sick yesterday, but he is somewhat better today."

92. It is better not to add "in" or "up" to the verb "start." Do not say, "When did you start in to play in the orchestra?" Say, "When did you start to play in the orchestra?"

93. You do not say, "I stopped at the Blackstone Hotel." You say, "I stayed at the Blackstone Hotel." "Stop" means to arrest progress or movement or to cease activity.

94. Do not use "swell" to mean excellent. "Swell" means to grow larger or dilate.

95. Avoid adding "there" to "that" and "here" to "this." Say, "This [not this here] book has more pages than that [not that there] book."

96. Be extremely careful in using the article "the" before each of two or more connected adjectives or nouns to make the meaning clear. "*The* blue-and-red awnings" obviously does not mean the same as "the blue and the red awnings." "The blue, yellow, and brown banners" expresses one idea. "The blue, the yellow, and the brown banners" is another idea. "Exercises for boys and girls" and "Exercises for the boys and for the girls" convey different meanings.

97. "Together with" and "along with" do not require a plural verb. You say, "The professor, together with his class, was [not were] sent to another library." You also say, "The house, along with the furniture, was [not were] sold."

98. "Transpire" should not be used in the meaning of to happen or to occur. "Transpire" means to come to light, to become known, or to exhale. Say, "The airplane crash occurred [not transpired] last week." "The story of the airplane crash in Asia did not *transpire* for five days after it occurred."

99. Avoid using "way" as an abbreviation for "away." "The man lives away [not way] up the mountain."

100. Avoid the use of "can't seem to," as it is not a logical expression. Do not say, "I can't seem to open this door." Say, "I seem unable to open this door."

Chapter VI

BUILDING YOUR VOCABULARY

IF YOU have an idea, you can express it by speaking or writing. These are the only two methods by which you can convey ideas to others unless you are one of the few persons who use the sign language. But no idea can be expressed, regardless of method, without the use of words.

We communicate ideas by means of words. Your command of words will therefore largely determine the clarity with which you present your ideas. If you wish to converse well, or to make effective speeches, you must spend some time building your vocabulary. If you will spend only ten or fifteen minutes a day for a few months in adding words to your vocabulary, you will be well repaid in the confidence your increased vocabulary gives you in your business and social affairs.

In building your vocabulary it is not necessary to concentrate solely on learning long words. Your aim should not be to impress others with your command of long words which are seldom used. Your vocabulary should consist first of words which will help you in your particular surroundings, in your business, and with your friends. When you have done a good job in increasing the number of words you can use effectively in your own field, you can begin to reach into related fields. You will find reading one of the most helpful ways in which to learn new words. Chapter XV contains lists of a number of books that will not only greatly increase your knowledge but also will help build a rich vocabulary.

The first tool you will need is a good dictionary. From your reading each day you may select three or four words you do not know. Turn to the dictionary and find the exact meaning of each word, its spelling, and its pronunciation. You will note also whether the word is a noun, verb, adjective, or some other part of speech. Now see how the word was used in the place you found it. Then use the word in your own sentence. Keep these words in a notebook and review the list each week and each month. There is nothing difficult about it. Only ten or fifteen minutes each day will help to give you a decided advantage in the clarity and effectiveness with which you speak.

To assist you in finding words to add to your vocabulary, over six hundred are listed below. Take at least one word each day and with the help of a good dictionary you may add still more words to your vocabulary. If you know a word in this list, pass over it; in its place add a new word to the end of the list from strange words you find in your outside reading.

A List of Words to Help Increase Your Vocabulary

wanton	abject	vociferously
abysmal	vindictive	acclimate
vicarious	accolade	vapid
acquiesce	unison	acumen
unctuous	adept	ubiquitous
agile	tyro	ameliorate
taciturn	amenable	sycophant
amenity	surreptitious	amicable
supercilious	anathema	subversive
artifice	sublimate	askance
stoic	aspirate	specious
assiduously	soporific	assimilate
scurrilous	audacious	savoir faire
auxiliary	saturnine	awry
sardonic	banal	sadistic
beatific	rusticate	benign
repercussion	bestial	redundancy
blase	recrimination	blasphemy
rationalize	bourgeois	quixotic
bovine	penury	braggadocio
perfunctory	brusque	persiflage
buoyant	philology	cadaver
phlegmatic	caisson	pompous
canon	presumptuous	caprice
procrastinate	caricature	profligate
chagrin	punctilious	chasten

BUILDING YOUR VOCABULARY

pusillanimous	chicanery	pyromania
chirography	nostalgia	choleric
obsequious	coadjutor	obstetrician
cognomen	ominously	conjure
omniscient	construe	paranoia
contemplative	parsimonious	contemptuous
parvenu	contour	pediatrician
conversant	malediction	cortege
maudlin	dilatory	misanthrope
dilettante	monotheism	dishevel
moribund	divers	mulct
divers	nebulous	diverse
indict	docile	inhibited
dolorous	insomnia	dubious
credulity	dulcet	decrepit
egregious	demagogy	elusive
demoniacal	enervate	denouement
ennui	desultory	epicurean
intermittent	fatalism	introversion
fiasco	irascibly	flagrant
kleptomaniac	epitome	futilitarian
esoteric	lethargy	gesticulate
exemplary	loquacious	gourmet
exotic	macabre	gullible
explicable	gynecologist	magnanimous
hypochondriac	explicable	magniloquent
iconoclastic	explicit	idiosyncrasy
exponent	impasse	extirpate
inadvertently	eyrie	inane
facetious	formidable	incongruous
facile	flaccid	indefatigable
facsimile	fetish	frustrate
heinous	garrulity	harbinger
germane	grimace	gibberish
homogeneity	intrigue	ignominious
ingenue	imperturbable	indigent
impiety	impugn	importunate
imposture	importune	abortive
chauvinist	abstemious	carte blanche
acrimoniously	biped	adroitly
altruism	ascetic	ambiguity
archaeologist	ambivert	apotheosis

1001 WAYS TO IMPROVE YOUR CONVERSATION

amnesia	antipathy	analogous
anomaly	claustrophobia	animosity
cliche	animosity	compunction
effete	concomitantly	effervescent
crass	dogmatic	deprecate
facet	disparagingly	desultory
expiate	didactically	exhibitionist
diffidence	euphemism	egocentric
eulogy	emulate	etymology
equanimity	entomology	esoteric
aesthete	naive	piquant
nepotism	picayune	nihilism
peremptory	nomenclature	pedantic
omnipotent	pathos	onerous
panoply	orgies	panacea
placable	paladin	plebeian
palfrey	puerile	plenary
protege	poignant	promulgate
polyglot	probity	posthumous
pristine	precedence	prestidigitator
revocable	quandary	reticent
querulous	requiem	qui vive
renaissance	quiescent	refutable
raillery	recondite	redress
reconnaissance	sinecure	ribald
scintillate	robust	schematic
sacrilegious	satiety	salutary
sanguine	sobriquet	taciturn
sonorous	auspicious	sortie
surveillance	spontaneity	surmise
suave	supine	subtile
summarily	subtle	succinct
languish	undulatory	transference
proficient	traumatic	unctuous
truculent	ukase	turgid
warily	unguent	vizor
vacillate	vizier	vacuity
viscous	vestigial	viscid
vagary	virulent	opulent
vignette	zany	wraith
affable	collocate	allegory
attrition	collaborate	assiduous
collateral	arrogant	anneal

BUILDING YOUR VOCABULARY

appertain	abominate	annunciation
abrasive	appellation	adduce
apperceive	commensurable	emendation
commiserate	emanate	disaffected
elucidate	dissemble	dissuasion
disseminate	dissonance	dissertation
dissolute	eclectic	dissoluble
commodious	disassociate	connive
disarray	connote	corroborate
disannul	emetic	disservice
enounce	dissidence	eccentric
dissimulate	efface	ineffaceable
effervesce	ineffable	efficacy
erratic	effigy	effusion
effluence	inaptitude	inanimate
effulgent	inanition	inutile
inexorable	inure	inexpiable
inundate	inexplicable	inordinate
innate	inopportune	innervate
inoperable	innocuous	innutritious
innominate	innuendo	innovate
augury	ceramic	imbroglio
cynosure	indigenous	decimate
artificer	dolce	caprice
eclat	chicanery	felicitous
flaccid	placid	recreant
succulent	hierarchy	piquant
fistulous	flagitious	minutiae
otiose	requital	portentous
aphorism	elixir	exigency
seraphic	exorable	obnoxious
derisive	espouse	malfeasance
poser	resilient	transient
truism	usurp	amicable
blatant	flagrant	lackadaisical
pathos	cacophony	ellipses
euphony	supersede	consensus
dissension	desiccate	innuendo
appellation	malign	annihilate
soliloquy	beneficent	eleemosynary
obeisance	elicit	ingenuous
ingenious	irrelevant	precedence
precedents	choleric	decorous

abridgment	proselyte	committal
corroborate	ecstasy	exaggerate
grievous	harass	impinging
inoculate	intercede	iridescent
likable	millennium	noticeable
occurrence	peremptory	questionnaire
apropos	archives	commensurate
aspersion	clique	irresolution
desultory	embrasure	gourmand
fathom	flatulent	hirsute
homily	homologous	liaison
molybdenum	perforce	paroxysm
portent	portcullis	assuage
roseate	scion	sardonic
satiate	trichology	tenuity
aberrant	accost	ambidextrous
amenable	arraignment	automaton
bedizen	beneficent	cache
capricious	collusion	carnage
carnivorous	charlatan	translucent
commiserate	complaisant	correlate
credence	credulous	dais
deleterious	depreciate	desultory
dextrous	diaphanous	digitalis
ebullient	effete	endocrinology
ephemeral	esoteric	excoriate
facade	factious	factitious
satirical	fiasco	gynecology
hypercritical	impecunious	perspicacity
pith	precursor	pusillanimous
recitative	respite	sarcophagus
schism	scurrilous	surveillance
tourniquet	venal	viands
vicissitudes	elucidate	immobilize
repugnant	derisive	salient
sedentary	obsess	desensitize
integral	temporize	contortionist
distort	intractable	convene
subvert	imperious	evocation
avocation	circumvent	philanthropist
connoisseur	sardonic	amphibian
synchronize	cosmic	microcosm
criterion	antipathy	impassive

agoraphobia	cacophony	diathermy
sophisticated	absolve	attune
circumspect	exonerate	intransigent
ambivalent	hypochondriac	periphery
excruciating	congenital	symposium
grimace	entomology	lexicography

At the same time you make each word a part of your vocabulary, or after you have mastered all of them, prepare a list of the synonyms and antonyms for as many as possible of these words. This exercise will further increase your vocabulary and will enable you to use the word with exactly the right shade of meaning. A synonym is one of two or more words of the same language having the same or nearly the same essential meaning. An antonym is a word of opposite meaning. Synonyms for "distress" are grief, anxiety, anguish, and agony. Antonyms for "distress" are comfort, soothe, and gratify. Synonyms for "distant" are far and remote. Antonyms for "distant" are close, near, and cordial.

Another interesting method for increasing your vocabulary is to see how many homonyms you can find in the course of a month. A homonym is a word having the same pronunciation as another, but differing from it in origin, meaning, and often in spelling. Common examples are principal and principle, bear and bare, capitol and capital, cellar and seller, stationary and stationery.

There are a number of words whose use is very confusing. Sometimes confusion may result because words are similar in sound. Study the following words carefully with the aid of a dictionary until you know their exact meaning and use:

Confusing Words

respectably	respectfully	respectively
accept	except	
most	almost	
farther	further	
robbed	stolen	
pour	spill	

1001 WAYS TO IMPROVE YOUR CONVERSATION

formally	formerly	
leave	let	
adapt	adopt	
liable	likely	
beside	besides	
around	about	
allusion	illusion	delusion
instance	case	example
mad	angry	
disinterested	uninterested	
censor	censure	
allude	elude	
majority	plurality	
unique	rare	unusual
then	than	
common	mutual	
desert	dessert	
lose	loose	
carton	cartoon	
amazed	astonished	
Calvary	cavalry	
celery	salary	claim
cemetery	symmetry	seminary
consul	counsel	council
finally	finely	
prophecy	prophesy	
specie	species	
minister	minster	
ingenious	ingenuous	
emigrant	immigrant	
invent	discover	
lightening	lightning	
accent	ascent	assent
advice	advise	
aught	ought	
canvas	canvass	
choose	chose	
cite	sight	site
complement	compliment	
conscience	conscious	
corps	corpse	
decent	descend	descent
device	devise	

later	latter	
reverend	reverent	
straight	strait	
to	too	two
track	tract	

Earlier in this chapter it was suggested that you make lists of synonyms and antonyms for as many as possible of the words given. Now you may be ready to work with verbs, adjectives, adverbs, and nouns in special groups.

You will find below four lists of words, with their synonyms, in the following order: verbs, adjectives, adverbs, and nouns. You may be able to think of additional synonyms for each of the words. Study these lists carefully and use the words in sentences. Then each day select one word from your reading and find synonyms for the word. The dictionary and a book of synonyms will be helpful to you.

A verb is the part of speech that expresses action, occurrence, or a mode of being. You will note that verbs are often dynamic, live words that give your speech power. They help to give life to a whole sentence. "A person may merely *ask* for a book" or "he may *demand* it." "John may merely *say* [or he may *declare, maintain, assert,* or *complain*] that taxes are too high." Verbs offer an opportunity to make your conversation sparkle.

An adjective is a word used with a noun or pronoun to indicate a quality of the thing named or something attributed to it. A boy may be "a student," "a *dull* student," or "a *brilliant* student." Adjectives enable you to paint ideas in bright and striking colors. They help to keep your speech from being drab. You should not, however, use so many adjectives that your speech becomes flowery. You would not say, "On this memorable, auspicious, and significant occasion." Such ornamentation is inexcusable.

Adverbs modify or qualify verbs, adjectives, or other adverbs in somewhat the same way adjectives modify or describe nouns or pronouns. John may simply "walk to the store." John may also "walk *quickly* [or *leisurely*] to the store." The words "quickly" and "leisurely" paint the picture more vividly.

A noun is a word used as the name of a person or thing. "Blunder" may be a better noun for some "mistakes" than "oversight" or merely "error." Select nouns to convey the exact meaning you wish to express.

VERBS WITH THEIR SYNONYMS

abandon—leave, forsake, abdicate
abide—remain, stay, rest
adapt—suit, conform, regulate
alter—modify, vary, qualify
amend—change, rectify, correct
anger—arouse, inflame, irritate
announce—tell, inform, proclaim
baffle—check, frustrate, balk
banish—expel, dismiss, exile
bargain—negotiate, haggle, stipulate
bear—suffer, feel, tolerate
belittle—disparage, run down, decry
calculate—reckon, compute, count
call—summon, notify, demand
cancel—revoke, overrule, abolish
captivate—fascinate, delight, enchant
cast—hurl, throw, deposit
cheer—applaud, acclaim, encore
circumvent—frustrate, thwart, outwit
damage—harm, injure, impair
debar—check, obstruct, hinder
decline—wane, weaken, retrograde
dedicate—consecrate, devote, inscribe
defeat—refute, rebut, silence
define—explain, construe, expound
eclipse—obscure, cloud, conceal
educate—instruct, enlighten, edify
elude—evade, baffle, dodge
embarrass—hamper, encumber, complicate
falter—waver, vacillate, stagger
forecast—foretell, prophesy, project
gather—pick, pluck, cull
get—obtain, procure, gain
go—operate, work, run
grant—give, allot, bestow
hamper—obstruct, encumber, fetter
ignore—disregard, slight, omit
illustrate—exemplify, elucidate, explain
jostle—push, elbow, shove
last—wear, endure, continue
manage — handle, conduct, manipulate
narrate—relate, tell, recite
observe—respect, obey, follow
perplex—bewilder, disconcert, distract
quell—calm, quiet, still
ramble—stroll, saunter, wander
scatter—dispel, disperse, sow

BUILDING YOUR VOCABULARY 69

tamper—meddle, interfere, alter
understand — perceive, sense, learn
venture—risk, hazard, dare
withdraw—retreat, retire, depart
yearn—long, covet, crave
yield—concede, allow, acknowledge

ADJECTIVES WITH THEIR SYNONYMS

abject—degraded, despicable, vile
absolute—unrestricted, unqualified, unconditional
abundant — ample, plentiful, copious
admirable — excellent, commendable, estimable
alert—quick, prompt, spry
ambitious — aspiring, soaring, zealous
ancient—antique, archaic, antiquated
bad—wicked, sinful, imperfect
base—impure, debased, counterfeit
bashful—timid, shy, diffident
beneficial — valuable, helpful, salutary
best—choice, rare, exquisite
brisk—quick, nimble, alert
calm—impassive, placid, serene
candid — artless, unaffected, frank
capable—proficient, competent, qualified
captious—faultfinding, carping, hypercritical
careless—easygoing, nonchalant, heedless
charitable—generous, unselfish, liberal
dainty—pretty, exquisite, delicate
deep—profound, bottomless, abstruse
defective—faulty, bruised, deficient
definite—positive, clear, plain
delicious—pleasing, dainty, delectable
delightful—charming, enjoyable, attractive
earnest—zealous, fervent, ardent
easy—untroubled, unconcerned, comfortable
eccentric—odd, peculiar, irregular
elaborate—complicated, studied, finished
fabulous—extravagant, incredible, mythical
fantastic—unreal, illusory, fanciful
faulty—imperfect, defective, deficient
firm—rigid, solid, fast
fleet—swift, brief, evanescent
gay—blithe, lively, merry
genuine—sincere, frank, unaffected
glaring—brilliant, intense, dazzling
habitual—customary, usual, regular
harmful—injurious, detrimental, damaging

illustrious—famous, distinguished, eminent

just—impartial, fair, equitable

kind—benign, forbearing, generous

languid — listless, sluggish, heavy

main — foremost, leading, prime

natural—regular, normal, unaffected

obstinate—headstrong, perverse, firm

powerful — effective, strong, cogent

questionable—undecided, problematical, inconceivable

random — casual, accidental, haphazard

sarcastic — satirical, sardonic, cynical

talkative—loquacious, garrulous, chattering

unbiased—unprejudiced, uninfluenced, impartial

vague — obscure, ill-defined, ambiguous

woeful—wretched, deplorable, lamentable

young — youthful, juvenile, childlike

zealous—earnest, ardent, willing

Adverbs with Their Synonyms

above—overhead, on high, up

after—behind, aft, back

airily — breezily, vivaciously, gaily

almost—nearly, all but, approximately

also—likewise, too, furthermore

apart—asunder, alone, aloof

away—absent, elsewhere, out

before — forward, foremost, ahead

below—inferior, subordinate, beneath

beneath—under, down, below

besides—further, also, moreover

beyond—far, farther, yonder

commonly — generally, usually, equally

down—under, below, underneath

downright — bluntly, plainly, completely

easily—smoothly, readily

eminently — pre-eminently, supremely, notably

ever — perpetually, incessantly, always

exactly—precisely, absolutely, flat

far—widely, remotely, afar

forcibly—necessarily, perforce, by force

forever — always, eternally, constantly

formerly—heretofore, previously, of old

frontwards—forward, onward, before

gradually—by degrees, little by little

hardly—scarcely, rarely, barely

heartily—cordially, sincerely, earnestly
hence—therefore, so, thence
here—hither, hereabouts, in this place
hereafter—ultimately, eventually, subsequently
immediately—speedily, forthwith, straightway
immoderately—excessively, inordinately, extremely
less—to a smaller extent, not so much
meantime—meanwhile, in the interim
merely—simply, barely, solely
modestly—diffidently, demurely, quietly
notwithstanding — nevertheless, yet, although
now—at present, immediately, at this moment
nowise—noway, in no manner, not at all
offhand—impromptu, extempore

often—repeatedly, frequently, oftentimes
over—by, past, across
overhead—above, aloft, up
partially—partly, incompletely, somewhat
partly—partially, incompletely, somewhat
perhaps—haply, by chance, peradventure
posthaste—rashly, headforemost, apace
profitably—beneficially, productively, advantageously
quiet—wholly, completely, totally
rather—slightly, fairly, somewhat
since—subsequently, after, afterward
singly—individually, severally, separately
then—therefore, wherefore, consequently
very—extremely, exceedingly, absolutely

Nouns with Their Synonyms

abode—dwelling, lodging, residence
accident—mishap, casualty, mischance
admonition—warning, caution, exhortation
agony—torture, torment, suffering
allegiance—loyalty, obedience, homage
anecdote—tale, story, narrative
appeal—petition, prayer, entreaty

barrier—obstacle, impediment, fence
barter—exchange, truck, trade
beggar—solicitor, suppliant, mendicant
benefit—gain, profit, advantage
birth—origin, genesis, creation
calamity—disaster, affliction, casualty
caliber—gauge, bore, diameter
capacity—space, room, size
carriage—bearing, mien, demeanor

champion—defender, supporter, backer

competence—ability, proficiency, capability

confirmation—ratification, corroboration, verification

decision—purpose, resolve, decree

deed—performance, feat, exploit

defect—fault, flaw, imperfection

definition—meaning, explanation, description

disgust—offend, nauseate, repel

eagerness—zeal, ardor, enthusiasm

egotism—self-conceit, self-exaltation, vanity

emergency—crisis, necessity, exigency

fame—glory, distinction, reputation

fantasy—dream, illusion, fancy

foreboding—apprehension, dread, presentiment

fright—alarm, dread, terror

glory—grandeur, magnificence, brilliancy

grandeur—eminence, loftiness, stateliness

grievance—wrong, injustice, injury

happiness—felicity, bliss, rapture

impediment—obstruction, difficulty, obstacle

joy—delight, elation, gladness

kindness—benignity, graciousness, gentleness

knickknack—gewgaw, trinket, bauble

labor—work, toil, drudgery

lawlessness—unruliness, disorderliness

maze—labyrinth, network, perplexity

need—want, lack, requirement

noise—din, clamor, uproar

objection—criticism, exception, barrier

partiality—predilection, preference, bias

query—question, issue, problem

rebate—decrement, discount, decrease

satisfaction—amends, compensation, indemnification

tedium—tiresomeness, irksomeness, monotony

usurpation—assumption, seizure, dispossession

vacillation—irresolution, indecision, faltering

vivacity—animation, energy, liveliness

worry—care, anxiety, solicitude

yarn—story, tale, anecdote

zest—exhilaration, enjoyment, gusto

Master 14,000 Words

Many words in the English language are derived from the Latin and Greek languages. A knowledge of Latin and Greek roots, together with an acquaintanceship with some of the common prefixes and suffixes, is of great value in helping to increase one's knowledge of words.

A prefix consists of one or more letters or syllables combined with the beginning of a word to modify its meaning. "Mono" means *one, single,* or *alone;* this prefix helps you to understand "monoplane," "monopoly," "monologue," and "monograph." "Bi" means *two* or *doubly.* "Bi" is found in "bicycle," "bisect," "biannual," "bifocals," and "biped."

A suffix is similar to a prefix except it is used to end a word. For example, "graph" means *"to write," "something written,"* or a *"writing."* We find, therefore, such words as "telegraph," "autograph," "monograph," and "paragraph."

In an article on "Reading and Vocabulary," [1] James I. Brown has given the following interesting and profitable account of methods used at the University of Minnesota to increase greatly a student's vocabulary.

Would you like a way of getting acquainted with words, a thousand at a time?

A few minutes with each of the following fourteen words will help you master well over 14,000 words. These words, the most important in the language to speed you along a superhighway toward vocabulary and success, do even more. They furnish invaluable background for further word study and give you a technique, a master key, which has endless possibilities.

You see, most of our English words are not English at all, but borrowings from another language. Eighty per cent of these borrowed words come to us from Latin and Greek and make up approximately sixty per cent of our language.

Since this is so, the most important of these classical elements offer amazingly useful short cuts to a bigger vocabulary. The words in the list below contain twelve of the most important Latin roots, two of the most important Greek roots, and twenty of the most frequently used prefixes. Over 14,000 relatively common words, words of

---

[1] By permission. From "Reading and Vocabulary," by James I. Brown, first published in *Word Study,* copyright, 1949, by G. & C. Merriam Co.

Collegiate Dictionary size, contain one or more of these elements (or an estimated 100,000 from *Webster's New International*). (See table on page 75)

Now, how convert these words into keys to thousands of related words?

First, look up each word in the dictionary, noticing the varied relationships possible between derivation and definition.

Then look up each prefix. The dictionary entry will help fix meanings in mind and will often indicate assimilative changes.

Next, quickly list at least ten words containing the prefix, checking each with the dictionary to avoid mistakes. Some prefixes are as changeable as chameleons. *Com-* sometimes appears as *con-*stant, *cor-*relation, *col-*laboration, or *coun-cil*, to mention a few. That establishes a background for understanding similar changes in such prefixes as *sub-*, *ob-*, *ex-*, and others.

Now list at least ten words containing the root, checking each carefully with the dictionary. Try to discover less common forms by some intelligent guessing.

Take a root *plicare* as found in *complication*. It is relatively simple to think of *application*, *implication*, and *duplication*. But did *duplication* suggest *duplex* and open the way to *perplex* and *complex*? Did *complex* suggest *comply*, *reply*, *imply*, and others? Did *ply* lead to *pliant*, *supple*, *deploy*, and *employ*? Each discovery of a variant form adds to your background and understanding of the large family of words for which that root is key. The dictionary keeps guesses in line with facts.

So much for method.

Suggestions were then given for using this knowledge to improve spelling and supplement contextual clues to word meanings. Knowing only part of a word often opens the way to a definition. A student reading of a man's *pre-dilection* for novels need only notice the *pre-* to assume that novels are placed "befor " other books; that the man has a "preference" or "partiality" for novels.

The conclusion was that study of these fourteen words might arouse a curiosity about derivations that would

BUILDING YOUR VOCABULARY 75

THE FOURTEEN WORDS
Keys to the meanings of over 14,000 words

Words	Prefix	Derivations Common meaning	Root	Common meaning
1. Precept	pre-	(before)	capere	(take, seize)
2. Detain	de-	(away, from)	tenere	(hold, have)
3. Intermittent	inter-	(between)	mittere	(send)
4. Offer	ob-	(against)	ferre	(bear, carry)
5. Insist	in-	(into)	stare	(stand)
6. Monograph	mono-	(alone, one)	graphein	(write)
7. Epilogue	epi-	(upon)	legein	(say, study of)
8. Aspect	ad-	(to, towards)	spacere	(see)
9. Uncomplicated	un-	(not)	plicare	(fold)
	com-	(together with)		
10. Nonextended	non-	(not)	tendere	(stretch)
	ex-	(out of)		
11. Reproduction	re-	(back, again)	ducere	(lead)
	pro-	(forward)		
12. Indisposed	in-	(not)	ponere	(put, place)
	dis-	(apart from)		
13. Oversufficient	over-	(above)	facere	(make, do)
	sub-	(under)		
14. Mistranscribe	mis-	(wrong)	scribere	(write)
	trans-	(across, beyond)		

bring words to life and lead to an awareness and understanding of words reached by relatively few.

How well you build your vocabulary depends on you. If you wish a mastery of words that will enable you to express yourself clearly and effectively, the objective is not too difficult to attain. The time to begin is today.

Chapter VII

FIGURES OF SPEECH AND OTHER SPEECH TOOLS

IN THIS chapter there are presented a number of speech tools, speech ideas, and figures of speech—both good and bad—with which one who wishes to talk well should be thoroughly familiar.

METAPHORS

A metaphor is defined by the *Oxford Universal English Dictionary* as a "figure of speech in which a name or descriptive term is transferred to some object to which it is not properly applicable." *Webster's Collegiate Dictionary* gives as an illustration, "the ship *plows* the sea." Here an agricultural term is transferred to apply to a ship. Aristotle in the *Poetics* said that "the greatest thing in style is to have a command of metaphor . . . it is a mark of genius, for to make good metaphors implies an eye for resemblances." Joseph Addison, writing in the *Spectator* in 1712, said, "A noble metaphor, when it is placed to an advantage, casts a kind of glory round it, and darks a lustre through a whole sentence." One hears daily the use of such metaphors as "Henry's girl is a peach, but he's an egg." Metaphors can be employed effectively to give color to conversation and speeches.

To describe a situation in which a person faces many difficulties we may use the metaphor "The candidate for

FIGURES OF SPEECH & OTHER SPEECH TOOLS

governor had two strikes against him." In this sentence we applied a baseball term to a political candidate. We often speak also of someone "muffing the ball" when the situation has nothing to do with baseball. Someone may also "blow off steam," thereby taking on the quality of a steam engine.

Illustrations of Metaphors

Thou art the grave where buried love doth live. *Shakespeare*

The world is an old woman, and mistakes any gilt farthing for a gold coin. *Carlyle*

The day is done, and the darkness falls from the wings of Night. *Longfellow*

All the world's a stage. *Shakespeare*

Juliet is the sun. *Shakespeare*

Moneys are the sinews of war. *Fuller*

Music is the moonlight in the gloomy night of life. *Richter*

You may often change a metaphor into a simile by the use of "as" or "like." "John is a sly fox" is a metaphor. "John is like a sly fox," or "John is as sly as a fox," is a simile. In a simile one thing, action, or relation is likened or explicitly compared to something of different kind or quality. "As" and "like" are often used to make the comparison.

Confused or Mixed Metaphors

One must be very careful not to confuse or mix metaphors. In a mixed metaphor two or more ideas which are dissimilar or incompatible are brought together. The effect is confusing. You may remember Shakespeare asks in Hamlet's soliloquy whether it is nobler to suffer "the slings and arrows of outrageous fortune, or to take arms against a sea of troubles." His "take arms against a sea of troubles" is a mixed metaphor, but his language is so powerful that one may overlook the mixed metaphor.

One of the best-known mixed metaphors is found in a speech given in the Irish Parliament by Sir Boyle Roche about 1790. He said, "Mr. Speaker, I smell a rat. I see him floating in the air. But mark me, sir, I will nip him in the bud." Addison also mixed his metaphors when he said:

> I bridle in my struggling muse with pain
> That longs to launch into a bolder strain.

Here Addison combines a horse (bridle), a ship (launch), and music (strain). That's a good trick if you can do it.

Hyperbole

Webster's Collegiate Dictionary defines a hyperbole as an "extravagant exaggeration of statement: a statement exaggerated fancifully, as for effect." It is not intended that it will be taken literally. In his *Rhetoric*, Aristotle said, "Hyperboles are the peculiar property of young men; they betray a vehement nature." It would, however, be extremely difficult to prove that hyperboles are the peculiar property of young men or that they betray a vehement nature.

To illustrate the use of the hyperbole, you may say, "The dahlias were as tall as telephone poles." The dahlias may have been very tall, but hardly as tall as telephone poles. In the first verse of the Ninth Chapter of Deuteronomy, the author speaks of "cities great and fenced up to heaven." We also find in the Bible, in the twenty-fifth verse of the Twenty-first Chapter of St. John, the statement that "even the world itself could not contain the books that should be written." You may remember Mark Twain once wrote, "I scratch my head with lightning and purr myself to sleep with the thunder! When I'm cold, I bile the Gulf of Mexico and bathe in it." In these illustrations the authors are attempting to obtain the effect they wish by overstatement.

In his *Comus*, Milton says:

> I was all ear,
> And took in strains that might create a soul
> Under the ribs of death.

Note the exaggeration, "I was all ear." Yet the expression conveys the idea Milton wishes to give the reader. Such exaggeration is clearly not intended to be taken literally and often provides an effective figure of speech. It gives emphasis to an idea, but it must not be used repeatedly in conversation or it becomes tiresome and even leads one to question the truth of the speaker's other comments.

Here are several common illustrations of boring exaggerations: "Girls, the boss drives me crazy. He opens the window for ventilation, and I freeze to death. I have to go to lunch late and I get so hungry I could die. Sometimes he complains and growls so over small errors I'm scared stiff to ask him a question." In only four sentences this person was crazy, died, almost died, and was scared stiff, which would make the person a poor risk for any insurance company and a boring conversationalist.

Tautology

Webster's Collegiate Dictionary defines tautology as "needless repetition of meaning in other words," and gives as an example "audible to the ear." It could obviously not be audible in any other way!

The unnecessary repetition of a thought in different words should be carefully avoided. One of the most common illustrations of careless wordiness is the expression "this here." "This here book is mine" is wrong. Correct: "This book is mine." You would not say, "That would leave me with fifty cents left." You would say, "That would leave me fifty cents," or "I should still have fifty cents."

The following cases are typical instances of tautological expressions. The correct expressions are given in the column at the right.

Needless Repetition   *Correct*

Needless Repetition	Correct
ascend up	ascend
descend down	descend
modern houses of today	modern houses or houses of today

mingle together	mingle
eat up	eat
connect up	connect
consolidate together	consolidate
small in size	small
study up	study
swallow down	swallow
follow after	follow
meet up with	meet
many frequent	many or frequent
repeat again	repeat
repay back	repay

You will find it helpful now to correct the following tautologies:

circulated around	you all
discuss about	we all
divide up	just exactly
new beginner	three P.M. in the afternoon
link together	drink it up
as a usual rule	visible to the eye
more easier	mix together
large in size	recall back
hurry up	polish up
still continue	return back
adequate enough	revive again

"Back," "again," "up," "down," and "together" are often found in tautologies. If you wish to speak clearly and to the point, eliminate needless words.

IDIOMS

The *New College Standard Dictionary* defines an idiom as "a use of words peculiar to a particular language, especially if it be an irregularity." It cites such illustrations as "to come by," which means "obtain," and "to put up with," which means to "tolerate" or "endure." Idioms or idiomatic phrases are often figures of speech peculiar to a people or nation and sometimes to particular groups of persons or sections of a country. Idioms may even be characteristic of an author.

We recognize idioms more easily in other languages because they frequently do not follow the regular rules of grammar of the language. Imagine the difficulty of trying to explain to a person learning English the meaning of the words "It goes without saying," or "follow at close hand." An American might have some difficulty understanding why a Frenchman says, "It makes cold" instead of "It is cold." How would you explain "How do you do" to a foreigner or the difference between "upset" and "set up"?

Idioms find their way into a language from such sources as occupations, sports, the arts, and various types of activity. The sources of the following idioms are shown:

From farming

To let the grass grow under you feet
To put your hand to the plough
To live in clover

From sports

To be bowled over
To have your innings
To strike out

From the ocean

To be in the same boat
To put in your oar
To sail into someone
To stem the tide

From horses

To work like a horse
To put the cart before the horse

From birds

To be in fine feather
A swan song
A lark

From the Bible

Milk and honey
A thorn in the flesh
The wages of sin
The blind leading the blind
A voice in the wilderness

From dogs

To lead a dog's life
To go to the dogs
To let sleeping dogs lie

From soldiers

To draw someone's fire
To beat a retreat
To pass muster
Between two fires

From the head

    To have a swelled head
    To keep one's head
    To lose one's head

From poultry

    Like water off a duck's back
    A bad egg
    A lame duck

From music

    To blow your own horn
    To be fit as a fiddle
    To pay the piper

From the Weather

    To blow hot and cold
    To praise to the skies
    To be under a cloud

There are hundreds of idioms. They help to make a language rich and colourful. They may make conversation and speeches interesting. A careful student of the art of conversation and speech will avoid, however, many idioms because they have become hackneyed and overworked. For example, "To work like a horse" or "to blow your own horn" are used far too frequently.

ALLITERATION

Alliteration simply means repeating the same sound at the beginning of two or more consecutive words or of words near one another. Alliteration gives style to conversation provided—and this is important—it is not overdone. Swinburne used it in the sentence, "The *lisp* of *leaves,* and the *ripple* of *rain.*" Pope spoke of "Apt alliteration's artful aid." G. K. Chesterton often used alliteration effectively, and Winston Churchill is also a master of it. Few Americans, if any, in recent years have been the equal of Glenn Frank in his manipulation of alliteration.

ILLUSTRATIONS OF ALLITERATION

Penny wise, pound foolish.
The winnowing wind. *Keats*
Merger of radical politics and reactionary economics. *Glenn Frank.*

FIGURES OF SPEECH & OTHER SPEECH TOOLS

In a somer seson when soft was the sonne. *The Vision of Piers Plowman*
So many fashionable fallacies still stand firmly on their feet. *Chesterton*
The fair breeze blew, the white foam flew.
The furrow followed free. *Ancient Mariner*
A social revolution or a spiritual reversal. *Glenn Frank*
This mood of panic and patent-medicine politics must pass. *Glenn Frank*

Ellipsis

Ellipsis means the omission of one or more words, which are understood but are necessary to make an expression grammatically complete. Such omissions are frequent and are permissible in conversation as we use facial expressions, gestures, and tone to help make our meaning clear. In writing, however, care is necessary to be certain the meaning of an expression is obvious when words are omitted. Examples: "Tired?" meaning, "Are you tired?" "Hungry?" "Not now." These expressions obviously mean, "Are you hungry?" "I am not hungry now."

Euphemism

Euphemism is the use of an expression which is considered unobjectionable or mild compared to one that offends, is harsh or unpleasant. A common illustration is the use of "passed away," "gone to his reward," "gone to his rest," and "called home" for "dead." One must be careful not to use such substitution too freely or conversation will seem affected.

Verbosity

Verbosity means wordiness or the use of more words than are needed to express one's thoughts. In *Love's Labour Lost*, Shakespeare said, "He draweth out the thread of his verbosity finer than the staple of his argument."

One may use eight words to say, "There were ten men who built the wall." One may express the same thought effectively with only five words. "Ten men built the wall." The British Ministry of Health once reported "a cessation of house-building operation over a period of five years." A member of Parliament criticized such wordiness and remarked that it was sufficient to say, "No houses had been built in five years."

ANTITHESIS

Antithesis means an opposition or contrast of ideas. The *Oxford Universal English Dictionary* gives as an illustration, "*Thou* shalt *wax* and *he* shall *dwindle*."

Macaulay speaks of the old Cavaliers who had turned *demagogues* and the successors of the old Roundheads who had turned *courtiers*. One may say: "He came to *criticize* the work, but he remained to *praise* it." "It is a question of *life* or *death*." "In one face there was *hope*, and in the other *despair*." "This man was no *patriot*; he was a *traitor*."

By the use of this figure of speech we are often able to make striking and dramatic comparisons.

IRONY

Irony is a figure of speech in which the words mean the exact opposite of what is said. Irony may be used for ridicule, humor, or light sarcasm. A golf player misses the ball and you may say, "Henry, you made a very good shot." What you meant was that Henry made a poor shot. The use of irony in conversation may help you to lose friends and alienate people if you are not careful with whom and how you use it.

In *Julius Caesar*, when Shakespeare has Mark Antony say over Caesar's dead body, "For Brutus is an honourable man," he was using irony very effectively. When Job, speaking to his friends, said, "No doubt but ye are the people, and wisdom shall die with you," he was also using irony with striking effect. Billie is told to weed the

FIGURES OF SPEECH & OTHER SPEECH TOOLS 85

garden. He forgets to do it. Mother says, "Billie, I think the garden looks beautiful since you weeded it." Mother knows that is irony. So does Billie.

SARCASM

Sarcasm is not often spoken of now as a figure of speech. Whereas irony is frequently used as a means of expressing wit and light humor, sarcasm may have humor, but it is bitter and cutting. It may contain a rebuke. It is direct and sharp and may express a contemptuous feeling. The word "sarcasm" is derived from the idea of "flesh tearing." In *Sartor Resartus*, Thomas Carlyle said, "Sarcasm I now see to be, in general, the language of the devil."

When Voltaire said, "I know I am among civilized men because they are fighting so savagely," it was sarcasm. It would be considered sarcasm if you said, "We shall ask Mrs. Blank to explain the problems of the illiterate person, as she can speak from personal experience."

METONYMY

Metonymy is a figure of speech in which a word is used for another that it suggests or to which it is closely related. One may say, "Gray hair often tends to assure good judgment." By "gray hair" the speaker means "age" or "experience." When we say, "The *pen* is mightier than the *sword*," we mean the words and thoughts of men are mightier and accomplish more than war.

PUN

Webster's Collegiate Dictionary defines a pun as "a play on words of the same sound but different meanings or on different applications of a word, for the witty effect." Puns are found in both verse and prose. Punning was common in Shakespeare's time, and Shakespeare used the pun in his writing. Charles Lamb (1775-1834), Douglas Jerrold

(1803-1857), and Humbert Wolf (1885-1940) all used the pun.

Alexander Pope said, "He that would pun would pick a pocket," but Charles Lamb wrote, "A pun is a noble thing *per se*. It fills the mind; it is as perfect as a sonnet; better." Oscar Levant made this significant comment on punning, "A pun is the lowest form of humor—when you don't think of it first."

ILLUSTRATIONS OF PUNS

Ed Wynn, well-known American comedian, gave a good illustration of a pun in his comment, "A bun is the lowest form of wheat"—with his use of "bun" for "pun" and "wheat" for "wit."

A student spelled the word "weather" w h e t h e r. The teacher said, "That's the worst spell of weather we have had in years."

An old pun is the epigram:

> And in her wondrous eyes
> Love lies—and lies and lies.

Many human geese fall for a quack.

The dentist always has a drawing room in his suite of rooms.

The poor old man asked me for five dollars and I was touched.

The admiral knew gobs and gobs of men in the navy.

A college student swallowed a live frog on a dare and the doctor thought he might croak.

The four daughters called their mother "the mater." She found husband's for all of them.

A pun is most effective at the time when it strikes one.

Chapter VIII

TWO HUNDRED SIMILES

Absurd as giving bread-pills for a broken leg. *Kipling*
Adorable as is nothing save a child. *Swinburne*
Adventurous as a bee. *Wordsworth*
As excited as an eight-year-old boy at a five-ring circus. *Herbert V. Prochnow*

> Sweet are the uses of adversity,
> Which, like the toad, ugly and venomous,
> Wears yet a precious jewel in his head. *Shakespeare*

Affable as a wet dog. *Alfred Henry Lewis*

> Like mist upon the lea,
> And like night upon the plain,
> Old age comes o'er that heart. *Robert Nicol*

> Aimless as an autumn leaf
> Borne in November's idle winds afar. *P. H. Hayne*

> Amazed, as one that unaware
> Hath dropp'd a precious jewel in the flood.
> *Shakespeare*

Ambition is like hunger; it obeys no law but its appetite. *Josh Billings*

To reach the height of our ambition is like trying to reach the rainbow; as we advance it recedes. *W. T. Burke*
As barren of important news as the society column of a newspaper. *Herbert V. Prochnow*
As ambitious as Lady Macbeth. *James Hunekar*
April is like a child that smiles in waking. *Hugo*

> She walked in flowers around my fields
> As June herself around the sphere. *Emerson*

Avarice is like a graveyard; it takes all that it can get and gives nothing back. *Josh Billings*

Away, like wild pigeons startled in the wood. *Euripides*

Awful as the last trump that shall proclaim to mankind the end of the world. *Anatole France*

Beautiful as is the rose in June. *Emerson*

Her face as beautiful as though the rays of Paradise were there. *Sadi*

Blue as the overhanging heaven. *Shelly*

With all his tumid boasts, he's like the sword-fish, who only wears his weapon in his mouth. *Samuel Madden*

A house without books is like a room without windows. *Henry Ward Beecher*

His face was an expressionless as a concrete pavement *Herbert V. Prochnow*

> As the fading of a flower.
> As the falling of a leaf,
> So brief its day and its hour. *C. G. Rossetti*

Bright as fair sunshine after winter's storms. *Aeschylus*

Like a star glancing out from the blue of the sky! *Whittier*

Brisk as bees that settle on a summer rose's petal. *C. S. Calverley*

Brisk as a body louse. *Swift*

Brittle as glass that breaks with a touch. *Swinburne*

Calm as an autumn night. *Lord De Tabley*

> As calm as evening when caressed
> By twilight breezes from the west. *Sam Walter Foss*

> Calm as a child to slumber soothed,
> As if an Angel's hand had smoothed
> The still, white features into rest. *Whittier*

Careless as the young flower tossing on the summer breeze. *Ouida*

Catching like fire in dry grass. *W. D. Howells*

Exacting as a senior clerk. *Balzac*

Exhaustless as the ocean. *Ouida*

Expanded like the face of the sun when it mounts above the eastern hill. *Jeremy Taylor*

Human experience, like the stern lights of a ship at sea, too often illuminates only the path we have passed over. *Coleridge*

TWO HUNDRED SIMILES

Her eyes were like a butterfly's gorgeous wings. *James Lane Allen*

Languishing eyes like those of a roe looking tenderly at her young. *Amrilkais*

Eyes like live coals. *Dumas pere*

The eyes are the pioneers that first announce the soft tale of love. *Propertius*

An eye like Mars, to threaten and command. *Shakespeare*

> How brilliant and mirthful the light of her eye,
> Like a star glancing out from the blue of the sky.
> *Whittier*

A face like a smoked herring. *Anatole France*

He worked harder than a man with one tooth trying to eat an olive. *From a radio program by Fred Allen*

> Her little face is like a walnut shell
> With wrinkling lines. *W. E. Henley*

> Her face like roses blown,
> And in the radiance and the hush,
> Her thought was shown. *Jean Ingelow*

His face is like a squeezed orange. *Ben Jonson*

'Tis not that she paints so ill but, when she has finished her face she joins so badly to her neck, that she looks like a mended statue, in which the connoisseur may see at once that the head is modern, though the trunk's antique. *R. B. Sheridan*

Faith, like light, should ever be simple and unbending, *Martin Luther*

Faith is like a lily lifted high and white. *C. G. Rossetti*

> Like a leaf that quits the bough,
> The mortal vesture falls. *O. W. Holmes*

Like a city without walls, the grandeur of the mortal falls who glories in his strength and makes not God his trust. *Macaulay*

Fast as autumn days toward winter. *Swinburne*

Fearlessly, like a happy child, too innocent to fear. *Southey*

Fresher than berries of a mountain-tree. *Keats*

Full as the summer rose. *James Thomson*

Harmless as the murmur of a mountain stream. *Herbert V. Prochnow*

Lingering gaze, like a peacock whose eyes are inclined to his tail. *Hood*

More gentle than the wind in summer. *Keats*

The glance of the eyes like the fawn's soft gaze. *Arabian Nights*

A glance like the sunshine that flashes on steel. *Whittier*

> Like shuttles through the loom, so swiftly glide
> My feather'd hours. *George Sandys*

Glimmer like a star in autumn's hazy night. *William Cullen Bryant*

Gold, like the sun, which melts wax and hardens clay, expands great souls and contracts bad hearts. *Rivarol*

> Gone was every trace of sorrow,
> As the fog from off the river,
> As the mist from off the meadow. *Longfellow*

> Like the dew on the mountain,
> Like the foam on the river,
> Like the bubble on the fountain
> Thou art gone, and forever. *Sir Walter Scott*

Gone, like the summer lightning's gleam. *Frank Waters*

Graceful as the willow-bough o'er the streamlet weeping. *Lover*

She is graceful as the greenly waving boughs in summer wind. *Gerald Massey*

Grim as a Swiss guard. *Robert Browning*

Groaned

> Like some sad prophet that foresaw the doom
> Of those whom best he loved, and could not save.
> *Dryden*

Groaneth, like a door on rusty hinges. *Tupper*

Grow like weeds on a neglected tomb. *Shelley*

His heart

> Gush'd like a river-fountain of the hills,
> Ceaseless and lavish, at a kindly smile,
> A word of welcome, or a tone of love. *Whittier*

A baby's hands, like rosebuds furled. *Swinburne*
Hung like an icicle on a Dutchman's beard. *Shakespeare*
Happy as a fish in water. *Victor Cherbuliez*
As restful as the quiet murmur of a hidden brook. *Herbert V. Prochnow*

Happy as birds that sing on a tree. *Sir James Carnegie*

Happy as the Bird whose nest
Is heaven'd in the heart of purple hills. *Gerald Massey*

Harmless as the turtle-dove. *Patrick Bronte*
Harsh as truth. *William Lloyd Garrison*
Haunts like a wild melody. *Thomas Moore*
Vex and haunt me like a tale of my own future destiny. *Schiller*
Health is like munny, we never hav a true idea ov its value until we lose it. *Josh Billings*

My heart is like the fair sea-shell,
There's music ever in it. *Eliza Cook*

Heart as calm as lakes that sleep,
In frosty moonlight glistening. *Wordsworth*

Heavy as remembered sin
That will not suffer sleep or thought to ease. *Kipling*

Helpless as a turtle on its back. *O. Henry*
Hesitating like a bather about to make his plunge. *Thomas Hardy*
Higher than the price ov gold. *Josh Billings*
As hollow as an egg shell. *P. J. Bailey*
Hope is like the sun, which, as we journey towards it, casts the shadow of our burden behind us. *Samuel Smiles*
A house without woman or firelight is like a body without soul or spirit. *Franklin*
Howled like a pack of famished dogs. *Lamartine*

Happy as a cat with a pan of fresh milk. *Herbert V. Prochnow*

Hushed, as in waiting for a bird to sing. *Richard Hovey*
How close-packed the mob is, they hustle like a herd of swine. *Theocritus*
Ideas are like beards; men do not have them until they grow up. *Voltaire*

As idle as a dial when the sun
Sulks in the clouds. *Alfred Austin*

Immovable, as if it were painted on the wall. *Hawthorne*
Impassive as the copper head on a penny. *Kipling*
Truth is as impossible to be soiled by any outward touch as the sunbeam. *Milton*
Independence, like honor, is a rocky island without a beach. *Napoleon*
Indestructible as are the stars. *Schiller*
Indifferent as rain. *G. K. Chesterton*
Indolent as a lazy breeze of midsummer. *James Whitcomb Riley*

> A small drop of ink,
> Falling like dew, upon a thought, produces that which makes thousands, perhaps millions, think. *Byron*

Innumerable as the stars of night. *Milton*
Intermittently, like the click of a blind man's cane. *Irvin S. Cobb*
Invisible as thought. *George Eliot*
Jingle like a crate of broken crockery. *W. J. Locke*
Joyfully as the shepherd bears a strayed lamb to the fold. *Charles Reade*

> 'Tis with our judgments as our watches,—none
> Go just alike, yet each believes his own. *Pope*

Lasting as the pyramids. *Agnes Repplier*
Her laff is like a singin' brook that bubbles as it passes. *Sam Walter Foss*
Gave a short laugh like the closing of a padlock. *O. Henry*
He laughed like the screech of a rusty hinge. *James Whitcomb Riley*
Laziness is a good deal like money—the more a man has of it, the more he seems to want. *Josh Billings*
Light as cobwebs. *R. D. Blackmore*
Light as winds that stir the willow. *Alice Cary*

> My life is like the summer rose
> That opens in the morning sky,
> But, ere the shades of evening close,
> Is scattered on the ground—to die. *R. H. Wilde*

A quiet smile played around his lips,
As the eddies and dimples of the tide play round the bows
　of ships. *Longfellow*

Hard as the palm of a dock worker. *Herbert V. Prochnow*

Lively as a squirrel. *O. W. Holmes*

She looks like an old coach new painted, affecting an unseemly smugness, whilst she is ready to drop to pieces. *Vanbrugh*

　　　Hang loose about him, like a giant's robe
　　　　Upon a dwarfish thief. *Shakespeare*

Love, like death, levels all ranks and lays the shepherd's crook beside the sceptre. *Bulwer-Lytton*

Love's like the measles—all the worse when it comes late in life. *Douglas Jerrold*

Love, like death, makes all distinction void. *Mathew Prior*

Lovely as the budding rose. *Southey*

Man is like a tree which is shaken that its fruit may drop to the ground. *Lamartine*

Mean as dust, and dead as dreams. *William Watson*

Marriage to maids is like a war to men; the battle causes fear, but the sweet hope of winning at the last still draws them on. *Nathaniel Lee*

Meek as a saint. *Pope*

　　　A melancholy strain,
　　　　Like the low moaning of the distant sea. *Poe*

Melt away into the darkness like a snowflake in the water. *Hugo*

Merry as a kitten. *Burns*

Merry as a marriage bell. *Byron*

Merry as birds on the bough. *Frederick the Great*

Mild as any lamb that ever pastured in the fields. *Dickens*

A wise man's mind, as Seneca holds, is like the state of the world above the Moon, ever serene. *Robert Burton*

A weak mind is like a microscope, which magnifies trifling things, but cannot receive great ones. *Chesterfield*

　　　Moan, like the voice of one who crieth
　　　　In the wilderness alone. *Longfellow*

A wild and desolate moan,
As a sea heart-broken on the hard brown stone.
Joaquin Miller

Modest as the violet in dewy dell. *F. A. Fahy*

She mourns, like the sweet wind grieving in
The pines on an autumn night. *Barry Cornwall*

Murmured like a whispering priest. *Aubrey de Vere*
Murmur like the wind in the leaves. *Mary Johnston*
As mute and motionless as statues. *Goldsmith*
Make a noise like an assessment. *O. Henry*
Noiseless as the sunlight. *Thomas Ashe*
Nodded in bright array, like hollyhocks heavy with blossoms. *Longfellow*
Noiseless as night's soft shade. *Aaron Hill*
Obnoxious as an alligator. *Tom Taylor*
Opened inertly like the hands of the dead. *Hugo*
Pale as a moon that moves alone through lonely space. *Alfred Austin*
Passed away like waves. *Hugo*
Little troubles pass like little ripples in a sunny river. *W. S. Landor*

Pass'd by me
As misers do by beggars. *Shakespeare*

Patient as sheep. *Macaulay*
Patient as a gentle stream. *Shakespeare*
Peaceful as summer woods. *George MacDonald*
Plain as the plain bald pate of Father Time himself. *Shakespeare*
Points like death's lean lifted finger. *Robert Browning*
Quiet as a heart that beats no more. *Longfellow*
Rebellious as the sea. *Thomas Heywood*
Red as an angry sunset. *Jean Ingelow*
The reputation of a man is like his shadow; it sometimes follows and sometimes precedes him, sometimes longer and sometimes shorter than his natural size. *French Proverb*
Restless as the sea. *Alfred Austin*
Rose like dust before the whirlwind's force. *Bayard Taylor*

Sad as raindrops on a grave. *George P. Lathrop*
Sad as the tears the sullen Winter weeps. *George MacHenry*
Scared as a jack-rabbit that has heard the howl of a wolf. *Alfred Henry Lewis*
Secure as the firmament. *George Meredith*
Serene as the dawn. *Hugo*
The pile of fish ... shone like a dump of fluid silver. *Kipling*
Ships are like flies in the spider's web of the sea. *Hugo*
A sigh like the long-drawn breath of a fog-horn. *Edgar W. Nye*
Silent as the depth of night. *James Montgomery*

Time

> Slept, as he sleeps upon the silent face
> Of a dark dial in a sunless place. *Hood*

Slowly, as a man in doubt. *E. B. Browning*
Slowly like the heave and roll of a glassy sea. *John C. Van Dyke*
Smiles like a May morning. *Allan Ramsay*
Snarled like an old dog. *Maurice Hewlett*
Soft as moonlight. *Miss Mitford*
Stately as a palm-tree standing before the moon. *George Meredith*
Still as a graveyard. *O. Henry*
Struggled instinctively like an animal under a net. *Joseph Conrad*
Sweet as the song of the wind in the rippling wheat. *Madison Cawein*
Sweet as are the orchards, when the fruit is hanging ripe. *Paul Laurence Dunbar*
Sweet as the twilight notes of the thrush. *Helen H. Jackson*
He talks as a piano-organ grinds out music—steadily, strenuously, tirelessly. *J. K. Jerome*
Tender as a youthful mother's joy. *Southey*
Thick as London fog. *Hood*
Great thoughts, like great deeds, need no trumpet. *P. J. Bailey*
Time is like money; the less we have of it to spare, the further we make it go. *Josh Billings*

Tranquil as a child who goes to gather flowers. *Fernan Caballero*

Twinkling like fireflies in the emerald grass. *Fanny Forester*

Unstained and pure as the lily or the mountain snow. *James Thomson*

Upright as a tower. *Charles Reade*

Useless as to enlarge upon the obvious. *Epictetus*

Vanish like an echo or a dream. *Goethe*

Voice like a coyote with bronchitis. *O. Henry*

A voice like a strained foghorn. *W. W. Jacobs*

Wagging like bell-clappers. *Edward Robins*

Walks like he had gravel in his shoes. *George Ade*

Great warriors, like great earthquakes, are principally remembered for the mischief they have done. *C. N. Bovee*

Weatherbeaten as a fisherman's oar. *Thomas Wade*

White as frost on field. *W. E. Aytoun*

White as the face of the dead. *Camille Lemonnier*

Wrinkled like a last year's apple. *Guy de Maupassant*

Yawn and stretch like a greyhound by the fireside. *Vanbrugh*

Yellow like canned corn. *Carolyn Wells*

Zigzag like lightning. *Southey*

Chapter IX

TWO HUNDRED AND FIFTY HACKNEYED EXPRESSIONS

IF YOU are looking for some way to make conversation dull, memorize the phrases in this chapter and use them repeatedly in your conversation. They are trite, stereotyped expressions. They have died from overwork. They are cliches.

TWO HUNDRED & FIFTY HACKNEYED EXPRESSIONS

If you wish, however, to improve your ability to speak, you will avoid the use of these phrases. Make a list also of other cliches you are using. Study the cliches below carefully to see how many you may be using. All of us are guilty at times of using some of these expressions.

agree to disagree
all work and no play
better late than never
brave as a lion
clear as crystal
Grim Reaper
fools rush in
equal to the occasion
all in all
as luck would have it
course of true love
breathless silence
clinging vine
briny deep
busy as a bee
green as grass
easier said than done
footprints on the sands of Time
enjoyable occasion
partake of refreshments
he-man
order out of chaos
mad as a wet hen
no sooner said than done
royal reception
seething mass of humanity
silence reigned supreme
strong as a lion
the plot thickens
where ignorance is bliss
after all is said and done
budding genius
be that as it may
exception proves the rule
hoping you are the same

none the worse for wear
psychological moment
sadder but wiser
sigh of relief
sturdy as an oak
take my word for it
wee small hours
fine and dandy
doomed to disappointment
filthy lucre
ignorance is bliss
too numerous to mention
tired business man
bitter end
bolt from the blue
sweat of his brow
accidents do happen
age before beauty
alive and kicking
at a tender age
at one's wit's end
at long last
bag and baggage
put it across
die is cast
by and large
last but not least
staff of life
the acid test
adding insult to injury
all in a lifetime
all in the day's work
as a matter of fact
as the crow flies
his better half
you said it

the beginning of the end
better left unsaid
blissful ignorance
bored to death
bright and early
a burning question
by no manner or means
captains of industry
to cry over spilt milk
cut off one's nose to spite one's face
a dead certainty
to beat about the bush
one's better half
between two fires
to bite off more than one can chew
a blessing in disguise
to blow one's own horn
a bone of contention
to break the ice
brute force
by leaps and bounds
by word of mouth
crocodile tears
to make a long story short
to cut to the quick
in deadly earnest
the die is cast
a distinction without a difference
a dog in the manger
each and every one
to engage in conversation
to face the music
far from accurate
a feather in one's cap
to fight tooth and nail
a flash in the pan
a friend in need
generous to a fault
to die in harness

to do or die
done to a turn
dyed in the wool
East is East, and West is West
even if the worst happens
to express one's appreciation
fast and furious
to feather one's nest
few and far between
fit for a king
a fly in the ointment
a foregone conclusion
from bad to worse
give and take
to go to the dogs
the great open spaces
to hit below the belt
if the truth were known
in a nutshell
scared to death
in the last analysis
it might be worse
to keep a stiff upper lip
a land of milk and honey
the last straw
to leave no stone unturned
to let the cat out of the bag
good for nothing
the heart of the matter
to heave a sigh of relief
high and dry
to hit the nail on the head
ill-gotten gains
in less than no time
the incident was closed
an irreparable loss
it hurts me more than it does you
it stands to reason that

TWO HUNDRED & FIFTY HACKNEYED EXPRESSIONS

to keep body and soul together
to be on one's last legs
to lay one's cards on the table
leaves much to be desired
to lend an ear
life in the raw
the long arm of the law
to look for a needle in a haystack
to make hay while the sun shines
the man in the street
monarch of all one surveys
more or less
the naked truth
neither rhyme nor reason
to nip it in the bud
not wisely but too well
of the first water
on more than one occasion
a picture of health
the primrose path
little dreaming that
lock, stock, and barrel
to make no bones about it
the matter is receiving the closest attention
more than meets the eye
the more the merrier
much as I hate to say it
neither here nor there
a new lease on life
not the only pebble on the beach
off the beaten track
on pins and needles
once and for all
a place in the sun
a pretty kettle of fish
rain or shine
really and truly
to ring down the curtain
the salt of the earth
ships that pass in the night
slow but sure
a snake in the grass
sour grapes
spick and span
a step in the right direction
straight from the shoulder
stung to the quick
to take immediate steps
to take the bull by the horns
to talk through one's hat
a red-letter day
the root of all evil
sackcloth and ashes
safe and sound
short and sweet
signed, sealed, and delivered
to sink or swim
to skate on thin ice
to smell a rat
so to speak
to sow one's wild oats
to stem the tide
stranger than fiction
to take with a grain of salt
to tell tales out of school
this vale of tears
through thick and thin
tried and found wanting
to turn over a new leaf
to be up and doing
up to the hilt
to voice an opinion
to walk on air
wear and tear
well-earned rest
when one's ship comes home
with flying colors

words fail me
worked to death
you know what I mean
thanking you in anticipation
to tighten one's belt
to tell the truth
to toe the mark
under the thumb of
up in arms
a vicious circle
when all is said and done
the wide open spaces
to work one's fingers to the bone
worldly wisdom
you could have knocked me down with a feather
at your earliest convenience
fresh as a daisy
smooth as silk
it goes without saying
nipped in the bud
combine business with pleasure
dead as a doornail
skinny as a rail
dressed to kill
took the words out of my mouth
truth is stranger than fiction
permit me to say
hanging in the balance

Chapter X

FOUR HUNDRED EPIGRAMS

FROM the standpoint of cost to you it doesn't make much difference whether you give or lend someone $10.

Indigestion is a term synonymous with wealth.

Money is the only perfect linguist. It speaks all languages.

Many a woman's hat looks like a forced landing of a Blue Plate luncheon or the Chef's Special Tossed Salad.

Diplomacy is the mother of invention.

To make good a person has to be good.

The big idea in golf is not to stand too close to the ball after you have hit it.

A friend is a person who will share your lot with you without asking the size of it.

A reception is a crowd of bored people eating indigestible food and exchanging malicious gossip while they look in vain for the host to whom to express their appreciation.

Nothing makes a man hustle to get ahead like marriage and a family.

Humility is a quality only the great possess.

Life is the only thing a person possesses until he dies.

In booms the buyer gives the sales talk. In depressions the salesman does it.

No man is disillusioned like the one who reaches his goal.

A person who doesn't gossip is one who hasn't heard the rumor.

It's the head of a business who gets the headaches.

Everyone has fun at the fat man's expanse.

When a man says he can't be flattered, he wants you to flatter him by agreeing with him.

Fashion is vanity in reality.

No man is educated, experienced, or wise who has not learned enough about some subject to know how little he knows.

Wars may come and wars may go, but a politician never forgets the new sources of revenue that are discovered.

First you have to teach a child to talk; then you have to teach it to keep quiet.

It looks like eventually we will all make our living by collecting taxes from each other.

A radical is a person who feels he might get a little more if he howled a little louder.

The disgusted professor: "Class is dismissed. Please don't flap your ears as you pass out."

It's remarkable when you think that under the American system a man can have a savings account and an automobile at the same time.

Intelligence tests may be a means of grading intelligence, but there is nothing that equals a grade crossing for effectiveness.

The genius of another world war will be the fellow who figures out how to run it on a cash instead of an accounts-payable basis.

Classical music is music that threatens every other bar to develop a tune and then disappoints you.

The life of man: School tablet, aspirin tablet, stone tablet.

As a rule, government experiments end up with a "please remit" notice to the taxpayer.

The greatest undeveloped resources of any nation are its people.

Gambling is not only a means of getting money for nothing but also of getting nothing for your money.

All you have to do in business is to stand and watch the world go by—and, brother, it sure will.

There is no individual conceit greater than the idea that the world would be perfect if everyone were like us.

It's remarkable how a man can stand up under it when his competitors have hard luck.

When you look for trouble, you don't need a search warrant.

Any government depending upon checks and balances will face trouble if it runs short on balances and long on checks.

There may be a closer relationship between the unread and the Red than we think.

The worst thing about the fellow in the end seat is that he got there before we did.

A fool and his money may part, but they were lucky to get together in the first place.

Guests of a night club were held up on the way home. After all, these are days of keen competition.

A man who pays his family's living expenses and taxes deserves a badge of merit, but he gets a barrel.

Every automobile should have a small compartment in which to keep the instalment-loan contract.

No married man ever pokes fun at a woman for shopping all day and buying nothing.

There are days in the office when a man finds it hard to believe the telephone was once a convenience.

In September many people return from the summer resorts for a greatly needed rest.

The easiest way to remain poor is to pretend to be rich.

The world hasn't a broken heart, but a cracked head.

The quietest affair in the life of the average family is Dad's birthday.

As an inducement to hard work and economy nothing beats a big family.

The Internal Revenue Department apparently works on the theory that "Man wants but little here below."

Fathers who have hobbies rarely lose their minds. However, you can't say the same thing of their families.

Civilization is a slow process in which advertising men create new wants to be satisfied.

A man doesn't have to live as long as Methuselah to learn there is nothing common about common sense.

A lawyer is the fellow who steps in when an irresistible force meets an immovable object.

In a concert of nations there is the question of who plays the wind instruments and who plays second fiddle.

An egotist is a person of questionable taste more interested in himself than in me.

Satisfaction is a state of mind produced when you witness another person's discomfort.

A statesman thinks he belongs to the nation, but a politician thinks the nation belongs to him.

Hunger is an instinct placed in man to make certain that he will work.

A conviction is that commendable quality in ourselves which we call bull-headedness in others.

Tolerance is the patience shown by a wise man when he listens to an ignoramus.

We like Spring, but there is one thing gloomy about it. Everything seems to come back except us.

As a rule the fellow who blows his horn the loudest is in the biggest fog.

When a diplomat puts his cards on the table, he still has a deck up each sleeve.

The greatest misfortune in government is that those out of office always know the answers to the nation's problems.

Someone said there is no simple word which expresses what the American people want. We could suggest "more."

Scientists are men who prolong life so we can have time to pay for the gadgets they invent.

Unfortunately there are ten thousand ways for a government to spend money and only one way to save it.

Too often we live beyond our means to impress people who live beyond their means to impress us.

Economists now say we move in cycles instead of running around in circles. It sounds better, but it means the same thing.

It often takes a speaker twice as long to tell what he thinks as to tell what he knows.

When the people aren't sure of what they want in democracy, they vote for something different from what they have.

Someone wants to know where the population is most dense. Well, one answer might be—from the neck up.

It is remarkable how large a part ignorance plays in making a man satisfied with himself.

When a man thinks he is important he should ask what the world would miss if he were gone.

Football makes a nation hardy. You build up a lot of strong resistance sitting on a cold concrete seat.

It's strange how a man will demand a home atmosphere in a hotel and hotel service at home.

If the expenses of a government couldn't vote, it would be easier to balance budgets.

The one drawback to lovely autumn scenery is that you have to rake it up.

A middle-aged man's waistline is his line of least resistance.

Photographer's sign—"Come in and be enlarged, tinted, and framed for only $4.49."

Winter is the difficult period when the hair on your dog is thick and on your wife's fur coat is thin.

It is said some nations do not know what we stand for. Just about everything is probably the answer.

Fashion experts say waistlines will be lower. A little later they announce they will be higher. Remarkable how nature changes.

There are said to be prunes six inches in diameter. Well, we've seen some even larger.

When one fisherman calls another fisherman a liar, that's what the philosophers call truth.

There is something wrong in international relations when a diplomat is called courageous if he speaks the truth.

We never could understand why nations hold so many conferences to decide to live in peace and go back to work.

The first step in national defense is a nation of citizens who vote in elections.

Attention, fathers! In Mexico the donkey is the beast of burden.

It is an interesting fact that of all the comedians and humorists who get off wise cracks on Communism not one lives in Russia.

Under the heading of inflammatory literature we would include the spring seed-and-flower catalogs.

Rolling pins are no longer used on husbands, but they aren't used for much of anything else either in the modern home.

Most speeding is done by people who aren't going anywhere in particular.

When you look at the world's debt you are inclined to think that they who take the sword shall perish by the tax.

We're waiting for some scientist to invent an indestructible shirt collar that can meet an irresistible laundry machine.

Some persons have eyes that see not and ears that hear not, but there are few persons who have tongues that talk not.

When a bee comes in the side window, stop the car instead of relying on a telephone pole.

A great many foreign statesmen visit the U.S. Treasury to have a rendezvous with debt:

A Latin American insect has a white light at the head and a red light at the tail. That's more than you can say for some of our cars.

A professor says that the world will soon have more people than it can sustain. If work continues to be unpopular, it won't take very long.

When there is too much stall in stallment, a boom has gone too far.

The main difference between Swiss cheese and Camembert is that the ventilation is a little better.

Your grandfather, when he was a boy, would have thought it silly to ask how many pairs of sheer stockings could be made out of a ton of coal and some water and sunshine.

Patience may often be simply the inability to make a decision.

Gardening is simply a matter of your enthusiasm holding up until your back gets used to it.

When you meet a really great man, he seems so simple and modest that you almost have a new faith in your own possibilities.

To err may be human, but to admit it isn't.

When the elections approach, the politicians come out on platforms advocating good weather, eight hours' sleep, and strictly fresh eggs.

A monopolist is a fellow who manages to get an elbow on each arm of his theater chair.

As a man gets older, he suspects that nature organized him for the benefit of the dentists and doctors.

A happy marriage results when both parties get better mates than they deserve.

The difficult part about making good is that you have to repeat it every day.

Middle Age: The period when a man believes the thinning of his hair is only a temporary matter.

A philosopher says man must live life dangerously. Well, forty-eight million automobile drivers are doing their best.

Experience may be a good teacher but not many pupils bring her bright red apples.

Married men are said to be more inventive than single men. Well, what's that one about necessity being the mother of invention?

We are gradually reducing the number of illiterates in this country, which makes it harder and harder for the popular-song writers.

Whenever a foreign ruler plans a visit to this country, it generally means we are going to come across if he does.

There is an unconfirmed rumor that an American motorist recently stopped his car at a railroad crossing and waited for the train to pass.

A well-known businessman said his success was due to luck. That certainly makes it hard on the speakers at commencement exercises.

We used to see a great many advertisements about keeping that schoolgirl complexion. But what we would like is that schoolboy stomach.

Success is a matter either of getting around you better men than yourself, or getting around better men than yourself.

Advice to young men: If you manufacture something the people need, you will make a living. If you manufacture something they don't need, you will make a fortune.

We are concerned not only about where our taxes are going to, but where they are coming from.

The problem of the middle class is trying to save while spending as much as the rich do.

The ant may be industrious but he never gets on the front page as often as the butterfly.

If the world is waiting to hear the still small voice, it will either have to provide an amplifier or quiet down.

The next time you hear a nation called Shylock remember that a smart lawyer talked Shylock out of the principal and interest of the loan.

Maybe the reason so many people don't vote is that they vote the way they think.

Many persons are so busy telling the world what is wrong with it that they haven't time to improve themselves.

Little things count. Frequently they count better than the Dads who work their arithmetic problems wrong.

Nothing makes a modern girl blush like the corner drug store.

A polite man today is one who offers a lady a seat when he gets off the bus.

The only thing more expensive than education is ignorance.

To be fair you have to admit it's remarkable how many of our people escape being run over by cars.

Instalment-financing plans for automobiles might include a combination covering automobile, hospital, and funeral expenses with the down payment.

Splitting an atom would not be too difficult for a salaried man who divides his income between the Treasury and his family.

An after-dinner speaker is a person who doesn't talk in his own but in other people's sleep.

With so many persons on the Federal payroll, we presume Congress will soon have to relax the immigration laws to let in some prospective taxpayers.

Women are steadily growing more beautiful. Well, they have been steadily trying for several thousand years.

What the United States needs is less paternalism in Washington and more in American homes.

The problem in this country has been whether to participate actively in the United Nations Organization or just butt into the world's arguments from time to time.

Winter is the time of the year when it gets later earlier.

You can read the record of man's progress in better burglar alarms, combination locks, and bullet-proof, armored money trucks.

The way many persons measure success in the world there is a reasonable doubt whether men should be born acquisitive or inquisitive.

The publication of the names of large salary earners never has impressed us. What we are interested in is not how much they make, but how they make it.

A luxury is anything the neighbors have which we can't afford.

We have often wondered what appeal crossword puzzles have to a man of few words.

Someone has asked what becomes of those folks in the winter who run roadside vegetable stands in the summer. We assume they become holdup men.

If all men are equal, why do government make so many laws to cramp the able?

It may be that the saying "The good die young" grew out of the fact that you meet so few grown-ups who qualify.

Someone has said the secret of a long life is hard work. Well, we always knew it wasn't so simple.

When it follows a spending philosophy a nation finally reaches the point where it must decide whether the government or the people should spend the money.

We think education should not only broaden the minds of our youth but do a little something about their depth.

A combination of bright lights on a car with a driver who is all lit up is a sure way to collect collision insurance.

The world never recognizes a poet until after he is dead and then the fellow is safe.

There is a great deal of difference between a flat head and a level head.

What the peoples of various nations would like to have for a while is some rulers under whose administration nothing would happen but the expected.

About the nearest thing to being President is to umpire a game for the Brooklyn Dodgers.

The danger in driving a car is that some other motorist may be as reckless as you are.

A coal strike shows that when the miner isn't in the hole the consumer is.

A nation has reached financial maturity when it realizes there just ain't no such thing as Santa Claus.

It takes all kinds of people, and lots of them, to keep some European nations in Cabinets.

Disillusionment is what takes place when your son asks you to help him with the algebra.

When a nation reaches the point where no one buys real estate with the intention of keeping it, a speculative boom is nearing its end. *Banking*.

It's a strange fact that next month, not this month, is always the time some persons expect to start saving. *Banking*

Theme song for the fellow who buys everything on instalments: "Backward, Turn Backward, O Time in Your Flight."

We can never understand why the amateur who mistakes a guide for a deer always hits him.

Advertising is the fine art of making you think you have longed for something all your life that you never heard of before.

When we look at the headlines in the day's newspapers, we think it's a shame to break the mailman's back carrying that stuff.

No one is up in the air more of the time than a person with an inflated ego.

When one hears some of the programs forced through a radio, it's no wonder it protests with static every once in a while.

We may not be eating as much as our grandparents, but we're paying twice as much for it.

An optimist is a fellow who looks at the down payment. A pessimist looks at the last instalment and the upkeep.

The secret of success in politics is never to build your fences so high they can't be comfortably straddled.

Every man in France sooner or later gets a chance to enter the Cabinet.

It may be debatable whether a nation would raise its standard of living more by a five-day week or a forty-day month.

If you make it a point always to park alongside a brand-new car, you can be sure you will never get any bumps.

On our recent vacation trip by car the scenery ran mostly to tooth paste and shaving cream.

Some persons think too many young people are going to college. But what are parents going to do with the youngsters during that period when they don't have sense enough to do other things well?

Headline: "Holding the breath for fourteen minutes is the new record." Obviously a married man.

The fellow who never worries may not be smart enough to know what it's all about.

Some nations that fought for what they thought was right have gone left.

Life is not so much getting what you like as liking what you get.

Knowledge may have its limits, but ignorance has no such restrictions.

The lack of a sense of humor may make a person very funny.

Nothing dies faster than a new idea in a committee meeting.

Marriage is an association of two persons for the purpose of making one the beneficiary.

The difference between most of us is that we are ignorant on different subjects.

Imagination is what makes a politician think he is a statesman.

A great many public speakers have a terminological blind spot.

The minority is always wrong—at the beginning.

FOUR HUNDRED EPIGRAMS

He who hesitates is lost—except a bachelor.

Marriage is the one business that always has one silent partner.

When you have hot water in the summer and cold water in the winter, you are in a resort hotel.

The person who is in love with himself ought to get a divorce.

Marriage is an institution in which a man constantly faces the music, beginning with "Here Comes the Bride."

There are cases where a majority simply means all the fools are on one side.

It is reported by scientists that man's jaw has dropped half an inch in several thousand years. That's not so bad when you consider the government budgets he has faced.

There are still several million people in this country who cannot read or write. But why do they all devote themselves to writing our popular songs?

In Japan speeches at public dinners are made before the dinner. Who said we know everything?

A good politician is a fellow who has prejudices enough to suit the needs of all his constituents.

A diplomat leads a terrible life. When he isn't straddling an issue, he is dodging one.

We wonder whether the University of Chicago includes a pass book in its list of 100 great books.

Some speakers electrify an audience, others gas it.

Our government is one of checks and balances, that is, checks on your and my balances.

Peace is the short interval when nations toil to pay the costs of past and future wars.

Death Valley is the distance from curb to curb.

When all is said and done, the haircut is over.

Someone says the most essential things in life are the smallest, which exactly describes our bankroll. *Banking*

Women are advised to take bending exercises to reduce, which is a modern version of she stoops to conquer.

We suppose it is only on matters of great principle that a diplomat lies with a clear conscience.

The kind of a little lamb that could follow Mary in her modern car would be a Rocky Mountain goat that could run sixty miles an hour.

Easy street is always a dead end street or a blind alley.

When some people are afraid of an issue, they say there isn't one.

A music school announces they can teach anyone to play any brass instrument in a few lessons. It sounds to us like a national catastrophe.

When all is said and nothing done, the bridge party is over.

Automobile manufacturers have produced a relatively permanent finish for cars, but even yet nothing beats a locomotive.

We imagine every time a golf champion plays he must feel it's another uneasy lie for a crowned head.

Middle age is that period in life when your idea of getting ahead is staying even.

Many an argument is sound—just sound.

Every banker knows some men who spend half their lives borrowing money and the other half in not paying it back.

When a banker lends money to a going concern, he ought to know which way it is going. *Banking*

A bank robber was sentenced to 199 years in California. There is apparently nothing in the climate out there to prevent him from serving out his time.

The next thing you know somebody will debunk vitamin pills, and then nothing will be sacred.

Ten thousand cemeteries are filled with people who thought the world couldn't get along without them.

In order to go to sleep at night now, a Congressman must have to count his sheep in billions.

Be generous to a fault—especially your own.

It isn't necessary for politicians to fool all the people all the time. A majority will do.

There is no fool like an oiled fool.

Good municipal government pays. The other kind does also, but not the same people.

This country is so poor we can't eat more than a couple of hundred millions of dollars' worth of ice cream each year.

The eminent scientist who once said that we all behave like human beings obviously never drove a car.

It may be that the reason youngsters don't stay at home nights is that they're afraid to be alone in the house.

With absenteeism from work, together with a five-day week, we may reach the point where our week ends meet.

A philosopher refused to marry because it might interfere with his work. That isn't anything compared to what it will do to his philosophy.

The modern woman doesn't weep as much as her grandmother. After all, what is there left for her to cry for?

A friend is a person who can't understand how you get there, but still doesn't knock you.

Truth in the news: "After the collision Mr. Smith's car was brought to the local garage for repairs and was badly damaged."

It may be that the wheel that squeaks gets the grease, but it's also true that the dog that scratches has the fleas.

Maybe the cause of the rising juvenile crime is that too many parents' slippers are being worn out on the nightclub floors.

Just why is it that you convince a man but persuade a woman?

We imagine a President of the United States is never happier than when there is some matter before him requiring a hands-off policy.

Women take men's places in many ways, but they never try to fill their shoes.

What some nations want is not a loan but an endowment.

There never have been any idle rich. They were always kept busy dodging people who wanted to get some of it with as little work as possible.

A Chicago doctor says prehistoric man was neither stoop-shouldered nor bowlegged. Then came taxes.

Many women are getting men's wages nowadays, but then, they always have.

When a self-made man marries, his wife usually makes some alterations.

Nothing recedes like success.

Our grandchildren will certainly have a great time paying for the good times we didn't have

The world has ample facilities for transmitting intelligence rapidly. What is needed is more intelligence to transmit.

The man who really enjoys life is not the man who thinks, but the one who thinks he thinks.

It seems incredible—35,000,000 laws and no improvement on the Ten Commandments.

It is also the duty of a just democracy to see that the rich get every consideration afforded the poor.

Very few persons are as tolerant and broad-minded as you and I think we are.

Money sometimes makes fools of important persons, but it may also make important persons of fools.

Many a husband has wondered why his wife complains she has nothing to wear and needs five closets to keep it in.

We suppose that if people didn't get married for such silly reasons they wouldn't get divorced for such silly reasons.

We have often wondered what kind of terrible homes the homemade pies you buy came from.

We seem to have reached a stage in civilisation when our people have better homes and spend less time in them than ever before in history.

The reason some nations can't reach deeper in their pockets to pay off debts is that they have swords in their hands.

There are two groups who never know what the people want: Congress and the people.

We sometimes wonder if there is any connection between the increase in books on child psychology and the increase in juvenile crime.

The way for a married man to hide something from his wife is to put it in the basket with the undarned socks.

The reason history has to repeat itself is that no one heard it the first time.

A budget tells you what you can afford to spend, but it doesn't keep you from spending more.

Many people pay for their automobiles as they use them, but no so rapidly.

An optimist is a person who looks forward to enjoying the scenery on a detour.

A short speech may not be the best speech, but the best speech is a short one.

A streamline train not only has the right of way at a crossing but can prove it.

There is nothing raises a man's hope more in vain than the first spring cantaloupes.

In a Presidential campaign the party platform is first planned, then panned, and finally canned.

A national political issue is an issue that has become so important all candidates avoid discussing it.

There is no cure for insomnia like listening to yourself talk.

More money is spent on chewing gum than books. After all you can borrow a book.

When the engineers introduce standardization into the hotel business, we suggest that they start with reducing French pastry to a couple of models.

A college education helps a person to get involved in so many more complicated kinds of trouble.

An intelligent woman is one who has brains enough to tell a man how wonderful he is.

In nonstop flights across the United States a person at least doesn't take the risk of not getting a hotel room en route.

Figures don't lie—which is one reason why tailoring is so difficult.

The line is too often busy when conscience wishes to speak.

Cars are being made that will withstand harder and harder bumps. Pretty soon one will be made that will knock down a pedestrian without jarring the driver.

Man's inhumanity to man makes prize fights, wars, and buffet suppers.

We understand there are some horses that are trained to know a green light means go and a red light, stop. There may still be hope for some motorists.

Admiring oneself in a mirror may be more a matter of imagination than vanity.

A political candidate must be well balanced to run for office on the fence.

A great national or international problem is anything that requires a large appropriation from Congress.

A famous citizen reports that when he sends his shirts to the laundry they steal them for souvenirs. Guess we're fortunate, as they only take parts of ours.

A decathlon is any combination of athletic events like taking off the screen doors, putting up the storm windows, and scraping the leaves out of the eave troughs.

Marriage is like a railroad sign. You see a lovely girl and stop; then you look; and after you are married, you listen.

A few parents have claimed the babies they were given at the hospital were not theirs. A great many more parents have come to the same conclusion seventeen or eighteen years' later.

Most men in court are presumed innocent until they are proved guilty. Occasionally some are guilty after they are proved innocent.

Truth in advertising—"The latest in antiques."

A radical is a person who thinks you are a reactionary if you don't get as excited as he does about everything.

Scientists say mankind may have to make war against insects. Apparently appeasement through picnics hasn't worked.

Beauty experts say it is easy to lift a face. But it's difficult to keep it lifted after the bill comes in.

A Christian is a person who is as horrified by his own sins as he is by his neighbor's.

If men talked only about what they understand, the silence would become unbearable.

We suggest that the United Nations acquire a number of movable boundary partitions for use from time to time.

Definition of a road hog: Any other driver.

Newspaper advertisement: Position with good pay, open for a stenographer. Would prefer one who can take dictation.

The more laws, the more lawbreakers; the more lawbreakers, the more laws. This thing can go on forever.

After science invents an electric can opener, what else is there to do for the kitchen?

The armistices for two world wars were signed in a dining car, which probably explains why they were so expensive.

Those scientists who are always looking for dead civilizations should visit some of our busy traffic centers.

Sales resistance is a bad thing. Finally when you buy, you have to pay for all the effort that has been used to get you to buy.

Just how much credit would the busy bee get if he stored up something man couldn't use?

Even the men who aren't born meek get married and get that way.

What's confusing in traffic is the driver who signals that he is turning right and does so.

Wind is simply air that is in a hurry to go some place. In a speech it is often air that isn't going any place.

Bubble gum certainly made this a country of the wide-open faces.

The world is a globe which revolves on its taxes.

Economics simplified—Prosperity is the period when it is easy to borrow money to buy things which you should be able to pay for out of your own income.

Something ought to be done to improve sandwiches sold in depots. A coat of clear shellac would make them more attractive and easier to dust.

Whatever isn't worth saying will be made into a popular song.

No man has greater courage than the man who boasts that he is self-made.

No man is so complete a crackpot that he can't obtain some followers.

What the income-tax form needs is a new section which will explain the explanations.

A public speaker is a person who will sit up all night writing a speech that will put an audience to sleep the next day.

No man is worth less to a business than the one who always agrees with the boss.

Many homes are unionized. They have an eight-hour-a-day husband and a sixteen-hour-a-day wife.

It is getting so a good barber can earn as much per word as an author.

With two and a half million youngsters in college, education may be passing from a luxury to a necessity. Then nobody will want it.

Some universities now have 25,000 students, which means they have almost as many in the classrooms as in the stadiums.

Trying to solve a problem by verbal argument is like trying to clear up a traffic jam by honking your horn.

Experience is not only a dear teacher, but by the time you get through going to her school, life is over.

You can judge a man pretty well by whether he would ask for a light burden or a strong back if he were given a choice.

An opinion is a minimum of facts combined with prejudice and emotion.

Thousands of young people graduate from institutions of higher learning each year and enter businesses of higher yearning.

The fellow who owns a summer cottage meets all his relatives.

We'll bet the same fellow invented the telephone booth, breakfast nook, and upper berth.

It's slow business making a man out of a monkey, but it's easy to reverse it.

A squirting grapefruit is bad, but one that doesn't is worse.

Think of legs like those of a kangaroo being wasted in prairies instead of used on street corners.

Between wars nations need armament to show what they could do if they went to war.

Dishwater helps to keep a wedding ring bright.

When will the dictionaries start calling the locomotive cowcatcher the carcatcher?

The only successful substitute for brains is silence.

The road of the modern transgressor is hard-surfaced.

Unchanging morals: In the old days a twelve-year-old boy was six so he could travel at half fare; now he is sixteen so he can drive a car.

No automobile has ever licked a train at a crossing, but you have to give them credit, they keep on trying.

The steady bang of your hammer means you will succeed. The steady bang of other hammers means you have succeeded.

It might just be that the more a government cost, the less it is worth.

The great virtues seem to be among the few antiques which are not highly prized today.

No woman ever makes a fool out of a man without his full co-operation.

No one can define happiness. You have to be unhappy to understand it.

A person who brags is the one who puts his feat in his mouth.

Some persons spend half their lives not doing anything and the other half telling about it.

A blackberry is a purple berry that was red when it was green.

Divorces are cases where the blind have led the blind.

A bird in the hand is worth two in the bush, but not if you're a bird.

Experience may make a person better or bitter.

It's an impossible job to convince your wife you make as little as you do and the government that you make no more than you do.

An autobiography is the story of how a man thinks he lived.

Many a client wonders after he pays the lawyer his fee who it was that got hit by the truck.

Everything evens up. As you have less hair to comb you have more face to wash.

Economy is anything for which your wife wishes to spend money.

Judging from the amount of make-up she wears, the average girl believes Shakespeare's "all the world's a stage."

There is nothing that makes a man more self-satisfied than a poor memory.

The mathematician who said the lesser can not contain the greater never worked in a shoe store.

Famous last words: "I wonder how much this car will do?"

When these scientists get through working on the atomic bomb, we wish they would find an easy way to put a license plate on a car.

Vanity: A parent trying to make his child like him.

We wish the same fellow who helps make automobiles

faster and more durable would work on pedestrians for a while.

When a conference of diplomats states the diplomats have agreed "in principle," it means nothing has been accomplished.

Whatever else may be wrong with the domestic scene, it isn't cheap politics.

War or no war, one of the places substitutes for food are always used is in the hors d'oeuvres at cocktail parties.

In the old days we suppose there were pedestrians who tried to get across the road ahead of the dinosaur.

A middle-of-the-road policy may be all right in politics, but it's suicide on a highway.

About the only thing that compares with an atom bomb is a dominating personality driving a five-ton truck.

There is a vast difference between saturation in the automobile market and in the driver.

In every election some good candidate receives the solid backing of all the good people who don't vote.

The sun never sets on the British possessions or the American tourist.

All the President of the United States has to do is to pacify the taxpayers, consumers, farmers, businessmen, and union labor.

No matter what side of an argument an intelligent man gets on, he always finds some people with him he wishes were on the other side.

A conservative says that a radical may sometimes be right, but when he is, he is right for the wrong reasons.

It seems easier to succeed when one doesn't have the advantages others have.

The trouble with Opportunity is that it always comes disguised as hard work.

Progress is largely a matter of discarding old worries and taking on new ones.

The peak of a boom is reached when the average family is paying installments on five things instead of one.

Banking

We sometimes marvel when we think how little our parents knew of child psychology and how wonderful we are.

FOUR HUNDRED EPIGRAMS

The world is full of people who know how the other fellow should use his talents and resources.

One fourth of the cost of a car is in the engine and the rest is in the back seat.

A Communist in the United States is a person who says everything is perfect in Russia but stays in this country because he likes to rough it.

If you can believe all the people who appear before Senate and House Committees and say they represent ten million people, then the census bureau certainly underestimates our population.

One theory regarding the sudden development of that Mexican volcano is that somewhere near the American border a determined golfer was trying to get out of a sand trap.

The average person gets up in the morning feeling like a receipt marked paid in full and goes to bed at night feeling like the notice for the next instalment due.

Education used to consist of the three R's: Reading, 'Riting, and 'Rithmetic. It still features the three R's, but now they are Rah, Rah, Rah.

Some persons will go right on buying bread and meat and depositing money in a savings account when they don't have a fur coat in the house.

Any time you doubt whether any person is perfect, read a political advertisement.

Marriage encourages thrift, says a banker. Demands is the word. *Banking*

Someone says, "If you teach a boy to blow a cornet, he will never be bad." Well, you have to pay a price for everything.

Advertisement: "For rent—Large garage by man with two windows." Bay, we presume.

Strange how businessmen can time their new products to fit your last instalment payment.

Every four years in the United States is the year of the Big Wind.

If you think French is a difficult language, how about one in which applesauce and bologna mean the same thing.

It is better to breathe through the nose. Besides, it keeps the mouth shut.

The person who is all wrapped up in himself is overdressed.

Chapter XI

TWO HUNDRED HUMOROUS STORIES

Inquiry or Invitation

A candidate for sheriff called on a voter to ask his support at the coming election.

"Before I decide to give you my support," said the voter, "I would like to ask you a question. Do you partake of intoxicating beverages?"

"Before I reply," said the candidate cautiously, "is this an inquiry or an invitation?"

Putt

The schoolteacher was taking her first golfing lesson. "Is the word spelled 'put' or 'putt'?" she asked the instructor.

"'Putt' is correct," he replied. "'Put' means to place a thing where you want it. 'Putt' means merely a vain attempt to do the same thing."

Allergic

The speaker was annoyed by a man in the audience who coughed and sneezed and blew his nose almost constantly. Finally the speaker could stand it no longer. He suggested to the brother who was having so much discomfort that a visit to the open air might be good for his cold.

"I haven't any cold," came the answer. "I'm just allergic to applesauce."

Most Any Father Is

"I'm a self-made man."

"You're lucky. I'm the revised work of a wife and three daughters."

Absent-Minded

Houseowner—"Well, I see you brought your tools with you."

Plumber—"Yeah. I'm getting more absent-minded every day."

Experience

Willie—"Pop, there's a man at the circus who jumps on a horse's back, slips underneath, catches hold of its tail, and finishes up on the horse's neck!"

Father—"That's easy. I did all that the first time I ever rode a horse."

Modern Family

Officer (to man pacing sidewalk at 3 A.M.)—"What are you doing here?"

Gentleman—"I forgot my key, officer, and I'm waiting for the children to come home and open the door."

All Needed

Noah was checking off the pairs of animals when he saw three camels trying to get on board.

"Wait a minute!" said the patriarch. "Two each is the limit. One of you will have to stay behind."

"It won't be me," said the first camel. "I'm the camel whose back is broken by the last straw."

"I'm the one people swallow while straining at a gnat," said the second.

"I," said the third, "am the one that shall pass through the eye of a needle sooner than a rich man shall enter Heaven."

"Come on in," said Noah, "the world is going to need all of you."

He Thought it Through

Boss—"How is it that you're only carrying one sack, when the other men are carrying two?"

Laborer—"Well, I suppose they're too lazy to make two trips like I do!"

No Extra Charge

Customer—"Take a look at what you did to this!"
Laundryman—"I can't see anything wrong with that piece of lace."
Customer—"Lace, man, that was a sheet!"

Busy the Whole Year

"What is the principal occupation of this town?"
"Wall, boss," the man answered, yawning, "in winter they mostly sets on the east side of the house and follers the sun around to the west, and in summer they sets on the west side and follers the shade around to the east."

In Every Neighborhood

The neighborhood borrower approached Mr. Smith and inquired:
"Say, Smith, are you using your lawn mower this afternoon?"
"Yes," Smith replied warily.
"Fine. Then you won't be using your golf clubs—I'll just borrow them."

Sympathetic

"Poor, old Jordan tried to borrow five dollars from me today," the husband confessed.
"I hope you were sympathetic," said his wife.
"Yes. I was touched."

Obliging

"I wish you wouldn't whistle at your work," cried the employer.
"It's all right," said the office boy. "I'm not working."

Not Sleeping

When some women got on the car, every seat was already occupied. The conductor noticed a man who seemed to be asleep, and, fearing that he might miss his stop, he nudged him and said:
"Wake up!"
"I wasn't asleep," the man protested.

Modesty

A Hollywood actor, testifying in a case, was asked to identify himself.

"I am the world's greatest actor," he told the court.

One of his friends chided him next day:

"Don't you think that boost you gave yourself was a little too thick?"

"Usually I avoid self-praise," said the actor, "but this time they had me under oath."

Modern Youth

Our youngster tells us he got a zero the other day when he told his teacher the world revolved on its taxes. But we're wondering if maybe the kid doesn't have the right idea at that.

Two Gooses

Mr. Schultz, the tailor, decided to order new pressing irons. He wrote an order to the supply house for "two geese"; then he felt that this could hardly be correct, and amended it to "two gooses." That did not seem right, either. At last he took a new sheet of paper:

"Gentlemen: Please send me one 16-lb. goose.
                              Yours truly, Henry Schultz

"P. S. Please send another one, also."

A Little Help

The young lover, eloping with the only girl, climbed the ladder and rapped on her window. She opened the window softly.

"Are you ready?" he asked.

"Ssh! Not so loud!" she whispered. "I'm so afraid father will catch us."

"That's all right," said the youth. "He's down below holding the ladder."

Tragic Loss

Collegian—"What did you do with my shirt?"

Roommate—"Sent it to the laundry."

Collegian—"Man! The whole history of England was on the cuffs!"

He Had Experience

"See here," said the Indian inspector at a western reservation, "it is a violation of the law to have more than one wife, and the law must be obeyed. When you get back home, tell all of your wives except one that they can no longer look upon you as their husband."

"You tell 'em," suggested the Indian after a moment's reflection.

Particular

Customer—"I'll have some raw oysters, not too large nor too small, not too salty nor too fat. They must be cold, in the shell, and I want them quickly!"

Waiter—"Yes, sir. With or without pearls?"

Too Late

"I hear you have a little sister."

"Yes," answered the small boy.

"Do you like her?"

"I wish it was a boy, 'cause then I could play marbles, baseball, and other games with her."

"Then why don't you exchange her for a brother?"

"Can't," was the answer. "It's too late now. We've used her four days."

Observing

Dad—"You mustn't pull the cat's tail."

Sonny—"I'm only holding it. The cat is pulling."

It Makes a Difference

"I'm glad to find you as you are," said the old friend. "Your wealth hasn't changed you."

"Well," replied the candid millionaire, "it has changed me in one thing. I'm now 'eccentric' where I used to be impolite, and 'delightfully witty' where I used to be rude."

Emergency

Three Scotchmen were in church when the minister made an appeal for some worthy cause, hoping everyone would give at least one dollar. The three Scots became nervous as the collection plate neared them—when one fainted and the other two carried him out.

Lucky

McGarry—"Has anyone seen me vest?"
McNulty—"Sure, McGarry, and ye've got it on."
McGarry—"Right, I have, and it's a good thing ye seen it, or I'd have gone home without it."

The Best Man

Mike—"Where did ye get the black eye, Pat?"
Pat—"'Twas at Casey's wedding reciption. There was a big important-looking fellow swaggerin' around. 'An' who are ye?' says I. 'I'm the best man,' says he—an' he sure was!"

Almost Drowned

"Horses!" said Bill to Joe. "You can't talk to me about horses. I had an old mare that licked the fastest express train on a forty-mile run."

"That's nothing!" said Joe. "I was out about fifty miles from my house on my farm one day when a bad storm came up. I turned the pony's head for home and he raced the storm so close for the last ten miles that I didn't feel a drop, while my dog, only ten yards behind, had to swim the whole distance."

No Trouble

Steve—"Too bad about your falling off the ladder, Mike."
Mike—"Well, it could have been worse. I had to be coming down for nails, anyway."

Reasonable Pay

Once upon a time there was an Indian named Big Eagle employed as a missionary to his fellow Indians.

A white man encountering Big Eagle, asked him what he did for a living.

"Umph!" said Big Eagle, "me preach."
"What do you get for preaching?"
"Me get ten dollars a year."

"Well," said the white man, "that's awful poor pay."
"Umph!" said Big Eagle, "me awful poor preacher."

Plenty Nerve

Dentist—"Stop making faces, sir. I haven't even touched your tooth."

Patient—"I know you haven't, but you're standing on my corn."

Economy Size

Boasting of the farms in Texas a native said:

"We have some farms that are pretty good size. I've seen a man on a big farm start out in the spring and plow a straight furrow till fall. Then he harvested back. That's not all. It is the usual thing to send young married couples out to milk the cows, and their children come back with the milk."

Good as New

Golfer (to player searching for lost ball)—"What sort of a ball was it?"

Caddy (butting in)—"A brand new one—never been properly hit yet!"

Squelched

The old alumnus was disparaging the skill of modern football players.

"When I was in college," he boasted, "I helped Harvard beat Yale for three years straight."

"Is that so, sir?" said the quarterback. "And which team were you on?"

A Tale About Rover

They were discussing dogs, and each story got worse.

"Smith," one man said, "had a most intelligent dog. One night Smith's house caught fire. All was confusion. Smith and his wife flew for the children. Everyone was saved, but old Rover dashed back through the flames. Soon Rover reappeared, scorched and burned, with—what do you think?"

"Give up," cried the eager listeners.

"With the fire-insurance policy wrapped in a damp towel, gentlemen."

THAT'S DIFFERENT

A surgeon was asked out to dinner. The hostess felt that because of his training he would be the logical person to carve the chicken, so she asked him to do it.

All did not go well. The bird slipped off the platter and landed in the lap of the hostess. She was embarrassed, but attempted to pass it off quietly.

"Gracious, doctor," she said. "I don't know whether I would trust you to operate on me or not!"

The surgeon replied, "You, madam, are no chicken!"

THAT'S WHAT WORRIED HIM

"But, doctor," said the worried patient, "are you sure I'll pull through? I've heard of cases where the doctor has made a wrong diagnosis, and treated someone for pneumonia who has afterward died of typhoid fever."

"Nonsense," spluttered the doctor. "When I treat a patient for pneumonia, he dies of pneumonia."

SILENCE IN THE WIDE-OPEN SPACES

Dentist—"Open wider, please—wider."
Patient—"A-a-a-ah."
Dentist (inserting rubber gag, towel, and sponge)—"How's your family?"

HE KNEW WHICH ONE WAS FUNNY

"Did you like the famous ventriloquist?"
"Not much, but that little feller on his knee was funny!"

ALERT

Policeman: "Why didn't you stop when I yelled?"
Driver (with presence of mind): "I thought you said, 'Hello, Senator.'"
Policeman: "Well, you see, Senator, I was going to warn you about driving too fast in the next town."

UNEDUCATED

"Jones never completed his education, did he?"
"No, he lived and died a bachelor."

MODESTY

Calvin Coolidge had humor and sense enough to escape an exaggerated ego. Awakening from a nap in the middle of the day, he opened his eyes, grinned, and asked a friend, "Is the country still here?"

QUIET

Somebody once asked Professor Charles Townsend Copeland of Harvard University why he lived on the top floor of Hollis Hall, in his small, dusty old rooms, and suggested that he move.

"No," he said, "I shall always live on the top floor. It is the only place in Cambridge where God alone is above me." Then after a pause, "He's busy—but He's quiet."

TO HIS GOAL

"He drove straight to his goal," said the speaker. "He looked neither to the right nor to the left, but pushed forward, moved by a definite purpose. Neither friend nor foe could delay him nor turn him from his goal. All who crossed his path did so at their peril. What would you call such a man?"

"A truck driver," shouted someone from the audience.

HISTORY

A Bostonian was showing an Englishman the sights and finally took him out to the Bunker Hill Monument.

"This is where Warren fell, you know," he explained.

The Englishman looked up at the tall shaft. "Nasty drop! Killed him, of course?"

HALF DEAD

When Mackenzie fell in New York harbor a policeman rescued him.

"Thot mon saved your life," said Mrs. Mackenzie. "Shouldna we gie him a dollar?"

"I was half deed whin he pooled me oot," said Mackenzie. "Fifty cents is enough."

AS THE IRISHMAN TELLS IT

"Do you know the difference between the Irish, English, and Scotch?"

"No."

"Well, in leaving a train, an Irishman walks off without looking to see whether he has left anything behind; an Englishman looks back to see whether he has left anything; and a Scotchman looks back to see whether anybody else has left anything."

Perfectly Clear

An Englishman was trying to make himself heard over the phone:

"This is Mr. 'Arrison. No, 'Arrison . . . haitch, hay, two hars, a hi, a hess, a ho, and a hen . . . 'Arrison."

That Will Teach Him

Bus Conductor (helping stout woman aboard)—"Madam, to help you rise you should take yeast."

Stout Woman—"Take some yourself, lad, and then you will be better bred."

Success Assured

Mother: "What makes you think our boy is going to be a politician."

Father: "He says more things that sound well and mean nothing than any one I ever saw."

Stale News

Crook—"Did your paper say I was a liar and a crook?"
Editor—"It did not."
Crook—"Well, some paper in this town said so."
Editor—"It may have been our contemporary down the street. We never print stale news."

Correct

"If you get up earlier in the morning than your neighbor," said the town philosopher, "and work harder and scheme more and stick to your job more closely and stay up later planning how to make more money than your neighbor and burn the midnight oil planning how to get ahead of him while he is snoozing, not only will you leave more money when you die than he will, but you will leave it a lot sooner."

Smart Fellow

Jones was telling Smith he had gone to a lawyer for advice.

"Why spend money on a lawyer?" asked Smith. "Didn't you notice he read the advice out of a book?"

"Sure," replied Jones. "But he knows what page it is on."

Hard Guy

"You must think you are a pretty hard guy, Sergeant."

"Hard? Listen, recruit, I wasn't born. I was quarried."

Modern Youth

Mother: "Now, Junior, be a good boy and say 'ah-h-h' so the doctor can get his finger out of your mouth."

A Seat on the Aisle

The gentleman's attitude was polite but firm. "I'm sorry," he told the woman who was selling tickets for the charity concert, "but I won't be able to attend the concert. It's for a worthy cause, however, and I assure you I shall be with you in spirit."

"Fine," exclaimed the woman. "Where would you like to have your spirit sit? The tickets are one and two dollars."

The gentleman meekly replied: "I'll take a two-dollar one, please."

For Short Men

Oliver Wendell Holmes was small in stature. One day he was at a meeting attended by a number of rather tall men, thus making his diminutive size rather conspicuous in contrast.

An acquaintance waggishly remarked, "Well, Doctor Holmes, I should think you would feel rather small among these big fellows."

The genial but modest man replied, "I do. I feel like a dime among a lot of pennies."

Efficiency

A colonel was transferred to a new command. On reaching his depot, he found stacks of old documents in the archives, so he wired to headquarters for permission to burn them. The answer came back: "Yes, but make copies first."

Tough Decisions

A California laborer was sent to a psychiatrist, who asked him about his job.

The laborer replied, "I'm a sorter at an orange grove."

"What's that?" asked the psychiatrist.

"I stand at the foot of a sorting machine," the patient explained, "and sort the oranges as to size and quality."

"Why should an easy job like that trouble you?" inquired the psychiatrist.

"Doctor," shrieked the patient, slapping the palm of his hand against his forehead, "such terrific decisions."

Not a Bad Idea

Youth (to fair companion): "Have you ever tried listening to a play with your eyes shut?"

Voice (from row behind): "Have you tried listening to one with your mouth shut?"

Go to the Head of the Class

Teacher: "Now, Johnny, if I were to lay two eggs over here and three over there, how many will there be altogether?"

Johnny: "Personally, I don't think you can do it."

Tender

Farmer: "You can't go wrong on this mare, sir. She's sound, gentle, a good worker, and a fine saddle horse."

City Slicker: "What I want to know is, is she tender?"

Free Growls

A Russian wolfhound, exiled in London, lunched with an English bulldog.

"Can't offer you much," said the bulldog. "Since the food shortage, Master even keeps the bone. How's Russia?"

"All the food we want," said the wolfhound. "Big chunks of meat! Juicy bones!"

"How come you're here, then?" asked the English dog.
"Well, a fellow likes to bark once in a while, doesn't he?"

CONFUSED

Hold-up man: "Stick 'em up, or else!"
Victim: "Or else what?"
Hold-up man: "Don't confuse me—this is my first job."

FAVORITE BRITISH STORIES

Having ordered a plate of cabbage, a restaurant customer plastered it over his head. "What are you doing with that cabbage?" demanded the proprietor. "Is that cabbage?" said the customer. "I thought it was spinach."

The same joke has reappeared in many forms. Here's one of the variations:

A man enters a pub, orders a beer, drains it, and walks straight up the wall, across the ceiling, down the other side, and out of the door. "That's odd," said another man at the bar. "Yes," said the barmaid, "he usually orders ale."

Among other typical jokes that the British have found funny were these:

A friend met Harry Pollitt, British Communist leader, in brilliant sunshine with his umbrella up. "It's raining in Moscow," Comrade Harry explained.

Winston Churchill met Health Minister Aneurin Bevan in the House of Commons and the Socialist leader asked Mr. Churchill for twopence to ring up a friend. "Here's fourpence," said Churchill, "ring up all your friends."
United Press

OBSERVANT

Ardent Lover: "Your features are beautiful. Your hair is like spun gold. Your eyes are like limpid pools of water at dusk. Your lips—your—boy, what a mess you must make of the rim of a coffee cup!"

DIFFICULT TO FIND

Son: "Pop, gimme a hand, will ya, I'm trying to find the least common denominator."

Pop: "Good Heavens, son, hasn't that been found yet? They were looking for it when I was a kid."

SHE KNEW

Customer: "Waitress, what kind of pie is this—apple or peach?"
Waitress: "Well, what does it taste like?"
Customer: "Glue."
Waitress: "Well, then, that's the apple. The peach tastes like putty."

TRUTH

"You seem to have plenty of intelligence for a man in your position," sneered a lawyer, cross-examining a witness.
"If I wasn't under oath I'd return the compliment," replied the witness.

NOT CLOCKEYED

Employer—Are you a clock watcher?
Prospective Employee—No, I don't like indoor work. I'm a whistle listener.

NO ONE IS PERFECT

Wife: "You're lazy, you're worthless, you're bad tempered, you're shiftless, you're a thorough liar."
Husband: "Well, my dear, no man is perfect."

TOO TRUE

Storekeeper: "How is this fellow's credit?"
Credit Man: "Can't tell you. He always pays cash, so we don't know whether he's honest or not."

CAMPAIGN ORATORY

Two fellows came out of a campaign rally.
"Well, what do you think now?" one inquired.
"Think," was the reply. "I didn't come here to think. I came here to holler."

Quiet! He Did

The family was at the dinner table with a man who was a business acquaintance of the father, when the five-year-old blurted out: "Isn't this roast beef?"

"Yes," said the mother, noting his surprised look. "What of it?"

"Well, Daddy said this morning that he was going to bring a big fish home for dinner."

He Got the Idea

One of those old "grammatical" teachers heard a boy once say: "I ain't going." She said: "Don't say that. Say 'I am not going; you are not going; he is not going; we are not going; they are not going.' Get the idea?" "Oh, sure," he said, "there ain't none of them going."

Short Lesson

A teacher said to her students: "Tomorrow bring three sentences: interrogative, declarative, and imperative."

One boy brought this masterpiece:
Interrogative: "Was Carlo sick?" Correct.
Declarative: "Carlo is sick." Correct.
Imperative: "Sic 'em, Carlo."

Efficiency

"How are you getting on at home since your wife went away?"

"Fine. I've reached the highest point of efficiency. I can put my socks on from either end."

Too Easy

Said the scientist to the druggist: "Please give me some prepared white crystalline compound, the acetyl derivative, or the acetate, of salicylic acid."

"Do you mean aspirin?" asked the druggist.

"That's right! I never can think of that name."

Too Small

"How is your pan-fried steak, sir?" said the tip-eager waitress to a customer in a small restaurant.

Scowling at the small, overcooked piece of meat allotted him, the patron replied, "Let's not scold the chef for neglecting to turn it sooner. Maybe the poor fellow mislaid his tweezers and magnifying glass."

Radio Commercials

A writer of radio commercials entered a restaurant, called a waitress, and said:

"Give me some ham, piping hot and fragrant with the pleasant aroma of cloves, brown sugar, and steaming sauce. Serve it between slices of brown and crackly crusted bread. Draw me a cup of delicious, flavorful coffee and add to it some thick, rich cream."

The waitress turned toward the kitchen and yelled "Smoked pig on rye and Java with."

No Warning

The Smiths were on the balcony and could hear the young couple in the garden. Mrs. Smith nudged her husband and whispered, "I think he wants to propose. We ought not to listen. Whistle at him."

"Why should I?" her husband asked. "Nobody whistled at me."

Case Dismissed

"The reason I socked my wife, Your Honor, is that she keeps irritating me."

"Just how does she irritate you?"

"Why, she keeps saying: 'Beat me! Hit me! Go on, just hit me once and I'll have you hauled up before a baldheaded old reprobate they call a judge, and you'll see what he'll do to you!'"

"Case dismissed!"

Not True

Teacher: "The sentence 'My father had money,' is in the past tense. Now Jack, what tense would you be speaking in, if you said, "My father has money"?"

Jack: "Pretense."

Not Poverty

"I feel sure, my poor man," said the old lady visiting a state prison, "it was poverty that brought you to this."

"No, ma'am, quite the contrary," replied the prisoner. "I happened to be coining money."

It's Barely True

For the shaggy-dog-story connoisseurs, there's the one about the character who imagined that he saw a bear sitting a few rows ahead of him in the theater one night. He broached the matter to his wife, who shushed him impatiently, remarking that it was merely a woman with a fur coat. Unconvinced, our man tiptoed up the aisle and, sure enough, it was a bear, watching the picture intently, one paw curved lovingly around the man in the next seat. Said the tiptoer: "Is that your bear?"

"Yes, it is," admitted the seated one.

"Why on earth did you bring it to the movies?"

Replied the bear's friend: "Oh, he was just fascinated by the book." *Telephone Topics*

Just a Spot

A couple had a "love" spat and were driving down a country road in silence. A mule in a roadside pasture brayed.

"A relative of yours?" asked the husband.

"Yeah, by marriage," came the sweet reply.

They're All Alike

Husband (shouting upstairs to wife): "For the last time, Mary, are you coming?"

Wife: "Haven't I been telling you for the last hour that I'll be down in a minute?"

Truth

Bus Driver (to little girl): "You're only six? When will you be seven?"

Little Girl: "As soon as I get off the bus."

He Wouldn't Know

"Pardon me, sir," said the waiter, taking up the money, "but this includes nothing for the waiter."

"I didn't eat one, did I?" said the professor, glancing up from his book.

Not Easy

Visitor: "Has your baby learned to talk yet?"
Dad: "Yes, indeed. We're teaching him to shut up now."

No Faults

"Isn't it surprising that Mrs. Brown can never see any faults in her children?" said Mrs. Smith.

"Mothers never can," laughed Mr. Smith.

"What a silly thing to say. Just like a man. I'm sure I could see faults in our children—if they had any."

Otherwise O.K.

A credit-reporting agency in an eastern city made the following report concerning a debtor:

"We have a report that this party has no property, either real or personal; no credit, either actual or potential; no prospects, either present or future; and no hope, either now or next year."

That's what we call laying the cards face up on the table.

Too Busy

An immigrant was being examined for naturalization as a citizen of the U.S.A. The questioner demanded:

"Who is the President of the United States?"

The applicant answered correctly.

"And the Vice-President?"

Again he had the answer.

"Could you be President?"

"No, no."

"Why not?"

"Mister, you 'scuse me, please. I vera busy—worka da mine all day now."

American Language

English as spoken in America brings out some odd comments. There was the man who was talking about a certain political candidate. He said: "If Jones will only take this stand when he runs, he'll have a walkover."

Same Speech

A clergyman's daughter was once asked, "Jane, does your father ever preach the same sermon twice?"

After a moment's reflection Jane replied, "Yes, I think he does; but he hollers in different places."

In Debt

A new father, looking at the babies through the glass of the hospital nursery, noticed every baby was crying. "What's the matter?" he asked a nurse.

"If you were only a few days old, out of a job, and owed the government $2,050, you'd cry, too," she replied.

Helpless

The ladies were discussing the general helplessness of husbands.

"I declare," exclaimed Mrs. Jones, "I don't know what my husband would do without me! If I left him alone for a week, he would just die."

"You ought to see my husband," declared Mrs. Brown. "Without me, he is as helpless as a newborn babe."

"Girls," cried Mrs. Harrison, "you think your husbands are helpless, but you should see mine. Harry is so helpless that when he sews a button on his coat or darns his socks, I have to thread the needle for him!"

Ten Commandments

The kindly old lady handed a package to the post-office clerk. "Does this package contain anything breakable?" he asked.

"Nothing but the Ten Commandments," she sadly replied. "It's a Bible."

Flying Ice

During a snowstorm the foreman of the road crew, head bent against the below-zero gale, walked up to a halted bulldozer. Seeing only one man standing beside the machine, he yelled out: "Hey, Charlie, where's George?"

Charlie turned, hesitated, then bellowed: "He got knocked out by a piece of flying ice."

"Flying ice?" echoed the foreman.

"Yeah," Charlie shouted. "He tried to spit against the wind."

Proof

Judge: "Your age, madam?"
Lady witness: "Thirty years."
Judge: "You may have a hard time proving that."
Lady witness: "You'll have a difficult time proving the contrary. The church that had the record of my birth burned down in 1895."

They Guessed Wrong

"How about two of them?" asked the druggist of the man who was buying a toothbrush. "One for your wife?"

"No, thanks. When I buy a new one, I give her the old one."

Several customers in the store gasped, and then he added, "She uses it to clean her shoes."

A Great Experiment

A professor of English literature in a certain southern college included in his examination questions the query: "What did Shakespeare do in his experimental period?"

He naturally expected the students to provide the titles of some of the great master's early plays, but one knowing young lady removed the curse of dullness from her paper by replying, "He married Anne Hathaway."

There's a Reason

First Customer: "It's fellows like you who spoil it for the rest of us—giving that girl a dollar tip!"

Second Customer: "Well, look at the hat she gave me!"

WIDE EYES

If the quality and nature of restaurant fare varies in different parts of the country, so does the language in which it is characterized.

In a small roadside cafe in Mississippi, a northern tourist ordered from the simple bill of fare ham, eggs, cornbread, and coffee.

An ancient waiter took his order and shuffled off to the kitchen. In a little while he returned.

"Boss," said he, "How do you want dem eggs—blind, or lookin' up at ye?"

MODERN IDEAS

He: "Of course, I'll be liberal with my money after we're married, darling. I'll spend it on you as fast as I make it. Now what else do you want to know?"

She: "How fast do you make it?"

PUZZLE

On his way home, Mike stopped off at the post office to mail a letter to his fiancee, but the three letter slots, "City," "Domestic," and "Foreign" perplexed him. "Faith, and this is a fine problem," he exclaimed. "Maggie's a domestic, she lives in the city, and she's a foreigner. What beats me, is how I'm going to put this letter in three places at wanst!"

HOUSECLEANING

A patron came limping into the drug store.

"Give me some arnica," the cripple wearily demanded.

"What's the matter?" the druggist asked sympathetically.

"Oh, it's that spring housecleaning again," Smith rejoined.

"Oh, ho," laughed the pill pusher, "so your wife roped you into that again!"

"Nope," replied Smith. "It wasn't that. I came home tonight, and sat down where the sofa was yesterday."

Exactly

In a court recently a witness, on being asked "Which side of State Street do you live on?" made the remarkable statement, "Either side."

"Either side!" barked the attorney. "What do you mean by that?"

"Just what I said," the witness replied; "either side. When you're going north, it's on the right; but when you're going south, it's on the left."

"The witness is excused!" the lawyer cried.

Higher Mathematics

When the owner of a timber tract sent out a camp crew of fifty men with three women to cook for them, he said to the camp boss:

"Don't give me long reports about what you are doing. Instead of multiplying words, just give a few figures each week and I can tell how you are getting along."

The next week he received this note: "Two per cent of the men have married 33 1|3 per cent of the women."

Philosophy

Uncle Jake was eighty years old.
"Don't you hate to grow old?" he was asked.
"Man, no," he said. "If I wasn't old I'd be dead."

A Way of Looking at It

A friend watched a little girl pull out a big weed and, patting her on the head, remarked, "My what a strong girl you are!"

"Yep, I know it," the child agreed, "and the whole world was hangin' on the other end of it."

All Business

A piece of paper, slipped under the windshield wiper of the car parked in the no-parking zone, bore the words: "Attorney—am inside attending to business."

Below, very neatly written, appeared the note: "Policeman—am outside attending to business."

On the door handle was a parking ticket.

Two Heads Are Not Better

"There ought to be only one head to every family."

"You're right! I've just paid for hats for my wife and daughter."

Sad Recollection

A circus owner on tour wondered how he could increase the attendance. He decided to advertise that his elephant, Daisy, would play the piano. On the night of her first appearance, the tent was crowded with skeptical spectators.

Daisy came out, seated herself at the piano, gazed at the keyboard—then closed her eyes in an expression of profound sadness.

"A fake!" the people cried. "Why doesn't the elephant play?"

The manager came out and, motioning for silence, explained, "Poor Daisy is so overcome with grief she cannot play. She sits down to the piano, gazes at the keyboard—and what does she see? Daisy sees the teeth of her poor mamma!"

What's in a Name

"What's your name?" asked the recruit sergeant.

"Six-Six Jones," replied the recruit.

"That's a funny name, 'Six-Six.'" remarked the sergeant.

"That really isn't my name," declared the recruit. "As a matter of fact, it's Six-and-Seven-Eighths."

"I don't get you," said the somewhat bewildered sergeant.

"Well, when I was born, my parents didn't know what to call me," he explained, "so they put a lot of names in father's hat, and by mistake father pulled out the size of his hat."

Smile When You Say It

"Mother, are you the nearest relative I have?"

"Yes, dear, and your father is the closest."

Short Circuit

When visitors came, Sonny, age five, took them to see the pigs in their electric-fence enclosure, explaining, "When the piggies back into the 'lectric fence there'll be a short circus."

Time

A few years ago an ambitious clock peddler invaded a well-nigh inaccessible region.

He paused before a small ramshackle mountain cabin, and addressed himself to an ancient native sunning himself on the veranda. He was working around to the subject of clocks, when a boy came around the corner of the house and inquired: "Whut time is it, Paw?"

The aged native glanced at the shadow moving across the porch, and replied: " 'Bout fo' planks till dinnertime."

Poor Audience

Oscar Wilde, after witnessing a first performance of a play which was a complete failure, was greeted by his friends.

"How did your play go tonight, Oscar?" said one.

"Oh," said the playwright, "the play was a great success, but the audience was a failure."

A Good Provider

James Farley, addressing the Chicago Boys' Clubs, told the story of a Mrs. Murphy, whose husband fell off a boat and drowned. "Tell me," asked a friend, "did he leave you well provided for?" "That he did," replied Mrs. Murphy, "$100,000." "One hundred thousand dollars," whistled the friend. "That's marvelous for a man who could neither read nor write." "Nor swim either," replied the widow.

Different Situation

Teacher: "Bobby, can you tell me how many bones you have in your body?"
Bobby: "Yes'm. Nine hundred."
Teacher: "That's a good many more than I have."
Bobby: "Well I had sardines for lunch."

Traffic

Cowboy: "What kind of a saddle do you want—one with a horn or without?"

Dude: "Without, I guess. There doesn't seem to be much traffic on these prairies."

She Wasn't Mad

A teacher sent this note to the mother of an unruly pupil:

"Dear Mrs. Jones: I regret to inform you that your son idles away his time, is disobedient, quarrelsome, and disturbs other students who are trying to work. He needs a good thrashing and I urge that you give him one."

This was the reply she received:

"Dear Miss Smith: Lick him yourself. I ain't mad at him."

Bob Burns Describes a Hat

Her hat looked like a dish of chop suey with a choice of two vegetables. *Bob Burns*

Typical Sergeant

"When I was a little child," the sergeant sweetly addressed the men at the end of an exhaustive drill, "I had a set of wooden soldiers. There was a poor little boy in the neighborhood, and I gave them to him. Then I wanted them back and cried, but my mother said: 'Don't cry, Bertis. Some day you'll get your wooden soldiers back.'

"And, believe me, you lopsided, mutton-headed, goofus-brained set of certified rolling pins, that day has come."

Impossible

"Is it possible for a man to make a fool of himself without knowing it?"

"Not if he has a wife."

An Old Story

"Too bad that Jim and his girl aren't good enough for each other."

"What makes you say that?"

"I've been talking to both families."

No Dumbbell

Employer—Have you any references?

Applicant—No, sir. I tore them up.
Employer—That was a foolish thing to do.
Applicant—You wouldn't think so if you had read them.

Oil's Well

Filling-station operator up North: "I filled your tank with gas; now how's your oil?"
Southern boy: "We all's all right, how's you all?"

One Collar—Clean

A boy walked into the men's outfitting department of a large store. Addressing a salesman, he said: "A soft man's collar, please."

The other salesmen laughed, and the one serving said, "You mean a man's soft collar, my boy." Pointing to his own collar, he asked: "Do you mean one like this?"

The boy eyed it briefly. Then he replied: "No! A clean one."

Poor Aim

Mother: "When that boy threw stones at you, why didn't you call me instead of throwing them back at him?"

Junior: "What good would it have done to call you? You couldn't hit a thing."

Definition

The New York Times once referred to Noah Webster as that "astute scholar who wrote a perennial best seller by the efficacious expedient of placing words in alphabetical sequence."

Just Forget It

Private Doe wanted to slip out of the barracks, unofficially, to see his girl. He went to the sentry to state his case.

"Well," said the sentry, "I'll be off duty when you come back, so you ought to have the password for tonight. It is 'Idiosyncrasy.'"

"Idio what?"

"Idiosyncrasy."

"I'll stay in the barracks."

Speech in the Office

He had found fault with his secretary for altering a sentence in a letter he had dictated. She thought he meant what she had written.

"I don't want you to think," retorted the great man. "I want you to take down my words accurately and then type them, neither adding nor leaving out anything I may say."

Later in the afternoon the typist brought back the following letter for signature:

"Dear Smyth: Spell it with a y, although that's pure swank on his part. In answer to your letter of—look up the date. We can quote you—tell me, Walter, what's the most we can charge this old buzzard? Very well. We can quote you $50 a ton for the goods. If he accepts we shall have to make sure of our money beforehand, for I don't trust him. Awaiting the pleasure of your valued order, Yours faithfully."

Bright Boy

The question on a physiology examination read: "How may one obtain a good posture?"

The country boy wrote: "Keep the cows off it and let it grow a while."

Her Choice

Seth and Liz were married only a short time when he came home with a big wash tub, a washboard, and a handsome three-foot mirror.

Liz: "What is all that truck you are bringing?"

Seth: "You can take your pick. You can take the tub and washboard and go to work, or you can take the mirror and sit down and watch yourself starve."

He Should Know Better

A speaker was nearing the end of an address which had taken ninety minutes of shouting and table pounding. The audience was restless.

Finally, the speaker said, "In conclusion, I should like to ask myself a question." A voice in the balcony shouted, "Brother, will you get a lousy answer to that question."

High Finance

A man had barely paid off the mortgage on his house when he mortgaged it again to buy a new car. Then he sought out a banker to borrow money on the car so he could build a garage.

"If I do make you the loan," asked the banker, "how will you buy gas for the car?"

"It seems to me," the man replied with dignity, "that a fellow who owns his own house, car, and garage should be able to get credit for gas."

Generosity

The conductor was perplexed. "Who on earth," he sputtered, "would want to steal a Pullman ladder?"

Just then the curtain parted and a little old man poked his head through cautiously. "Porter," he whispered, "you may use mine if you like. I won't need it until morning."

Seesaw

The tramp approached a farmer and said, "Will you give me something to eat?"

"See that pile of wood?" asked the farmer.

"No," said the tramp.

"Why, I saw you see it," said the farmer.

"Well," the tramp said as he started away, "maybe you saw me see it, but you won't see me saw it."

Not Anonymous

One Sunday morning, just before service, a note was handed to the Reverend Henry Ward Beecher. The famous clergyman discovered it contained the single word: FOOL.

Mr. Beecher arose, described the communication to his congregation, and added, "I have known many an instance of a man writing a letter and forgetting to sign his name. but this is the first case I have ever known of a man signing his name and forgetting to write the letter."

Divided Affections

Bride: Will you think of me always, darling?
Bridegroom: I can't lie to you, dear. I'll try, but occasionally I might wonder if the Cubs win the pennant.

Seeing You Soon

"You've got a pretty place," said the departing guest "but it looks a little bit bare yet."
"Oh," explained the host, "it's because the trees are young. I hope they'll have grown to a good size before you come again."

Extended Terms

Proud Mother (walking into small-loan department): There! That's the last payment on our baby carriage.
Clerk: And how is the baby?
Mother: Oh, fine. She's getting married next week.

Just in Case

"Jones," remarked a neighbor, "I understand your boy is learning a trade. Do you think he'll work at it?"
"No, I don't think he will. He's just learning it so that when he is idle he will be able to tell people what kind of work he is out of."

Fair Question

"Could you," the specialist asked, "pay for an operation if I found one necessary?"
"Would you," countered the patient, "find one necessary if I couldn't pay for it?"

Came the Dawn

'Twas dawn when the new father whispered to his wife: "It must be about time to get up."
"How can you tell?"
"The baby's gone to sleep."

No Time to Waste

After several hours of poor fishing the little girl suddenly threw down her pole and cried, "I quit!"

"What's the matter?" her father asked.

"Nothing," said the child, "except that I can't seem to get waited on."

GET THERE FIRST

He was engaged in the task of reviewing the monthly household bills. They were terrible.

"I'm afraid we're on the road to the poorhouse," he observed to his wife.

"Well," retorted the little woman, "if we are, then there are a lot of other people who are on it, too."

"True, true!" he moaned, "but we're passing 'em on the road."

NEVER SANE

Mrs. Smith was boasting about the wholehearted devotion of her husband.

"I never worry about his paying attention to other women," she boasted; "he's crazy about me."

"That's wonderful, dear," said her friend, Mrs. Jones, "but aren't you afraid he has lucid intervals?"

SOUTHERN STYLE

Item on the menu in a New Orleans restaurant: Yankee Pot Roast—Southern Style.

IMPORTANT CASE

A young surgeon received a telephone call from a colleague, who invited him to make a fourth at bridge.

"Going out, dear?" asked his wife suspiciously.

"I'm afraid so," was the brave reply. "It's a very important case. There are three doctors there already."

INSANITY

Foreman: "We find the defendant not guilty."

Judge: "What possible reason can this jury have for such an astonishing verdict?"

Foreman: "Insanity, your Honor."

Judge: "What! All twelve of you?"

Turn It Down

Wife (trying on hats): Do you like this turned down, dear?
Hubby: How much is it?
Wife: Twenty-five dollars.
Hubby: Yes, turned down.

Business Is Better

"How's business, old man?"
"Picking up a little, I'm glad to say. As a matter of fact, one of our salesman came in yesterday with a $500 order."
"I don't believe it."
"It's true. I can show you the cancellation."

Don't Try This

Judge: "Did you see the shot that was fired?"
Witness: "No, I only heard it."
Judge: "That is not sufficient evidence."
The witness left the stand and while his back was turned to the judge he laughed out loud. The judge recalled him for contempt of court.
Witness: "Did you see me laugh?"
Judge: "No, but I heard you."
Witness: "Insufficient evidence, —Judge."

Unfair

Two labor leaders in a hotel lobby in Washington watched two pretty young girls kiss each other.
"There's another of those things that are so unfair," remarked one sadly.
"What do you mean?" asked his companion.
"Women doing men's work," came the answer.

Clear Profit

A bride-to-be was showing her friend a list of guests to be invited to the wedding. Her friend looked puzzled.
"What's the matter?" asked the bride-to-be.
"Isn't it strange," asked the friend, "you have only put down the names of married couples?"
"Yes, that was Jack's idea. Don't you think it's rather

clever? He says that if we invite only married people, the presents will be all clear profit."

SAFETY FIRST

Tommy: "Can you eat nuts, grandpa?"
Grandpa: "Oh, dear, no, I haven't any teeth."
Tommy: "Well, look after these till I come back from school."

SHE KNEW

Sue: "Mother, am I a canoe?"
Mother: "Certainly not!"
Sue: "Well, you are always saying you like to see people paddle their own canoes, and I thought I must be yours."

HARD TO UNDERSTAND

His mother had ordered Bill to bed. He had demanded to know why he had to retire so early, and she had told him. He turned to his father.

"Pop," he complained, "women are unreasonable!"

Papa watched Mamma out of the corner of his eye, and inquired:

"Why, son?"

"Well," explained Bill, "tonight Mom says, 'Bill, you are too young to stay up,' In the morning, she'll say, 'Get up, Bill—you're too big to stay in bed!' You can't win."

RAIN WATER

The tourist stopped at a hot-dog stand along the road and ordered coffee from a sour-faced waitress.

Just to be polite, he said, "Looks like rain, doesn't it?"

"Well," snapped the old gal, "tastes like coffee, don't it?"

DIDN'T KNOW

"I was so cold last night I couldn't sleep. I just shivered."

"Did your teeth chatter?"

"I don't know, we don't sleep together."

Fragile

Professor: "If molecules can be split into atoms and atoms can be broken into electrons, can electrons be split any further?"

Student: "Well, you might try mailing some in a package marked Fragile."

No Bathing, Either

The man had just brought a cigar in a department store and started to light it.

"Didn't you notice the sign?" asked the salesgirl.

"What!" exploded the customer. "You sell cigars in here but you prohibit smoking?"

The salesgirl smiled sweetly: "We also sell bath towels."

The Whole Truth

The personnel manager was interviewing a young lady for a bookkeeping position. "You understand, of course, young lady, that we are looking for a responsible person to fill this position."

"Oh, I'm responsible," the young woman replied eagerly. "On my last job, every time there was something they called a discrepancy, they always said I was responsible."

Time to Complain

One day Jones got fifty cents too much in his pay envelope, but he didn't say a word. During the week the paymaster found his mistake, and on the next payday deducted fifty cents.

"Excuse me, sir," said Jones, "I'm fifty cents short this week."

"You didn't complain last week."

"No, sir," said Jones. "I don't mind overlooking one mistake. But when it happens twice, then it's time to say something."

Testimonial

An unsolicited testimonial from an ardent golfer to a hosiery manufacturer: "Fifteen minutes after putting on a pair of your socks, I made a hole in one."

Now Will You Pipe Down?

Ida: "I hear you accepted him. Did he mention that he had proposed to me first?"

Ina: "Not specifically. He did say he had done many foolish things before he met me."

Just a Detail

The daughter was busy with the wedding plans when the bridegroom-to-be called. He watched the preparations for a while until his future wife noticed his look of annoyance.

"Darling, we have so much to do," she soothed, "and if we want to make our wedding a big success we mustn't forget the most insignificant detail!"

"Oh, don't worry about that," murmured the young man. "I'll be there all right."

Working Model

The dejected woman was describing her husband to the judge. "He neither drinks nor smokes. He never stays out late at night, and I have yet to catch him in a lie. In fact, your Honor, he is a model husband."

The perplexed judge gently asked: "Then why, madam, did you come here?"

"Well," she sighed, "he isn't exactly a working model!"

Lucky

The restaurant owner was sampling the meat loaf made by his newly hired cook. "You say you served in France?" he asked.

"Yes, sir," said the cook. "I was cook for a regiment for two years and was wounded three times."

"You're lucky," observed the owner. "It's a wonder they didn't kill you!"

Competition

Down in Alabama two bootblacks were working side by side, when they fell out. One of the boys vowed that he was going to revenge himself on the other.

"Is yoh goin' to fight?" the friend asked fearfully.

"Naw," the other boy replied. "Ah's gonna do wuss dan dat. When he gets through polishing de next gent's shoes, Ah's goin' ter say to dat gent jus' as he steps down from de chair: 'Shine, sah, shine?'"

We've Heard Him

A lady stalled her car at a traffic light and couldn't get is started. She tried and tried, while behind her an impatient motorist honked his horn steadily. Finally, she got out and walked back.

"I'm awfully sorry, but I can't start my car," she told the driver of the other car. "If you'll go and start it for me, I'll stay here and lean on your horn."

Bright Boy

Tommy came home from his first day at school.
"What did you learn in school?" asked his mother.
"Nothing," said Tommy; then, seeing the look of disappointment on her face, he added, "but I learned a lot during recess!"

Big Job

The baby had cried and fretted all day and the young mother was nearly frantic. When her husband came home in the evening, she described her experience.

"Remember," he told her cheerfully, "the hand that rocks the cradle rules the world."

About 8:30, with the baby crying again, she said to hubby:

"I'm going to a movie, darling, so for the next couple of hours you rule the world."

Observation

A four-year-old attended prayer meeting not long ago with his parents. When he knelt to say his prayers before going to bed, he prayed: "Dear Lord, we had a good time at church tonight. I wish you could have been there."

Prospect

Housewife (to salesman at door): "I am not in the market for a vacuum cleaner, but try the people in the next house. We borrow theirs and it is in terrible condition."

On the Menu

Waitress: We have practically everything on the menu.
Customer: So I notice. Would you bring me a clean one?

Signs

San Francisco coffee shop in middle of "up-all-night" belt: Breakfast—All Day.

In a Texas restaurant: "If our steak is too tough for you, GET OUT! This is no place for a weakling.

Yackson from Yale

Mr. Biggs wanted to know about the employees who worked in his business. One day he came upon a young male who was carrying out a large sack of the firm's cash.

"Where did you get your financial training, young man!" he asked.

"Yale," the young man answered.

Mr. Biggs was a staunch advocate of higher learning. "Good!" he said. "And what's your name?"

"Yackson."

Cured

Smith: "Your wife used to be so nervous. Now she seems cured."

Jones: "She is. The doctor told her her nervousness was a sign of old age."

That's Clear

With his wife sick in bed, pandemonium reigned supreme in the kitchen. The tea was missing. He looked high and low and finally called to his wife: "I can't find the tea, dear. Where do you keep it?"

"I don't know why you can't find it," came the peevish reply. "It's right in front, on the cupboard shelf, in a cocoa tin marked 'matches'!"

SALESMANSHIP

"What," exclaimed the lady, "you charge me five dollars for that pocket-book?"

"Yes, ma'am," replied the polite clerk, "that is the lowest price we can sell it for."

"How is it that I can get one just like it at Smith's for $4.50?"

"I cannot say, madam. Perhaps Mr. Smith has taken a fancy to you. He is a widower, and you are very beautiful and—yes, ma'am, five dollars. Thank you."

NOT GOING ANY PLACE

Hillbilly (to new bride, after he completed their cabin): "Wall, how d'ya like your new home, woman?"

Wife: "Not bad at all, husband, but I don't see no door!"

Hillbilly: "Door? Yew a-plannin' on agoin' somewheres?"

SAFETY

Concerned about her husband in the Navy, a young wife sent a note to her pastor. It reached the pulpit. It read, "John Anderson having gone to sea, his wife desires the prayers of the congregation for his safety." Looking over it hastily, the minister read aloud, "John Anderson, having gone to see his wife, desires the prayers of the congregation for his safety."

LET'S NOT GO TO ANY TROUBLE

The wife smiled at her husband when he got home. "Poor darling," she said, "you must be hungry. Would you like some tender chops with golden-brown potatoes and green peas, and some apple pie a la mode?"

"No, darling," was the weary reply. "let's save money and eat at home."

Don't Forget

Judge: "Now don't forget—you were a gentleman and a lady before you were man and wife."

Disillusioned

Just returned from summer camp, Willie was enthusiastically describing the many projects in which he had participated.

Mother smiled indulgently.

"I guess, after all, you were rather glad to get back home, weren't you?" she asked.

"Well, not 'specially," the youngster replied, "but some of the fellows were that had dogs."

Jackpot

Dr. Morris Fishbein tells about his colleague who wrote a prescription in his usual illegible hand. The patient must have recovered quickly, because he did not get it filled, and in due time he forgot what that little piece of paper in his card case was. "The patient used it for two years as a railroad pass," Dr. Fishbein says. "Twice it got him into Radio City Music Hall and once into Ebbets Field for a ball game. It came in handy as a letter from his employer to the cashier to increase his salary. And to cap the climax, his daughter played it on the piano and won a scholarship to a conservatory of music."

He Made it Easily

The Irishman was relating a story of his travels.

"I landed on the island and started to explore," he said. "When I got to the middle of the island I saw the biggest bear I've ever seen." He paused dramatically, then continued. "There was one tree on the island, and the lowest bough was twenty feet from the ground, and I jumped for it."

"Did you manage to grasp it?" asked one of his audience.

"I didn't grasp it going up," replied the Irishman, "but I caught it coming down."

A Veterinary Will Do

The car lay on its side. After turning several somersaults it was a complete wreck. It took the rescuers hours to extricate the driver. Finally they worked him free of the wreck and rushed him to the doctor.

"I'm sorry," said the doctor, "I can't do anything for him. You see, I'm a veterinary surgeon."

"That's all right," retorted the patient weakly, "I was a jackass to think I could do sixty on those tires."

Didn't Blow His Horn

The occasion was an amateur musical. The kind-hearted hostess, spying a lonely-looking little man huddled in a corner of the room, paused to make conversation.

"Tell me," she asked, "do you play any musical instrument?"

"Not away from home," the little man replied.

"How peculiar," remarked the hostess. "What instrument do you play at home?"

"Second fiddle," the little man replied.

Same as Usual

Entering the house just as her husband put down the telephone, the wife said, "Whom were you talking to, dear?"

"Miss Jones," he replied.

"And how is she?"

Wearily he answered, "About the same—unfair to meddling."

It Depends

Mother: "Where is Jimmy?"

Dad: "If he knows as much about canoes as he thinks he does, he is canoeing; but if he doesn't know any more than I think he does, he's swimming."

Best Wishes Too

A lovelorn sailor decided to celebrate payday by sending a telegram to his girl. He finally handed a message to the telephone clerk which read:

"I love you. I love you. I love you."

The clerk, reading it, said: "You're allowed to add another word for the same price."
The sailor thought a bit and then added: "Regards."

HELP!

In filling out an application for a factory job, a man puzzled for a long time over this question: "Person to notify in case of accident?"
Finally he wrote: "Anybody in sight."

GOOD AND DULL

"How's business?" a passer-by asked the scissors grinder.
"Fine," he aid. "I never saw things so dull."

Chapter XII

SIXTEEN HUNDRED QUOTATIONS FROM LITERATURE

ACTION

Every noble activity makes room for itself. *Emerson*
Mark this well, ye proud men of action! ye are, after all, nothing but unconscious instruments of the men of thought. *Heine*
The actions of men are the best interpreters of their thoughts. *Locke*
Every action of our lives touches on some chord that will vibrate in eternity. *E. H. Chapin*

> Trust no future, howe'er pleasant!
> Let the dead past bury its dead!
> Act,—act in the living Present!
> Heart within and God o'erhead. *Longfellow*

> Let us then be up and doing,
> With a heart for any fate;
> Still achieving, still pursuing,
> Learn to labor and to wait. *Longfellow*

I took the canal zone and let Congress debate, and while the debate goes on the canal does also. *Theodore Roosevelt*

He that is overcautious will accomplish little. *Schiller*

> Theirs not to make reply,
> Theirs not to reason why,
> Theirs but to do and die. *Tennyson*

ACTORS

The most difficult character in comedy is that of the fool, and he must be no simpleton that plays that part. *Cervantes*

ADVERSITY

Adversity is the trial of principle. Without it a man hardly knows whether he is honest or not. *Fielding*

God brings men into deep waters, not to drown them, but to cleanse them. *Aughey*

Prosperity is no just scale; adversity is the only balance to weigh friends. *Plutarch*

There is no education like adversity. *Disraeli*

Prosperity is a great teacher; adversity is a greater. Possession pampers the mind; privation trains and strengthens it. *Hazlitt*

> Sweet are the uses of adversity;
> Which, like the toad, ugly and venomous,
> Wears yet a precious jewel in his head. *Shakespeare*

> Be still, sad heart, and cease repining,
> Behind the clouds the sun is shining;
> Thy fate is the common fate of all;
> Into each life some rain must fall,—
> Some days must be dark and dreary. *Longfellow*

As threshing separates the sheaf from the chaff, so does affliction purify virtue. *Burton*

Affliction is not sent in vain from the good God who chastens those that he loves. *Southey*

It is not from the tall, crowded workhouse of prosperity that men first or clearest see the eternal stars of heaven. *Theodore Parker*

It is not until we have passed through the furnace that we are made to know how much dross there is in our composition. *Colton*

ADVICE

It is easy when we are in prosperity to give advice to the afflicted. *Aeschylus*

We ask advice: we mean approbation. *Colton*

Old men are fond of giving good advice, to console themselves for being no longer in a position to give bad examples. *La Rochefoucauld*

AGE

To know how to grow old is the master work of wisdom, and one of the most difficult chapters in the great art of living. *Amiel*

The evening of a well-spent life brings its lamps with it. *Joubert*

Youth is a blunder; Manhood a struggle; Old Age a regret. *Disraeli*

Age does not make us childish, as some say; it finds us true children. *Goethe*

At 20 years of age the will reigns; at 30 the wit; at 40 the judgment. *Franklin*

An aged Christian, with the snow of time upon his head, may remind us that those points of earth are whitest which are nearest to heaven. *E. H. Chapin*

If wrinkles must be written upon our brows, let them not be written upon the heart. The spirit should not grow old. *James A. Garfield*

In youth the days are short and the years are long; in old age the years are short and the days long. *Panin*

The old believe everything; the middle-aged suspect everything; the young know everything. *Wilde*

Whoever serves his country well has no need of ancestors. *Voltaire*

AGRICULTURE

Earth is here so kind, that just tickle her with a hoe and she laughs with a harvest. *Jerrold*

Let us never forget that the cultivation of the earth is the most important labor of man. When tillage begins,

AMBITION

When you are aspiring to the highest place, it is honorable to reach the second or even the third rank. *Cicero*

Hitch your wagon to a star. *Emerson*

> When that the poor have cried, Caesar hath wept:
> Ambition should be made of sterner stuff:
> Yet Brutus says he was ambitious;
> And Brutus is an honourable man. *Shakespeare*

> Ambition has but one reward for all:
> A little power, a little transient fame,
> A grave to rest in, and a fading name!
> *William Winter*

All you need in this life is ignorance and confidence, and then success is sure. *S. L. Clemens*

If a man write a better book, preach a better sermon, or make a better mouse-trap than his neighbor, though he build his house in the woods, the world will make a beaten path to his door. *Emerson*

Ambition is the spur that makes man struggle with destiny. It is heaven's own incentive to make purpose great and achievement greater. *Donald G. Mitchell*

Fling away ambition. By that sin angels fell. How then can man, the image of his Maker, hope to win by it? *Shakespeare*

Ambition is a lust that is never quenched, but grows more inflamed and madder by enjoyment. *Otway*

The noblest spirit is most strongly attracted by the love of glory. *Cicero*

AMERICA

> O beautiful for patriot dream
> That sees beyond the years
> Thine alabaster cities gleam
> Undimmed by human tears!
> America! America!
> God shed His grace on thee,

And crown thy good with brotherhood
From sea to shining sea! *Katharine Lee Bates*

Thou, too, sail on, O ship of State!
Sail on, O Union, strong and great!
Humanity with all its fears,
With all the hopes of future years,
Is hanging breathless on thy fate! *Longfellow*

In the United States there is more space where nobody is than where anybody is. This is what makes America what it is. *Gertrude Stein*

I was born an American; I live an American; I shall die an American. *Daniel Webster*

American liberty is a religion. It is a thing of the spirit. It is an aspiration on the part of the people for not only a free life but a better life. *Wendell L. Willkie*

ANGER

An angry man opens his mouth and shuts up his eyes. *Cato*

Beware the fury of a patient man. *Dryden*

Anger begins in folly, and ends in repentance. *Pythagoras*

The fire you kindle for your enemy often burns yourself more than him. *Chinese proverb*

Men often make up in wrath what they want in reason. *Alger*

Life appears to me too short to be spent in nursing animosity or registering wrong. *Charlotte Bronte*

APPEARANCE

O wad some power the giftie gie us
To see oursel's as ithers see us! *Burns*

All that glitters is not gold. *Cervantes*

Polished brass will pass upon more people than rough gold. *Chesterfield*

By outward show let's not be cheated.
An ass should like an ass be treated. *Gay*

APPLAUSE

Applause is the spur of noble minds; the end and aim of weak ones. *Colton*

O popular applause!—What heart of man is proof against thy sweet, seducing charms! *Cowper*

APPRECIATION

Next to excellence is the appreciation of it. *Thackeray*

He who receives a good turn should never forget it; he who does one should never remember it. *Charron*

To love one that is great, is almost to be great one's self. *Madame Necker*

The gratitude of most men is but a secret desire of receiving greater benefits. *La Rochefoucauld*

We must never undervalue any person.—The workman loves not to have his work despised in his presence. Now God is present everywhere, and every person is his work. *De Sales*

Gratitude is a duty which ought to be paid, but which none have a right to expect. *Rousseau*

Contemporaries appreciate the man rather than the merit; but posterity will regard the merit rather than the man. *Colton*

ARCHITECTURE

Architecture is frozen music: *Goethe*

Ah, to build, to build!
That is the noblest of all the arts. *Longfellow*

ARGUMENT

Arguments out of a pretty mouth are unanswerable. *Addison*

Men's argument often prove nothing but their wishes. *Colton*

Many can argue; not many converse. *Alcott*

There is no good in arguing with the inevitable. The only argument available with an east wind is to put on your greatcoat. *J. R. Lowell*

Strong and bitter words indicate a weak cause. *Victor Hugo*

Never argue at the dinner table, for the one who is not hungry always gets the best of the argument. *Whately*

When people agree with me, I always feel that I must be wrong. *Wilde*

No great advance has ever been made in science, politics, or religion, without controversy. *Lyman Beecher*

Men are apt to mistake the strength of their feeling for the strength of their argument. The heated mind resents the chill touch and relentless scrutiny of logic. *Gladstone*

ART

Art is the stored honey of the human soul, gathered on wings of misery and travail. *Dreiser*

A picture is a poem without words. *Horace*

The artist does not see things as they are, but as he is. *Alfred Tonnelle*

ATHEISM

Few men are so obstinate in their atheism, that a pressing danger will not compel them to the acknowledgment of a divine power. *Plato*

What can be more foolish than to think that all this rare fabric of heaven and earth could come by chance, when all the skill or art is not able to make an oyster? To see rare effects, and no cause; a motion without a mover; a circle, without a centre; a time, without an eternity; a second, without a first: these are things so against philosophy and natural reason, that he must be a beast in understanding who can believe in them. The thing formed, says that nothing formed it; and that which is made, is, while that which made it is not! This folly is infinite. *Jeremy Taylor*

AUTHORS

The pen is the tongue of the mind. *Cervantes*

The author who speaks about his own books is almost as bad as a mother who talks about her own children. *Disraeli*

AUTUMN

The melancholy days have come, the saddest of the year,

Of wailing winds, and naked woods, and meadows brown and sear. *Bryant*

O, it sets my heart a clickin' like the tickin' of a clock,
When the frost is on the punkin and the fodder's in the shock. *James Whitcomb Riley*

BEAUTY

A thing of beauty is a joy forever. *Keats*

The beauty seen, is partly in him who sees it. *Bovee*

Remember that the most beautiful things in the world are the most useless; peacocks and lilies, for instance. *Ruskin*

I pray thee, O God, that I may be beautiful within. *Socrates*

The saying that beauty is but skin deep is but a skin deep saying. *Ruskin*

There should be as little merit in loving a woman for her beauty, as a man for his prosperity, both being equally subject to change. *Pope*

BELLS

The tocsin of the soul—the dinner bell. *Byron*

Those evening bells! those evening bells!
How many a tale their music tells! *Moore*

Ring in the valiant man and free,
The larger heart, the kindlier hand;
Ring out the darkness of the land;
Ring in the Christ that is to be. *Tennyson*

Ring out the old, ring in the new,
Ring, happy bells, across the snow. *Tennyson*

BENEVOLENCE

To feel much for others, and little for ourselves; to restrain our selfish, and exercise our benevolent affections, constitutes the perfection of human nature. *Adam Smith*

There cannot be a more glorious object in creation than a human being replete with benevolence, meditating in what manner he may render himself most acceptable to the Creator by doing good to his creatures. *Fielding*

He only does not live in vain, who employs his wealth, his thought, his speech to advance the good of others. *Hindu maxim*

I truly enjoy no more of the world's good things than what I willingly distribute to the needy. *Seneca*

BIBLE

The Bible is a window in this prison world, through which we may look into eternity. *Timothy Dwight*

There never was found, in any age of the world, either religion or law that did so highly exalt the public good as the Bible. *Bacon*

A Bible and a newspaper in every house, a good school in every district—all studied and appreciated as they merit —are the principle support of virtue, morality and civil liberty. *Franklin*

It is a belief in the Bible, the fruit of deep meditation, which has served me as the guide of my moral and literary life. I have found it a capital safely invested, and richly productive of interest. *Goethe*

The English Bible—a book which, if everything else in our language should perish, would alone suffice to show the whole extent of its beauty and power. *Macaulay*

The longer you read the Bible, the more you will like it; it will grow sweeter and sweeter; and the more you get into the spirit of it, the more you will get into the spirit of Christ. *Romaine*

So great is my veneration for the Bible, that the earlier my children begin to read it the more confident will be my hopes that they will prove useful citizens to their country and respectable members of society. *J. Q. Adams*

All the distinctive features and superiority of our republican institutions are derived from the teachings of Scripture. *Everett*

A noble book! All men's book! It is our first, oldest statement of the never-ending problem,—man's destiny, and God's way with him here on earth; and all in such free-flowing outlines,—grand in its sincerity; in its simplicity and its epic melody. *Carlyle*

There is a Book worth all other books which were ever printed. *Patrick Henry*

BIOGRAPHY

Biography is the only true history. *Carlyle*

> Lives of great men all remind us
> We can make our lives sublime,
> And, departing, leave behind us
> Footprints on the sands of time. *Longfellow*

To be ignorant of the lives of the most celebrated men of antiquity is to continue in a state of childhood all our days. *Plutarch*

Every great man nowadays has his disciples, and it is always Judas who writes the biography. *Wilde*

BOASTING

Where boasting ends, there dignity begins. *Young*

Conceit, more rich in matter than in words, brags of his substance: they are but beggars who can count their worth. *Shakespeare*

The empty vessel makes the greatest sound. *Shakespeare*

BOOKS

The writings of the wise are the only riches our posterity cannot squander. *Landor*

Except a living man there is nothing more wonderful than a book! a message to us from the dead—from human souls we never saw, who lived, perhaps, thousands of miles away. And yet these, in those little sheets of paper, speak to us, arouse us, terrify us, teach us, comfort us, open their hearts to us as brothers. *Charles Kingsley*

A good book is the precious life-blood of a master-spirit, embalmed and treasured up on purpose to a life beyond life. *Milton*

Books are those faithful mirrors that reflect to our mind the minds of sages and heroes. *Gibbon*

Books are the legacies that genius leaves to mankind, to be delivered down from generation to generation, as presents, to those that are yet unborn. *Addison*

Books are the true levellers.—They give to all who faithfully use them, the society, the spiritual presence of the greatest and best of our race. *Channing*

BRAVERY

None but the brave deserve the fair. *Dryden*

At the bottom of not a little of the bravery that appears in the world, there lurks a miserable cowardice. Men will face powder and steel because they have not the courage to face public opinion. *E. H. Chapin*

True bravery is shown by performing without witness what one might be capable of doing before all the world. *La Rochefoucauld*

BUSINESS

Anybody can cut prices, but it takes brain to produce a better article. *P. D. Armour*

There are two times in a man's life when he should not speculate: when he can't afford it, and when he can. *Mark Twain*

We demand that big business give people a square deal; in return we must insist that when anyone engaged in big business honestly endeavors to do right, he shall himself be given a square deal. *Theodore Roosevelt*

That which is everybody's business, is nobody's business. *Izaak Walton*

Capital is that part of wealth which is devoted to obtaining further wealth. *Alfred Marshall*

Each needs the other: capital cannot do without labor, nor labor without capital. *Pope Leo XIII*

Capital is that part of the wealth of a country which is employed in production, and consists of food, clothing, tools, raw materials, machinery, etc., necessary to give effect to labour. *David Ricardo*

Capital is dead labor that, vampire-like, lives only by sucking living labor, and lives the more, the more labor it sucks. *Karl Marx*

CAUTION

A wise man does not trust all his eggs to one basket. *Cervantes*

Be slow of tongue and quick of eye. *Cervantes*

Among mortals second thoughts are wisest. *Euripides*

Caution is the eldest child of wisdom. *Victor Hugo*

It is a good thing to learn caution by the misfortunes of others. *Syrus*

Change

Earth changes, but thy soul and God stand sure. *Browning*

History fades into fable; fact becomes clouded with doubt and controversy; the inscription moulders from the tablet; the statue falls from the pedestal. Columns, arches, pyramids, what are they but heaps of sand, and their epitaphs but characters written in the dust? *Washington Irving*

> All things must change
> To something new, to something strange. *Longfellow*

Remember the wheel of Providence is always in motion; and the spoke that is uppermost will be under; and therefore mix trembling always with your joy. *Philip Henry*

The old order changeth, yielding place to new. *Tennyson*

Everything changes but change. *Zangwill*

Character

It is in general more profitable to reckon up our defects than to boast of our attainments. *Carlyle*

Character is perfectly educated will. *Novalis*

Talent is nurtured in solitude; character is formed in the stormy billows of the world. *Goethe*

Men best show their character in trifles, where they are not on their guard. It is in insignificant matters, and in the simplest habits, that we often see the boundless egotism which pays no regard to the feelings of others, and denies nothing to itself. *Schopenhauer*

Only what we have wrought into our character during life can we take away with us. *Humboldt*

The great hope of society is in individual character. *Channing*

> Not in the clamor of the crowded street,
> Not in the shouts and plaudits of the throng,
> But in ourselves are triumph and defeat. *Longfellow*

Character is higher than intellect....A great soul will be strong to live as well to think. *Emerson*

It is by presence of mind in untried emergencies that the native metal of a man is tested. *Lowell*

You cannot dream yourself into a character; you must hammer and forge one for yourself. *Froude*

> In men whom men condemn as ill
> I find so much of goodness still. *Joaquin Miller*

CHARITY

As the purse is emptied, the heart is filled. *Victor Hugo*

Charity is the perfection and ornament of religion. *Addison*

Charity gives itself rich; covetousness hoards itself poor. *German proverb*

My poor are my best patients. God pays for them. *Boerhaave*

To pity is but human; to relieve it is Godlike. *H. Mann*

Better to expose ourselves to ingratitude than fail in assisting the unfortunate. *Du Coeur*

We are rich only through what we give; and poor only through what we refuse and keep. *Madame Swetchine*

You are indeed charitable when you give, and while giving, turn your face away so that you may not see the shyness of the receiver. *Kahlil Gibran*

Be charitable and indulgent to every one but thyself. *Joubert*

I will chide no heathen in the world but myself, against whom I know most faults. *Shakespeare*

CHEERFULNESS

A light heart lives long. *Shakespeare*

He who sings frightens away his ills. *Cervantes*

The true source of cheerfulness is benevolence—The soul that perpetually overflows with kindness and sympathy will always be cheerful. *P. Goodwin*

A cheerful look makes a dish a feast. *Herbert*

If I can put one touch of a rosy sunset into the life of any man or woman, I shall feel that I have worked with God. *G. Macdonald*

Cheer up, the worst is yet to come. *Philander Johnson*

Let us be of good cheer, remembering that the misfortunes hardest to bear are those which never happen. *Lowell*

A good laugh is sunshine in a house. *Thackeray*

CHILDREN

A little curly-headed, good-for-nothing,
And mischief-making monkey from his birth. *Byron*

Childhood shows the man, as morning shows the day. *Milton*

Children should be seen and not heard. *English proverb*

I love these little people, and it is not a slight thing, when they, who are so fresh from God, love us. *Dickens*

Spare the rod and spoil the child. *English proverb*

Children have more need of models than of critics. *Joubert*

> Wynken, Blynken and Nod one night
> Sailed off in a wooden shoe—
> Sailed on a river of crystal light
> Into a sea of dew. *Eugene Field*

Call not that man wretched, who, whatever ills he suffers, has a child to love. *Southey*

> There was a little girl,
> And she had a little curl,
> Right in the middle of her forehead;
> When she was good she was very, very good,
> When she was bad she was horrid. *Longfellow*

What gift has Providence bestowed on man that is so dear to him as his children? *Cicero*

A torn jacket is soon mended, but hard words bruise the heart of a child. *Longfellow*

How dear to this heart are the scenes of my childhood,
When fond recollection presents them to view. *Samuel Woodworth*

When a child can be brought to tears, not from fear of punishment, but from repentance for his offence, he needs no chastisement. When the tears begin to flow from grief at one's own conduct, be sure there is an angel nestling in the bosom. *A. Mann*

CHOICE

God offers to every mind its choice between truth and repose. *Emerson*

Choose always the way that seems the best, however rough it may be; custom will soon render it easy and agreeable. *Pythagoras*

CHRIST

All history is incomprehensible without Christ. *Renan*

The sages and heroes of history are receding from us, and history contracts the record of their deeds into a narrower and narrower page. But time has no power over the name and deeds and words of Jesus Christ. *Channing*

Jesus Christ, the condescension of divinity, and the exaltation of humanity. *Phillips Brooks*

All His glory and beauty come from within, and there He delights to dwell. His visits there are frequent, His conversation sweet, His comforts refreshing; and His peace passing all understanding. *Thomas a Kempis*

Jesus Christ is a God to whom we can approach without pride, and before whom we may abase ourselves without despair. *Pascal*

Alexander, Caesar, Charlemagne and I myself have founded empires; but upon what do these creations of our genius depend? Upon force. Jesus alone founded His empire upon love; and to this very day millions would die for Him. *Napoleon*

I believe Plato and Socrates. I believe in Jesus Christ. *Coleridge*

If the life and death of Socrates were those of a sage, the life and death of Jesus were those of a God. *Rousseau*

Though a great man may, by a rare possibility, be an infidel, yet an intellect of the highest order must build upon Christianity. *De Quincey*

To be like Christ is to be a Christian. *William Penn*

The only truly happy men I have ever known, were Christians. *John Randolph*

Whatever makes men good Christians, makes them good citizens. *Daniel Webster*

The only way to realize that we are God's children is to let Christ lead us to our Father. *Phillips Brooks*

Christianity, with its doctrine of humility, of forgiveness, of love, is incompatible with the state, with its haughtiness, its violence, its punishment, its wars. *Tolstoy*

Let it not be imagined that the life of a good Christian must be a life of melancholy and gloominess; for he only resigns some pleasures to enjoy others infinitely better. *Pascal*

The Christian needs a reminder every hour; some defeat, surprise, adversity, peril; to be agitated, mortified, beaten out of his course, so that all remains of self will be sifted out. *Horace Bushnell*

The best advertisement of a workshop is first-class work. The strongest attraction to Christianity is a well-made Christian character. *T. L. Cuyler*

Christianity is not a theory or speculation, but a life; not a philosophy of life, but a life and a living process. *Coleridge*

Christianity is the companion of liberty in all its conflicts—the cradle of its infancy, and the divine source of its claims. *De Tocqueville*

Christmas

O little town of Bethlehem,
How still we see thee lie!
Above thy deep and dreamless sleep
The silent stars go by. *Phillips Brooks*

No Santa Claus! Thank God, he lives, and he lives forever. A thousand years from now, Virginia, nay, ten times ten thousand years from now, he will continue to make glad the heart of childhood. *Francis P. Church*

I heard the bells on Christmas Day
Their old, familiar carols play,
And wild and sweet
The words repeat
Of peace on earth, good-will to men! *Longfellow*

'Twas the night before Christmas, when all through the house
Not a creature was stirring—not even a mouse:
The stockings were hung by the chimney with care

In hopes that St. Nicholas soon would be there
Clement C. Moore

> Hark the herald angels sing,
> "Glory to the new-born king."
> Peace on earth, and mercy mild,
> God and sinners reconciled! *Charles Wesley*

Church

I never weary of great churches. It is my favorite kind of mountain scenery. Mankind was never so happily inspired as when it made a cathedral. *Stevenson*

It is only when men begin to worship that they begin to grow. *Calvin Coolidge*

And what greater calamity can fall upon a nation than the loss of worship. *Emerson*

> Ay, call it holy ground,
> The soil where first they trod.
> They have left unstained, what there they found—
> Freedom to worship God. *Felicia D. Hemans*

Circumstance

> Man is not the creature of circumstances,
> Circumstances are the creatures of men. *Disraeli*

Circumstances alter cases. *Haliburton*

The circumstances of others seem good to us, while ours seem good to others. *Syrus*

Civilization

We think our civilization near its meridian, but we are yet only at the cock-crowing and the morning star. *Emerson*

The path of civilization is paved with tin cans. *Elbert Hubbard*

Clothes

Good clothes open all doors. *Thomas Fuller*
The clothes make the man. *Latin proverb*

Costly thy habit as thy purse can buy,
But not express'd in fancy; rich not gaudy;
For the apparel oft proclaims the man. *Shakespeare*

The soul of this man is his clothes. *Shakespeare*

She wears her clothes as if they were thrown on her with a pitchfork. *Swift*

A fashionable woman is always in love—with herself. *La Rochefoucauld*

I see that the fashion wears out more apparel than the man. *Shakespeare*

COMMERCE

Perfect freedom is as necessary to the health and vigor of commerce, as it is to the health and vigor of citizenship. *Patrick Henry*

Commerce tends to wear off those prejudices which maintain destruction and animosity between nations.—It softens and polishes the manners of men.—It unites them by one of the strongest of all ties—the desire of supplying their natural wants.—It disposes them to peace by establishing in every state an order of citizens bound by their interest to be the guardians of public tranquility. *F. W. Robertson*

Commerce defies every wind, outrides every tempest and invades every zone. *Bancroft*

COMMON SENSE

Common sense is very uncommon. *Horace Greeley*

The crown of all faculties is common sense.—It is not enough to do the right thing, it must be done at the right time and place.—Talent knows what to do; tact knows when and how to do it. *W. Matthews*

Common sense is in spite of, not the result of, education. *Victor Hugo*

One pound of learning requires ten pounds of common sense to apply it. *Persian proverb*

Common sense is instinct, and enough of it is genius. *H. W. Shaw*

COMMUNISM

From each according to his ability, to each according to his needs. *Louis Blanc*

What is a Communist? One who hath yearnings
For equal division of unequal earnings.
Idler or bungler, or both, he is willing
To fork out his copper and pocket your shilling.
Ebenezer Elliott

The theory of Communism may be summed up in one sentence: Abolish all private property. *Karl Marx and Friedrich Engels*

Communism is the exploitation of the strong by the weak. In communism, inequality springs from placing mediocrity on a level with excellence. *Proudhon*

CONCEIT

Wind puffs up empty bladders; opinion, fools. *Socrates*

The overweening self-respect of conceited men relieves others from the duty of respecting them at all. *H. W. Beecher*

If he could only see how small a vacancy his death would leave, the proud man would think less of the place he occupies in his lifetime. *Legouve*

Conceit may puff a man up, but can never prop him up. *Ruskin*

CONFESSION

The confession of evil works is the first beginning of good works. *Augustine*

Be not ashamed to confess that you have been in the wrong. It is but owning what you need not be ashamed of—that you now have more sense than you had before, to see your error; more humility to acknowledge it, more grace to correct it. *Seed*

CONFIDENCE

Trust men and they will be true to you; treat them greatly and they will show themselves great. *Emerson*

They can conquer who believe they can. *Dryden*

Conquest

I came, I saw, I conquered. *Julius Caesar*
Self-conquest is the greatest of victories. *Plato*

Who overcomes
By force, hath overcome but half his foe. *Milton*

There are some defeats more triumphant than victories. *Montaigne*

Conscience

Nor ear can hear nor tongue can tell
The tortures of that inward hell! *Byron*

He will easily be content and at peace, whose conscience is pure. *Thomas a Kempis*
Conscience is a sacred sanctuary where God alone may enter as judge. *Lamennais*
I feel within me a peace above all earthly dignities, a still and quiet conscience. *Shakespeare*
The soft whispers of the God to man. *Young*
What other dungeon is so dark as one's own heart! What jailer so inexorable as one's self! *Hawthorne*
No man ever offended his own conscience, but first or last it was revenged upon him for it. *South*
There is no witness so terrible, no accuser so powerful as conscience which dwells within us. *Sophocles*
Conscience tells us that we ought to do right, but it does not tell us what right is—that we are taught by God's word. *H. C. Trumbull*
Labour to keep alive in your heart that little spark of celestial fire called conscience. *Washington*
Many a lash in the dark, doth conscience give the wicked. *Boston*
Conscience doth make cowards of us all. *Shakespeare*
A quiet conscience makes one so serene. *Byron*

Conservatism

A conservative is a man who will not look at the new moon, out of respect for that "ancient institution," the old one. *Jerrold*

We are reformers in spring and summer. In autumn and winter we stand by the old. Reformers in the morning; conservatives at night. Reform is affirmative, conservatism, negative. Conservatism goes for comfort; reform for truth. *Emerson*

The conservative may clamor against reform, but he might as well clamor against the centrifugal force. He sighs for "the good old times." He might as well wish the oak back into the acorn. *E. H. Chapin*

Consistency

A foolish consistency is the hobgoblin of little minds, adored by little statesmen and philosophers and divines. *Emerson*

Shoemaker, stick to your last. *Pliny*

Contentment

It is right to be contended with what we have, never with what we are. *Mackintosh*

Great is he who enjoys his earthenware as if it were plate, and not less great is the man to whom all his plate is no more than earthenware. *Leighton*

True contentment depends not upon what we have; a tub was large enough for Diogenes, but a world was too little for Alexander. *Colton*

A man who finds no satisfaction in himself, seeks for it in vain elsewhere. *La Rochefoucauld*

Conversation

It is good to rub and polish our brain against that of others. *Montaigne*

Never hold any one by the button or the hand in order to be heard out; for if people are unwilling to hear you, you had better hold your tongue than them. *Chesterfield*

The first ingredient in conversation is truth; the next, good sense; the third, good humor; and the fourth, wit. *Sir W. Temple*

Silence is one great art of conversation. *Hazlitt*

One of the best rules in conversation is, never to say a thing which any of the company can reasonably wish had been left unsaid. *Swift*

A single conversation across the table with a wise man is worth a month's study of books. *Chinese proverb*

Know how to listen, and you will profit even from those who talk badly. *Plutarch*

The reason why so few people are agreeable in conversation, is, that each is thinking more of what he is intending to say, than of what others are saying; and we never listen when we are planning to speak. *La Rochefoucauld*

Conversation is an art in which a man has all mankind for competitors. *Emerson*

As it is the characteristic of great wits to say much in few words, so it is of small wits to talk much, and say nothing. *Le Rochefoucauld*

Our companions please us less from the charms we find in their conversation, than from those they find in ours. *Greville*

There cannot be a greater rudeness than to interrupt another in the current of his discourse. *Locke*

That is the happiest conversation where there is no competition, no vanity, but only a calm, quiet interchange of sentiment. *Johnson*

When in the company of sensible men, we ought to be double cautious of talking too much, lest we lose two good things—their good opinion and our own improvement; for what we have to say we know, but what they have to say we know not. *Colton*

Cooking

We may live without friends; we may live without books;
But civilized man cannot live without cooks.
Bulwer-Lytton

Too many cooks spoil the broth. *English proverb*

Courage

Often the test of courage is not to die but to live. *Alfieri*

Courage is, on all hands, considered as an essential of high character. *Froude*

Hail, Caesar, those who are about to die salute thee. *Suetonius*

No man can answer for his courage who has never been in danger. *La Rochefoucauld*

To see what is right and not to do it, is want of courage. *Confucius*

Courage consists not in hazarding without fear, but being resolutely minded in a just cause. *Plutarch*

COURTESY

The small courtesies sweeten life; the greater ennoble it. *Bovee*

Life is not so short but that there is always time enough for courtesy. *Emerson*

To speak kindly does not hurt the tongue. *French proverb*

COWARDICE

One who in a perilous emergency thinks with his legs. *Bierce*

At the bottom of a good deal of the bravery that appears in the world there lurks a miserable cowardice. Men will face powder and steel because they cannot face public opinion. *E. H. Chapin*

> He who fights and runs away
> May live to fight another day.
> But he who is in battle slain,
> Can never rise to fight again. *Goldsmith*

Cowards die many times before their death; the valiant never taste of death but one. *Shakespeare*

A cowardly act! What do I care about that? You may be sure that I should never fear to commit one if it were to my advantage. *Napoleon*

All men would be cowards if they durst. *Earl of Rochester*

CRIME

Disgrace does not consist in the punishment, but in the crime. *Alfieri*

Whoever profits by the crime is guilty of it. *French proverb*

CRITICISM

The rule in carving holds good as to criticism; never cut with a knife what you can cut with a spoon. *Charles Buxton*

It is ridiculous for any man to criticise the works of another if he has not distinguished himself by his own performances. *Addison*

Critics are the men who have failed in literature and art. *Disraeli*

Silence is sometimes the severest criticism. *Charles Buxton*

Even the lion has to defend himself against flies. *German proverb*

Of all the cants in this canting world, deliver me from the cant of criticism. *Sterne*

What a blessed thing it is that nature, when she invented, manufactured and patented her authors, contrived to make critics out of the chips that were left! *Holmes*

The strength of criticism lies only in the weakness of the thing criticised. *Longfellow*

It behooves the minor critic, who hunts for blemishes, to be a little distrustful of his own sagacity. *Junius*

CURIOSITY

Curiosity killed the cat. *American proverb*

Ask me no questions, and I'll tell you no fibs. *Goldsmith*

Curiosity is one of the permanent and certain characteristics of a vigorous intellect. *Samuel Johnson*

CYNICS

It will generally be found that those who sneer habitually at human nature, and affect to despise it, are among its worst and least pleasant samples. *Dickens*

DEATH

Call no man happy till he is dead. *Aeschylus*

Death has nothing terrible which life has not made so. A faithful Christian life in this world is the best preparation for the next. *Tryon Edwards*

> But whether on the scaffold high,
> Or in the battle's van,
> The fittest place where man can die
> Is where he dies for man. *Michael J. Barry*

Death expecteth thee everywhere, be wise, therefore, and expect death everywhere. *Quarles*

In the midst of life we are in death. *Book of Common Prayer*

Is death the last sleep? No, it is the last and final awakening. *Walter Scott*

Man that is born of a woman hath but a short time to life, and is full of misery. He cometh up, and is cut down, like a flower; he fleeth as it were a shadow, and never continueth in one stay. *Book of Common Prayer*

Let death be daily before your eyes, and you will never entertain any abject thought, nor too eagerly covert anything. *Epictetus*

> Death, so called, is a thing which makes men weep,
> And yet a third of life is pass'd in sleep. *Byron*

There is no better armor against the shafts of death than to be busied in God's service. *Fuller*

Every moment of life is a step towards death. *Corneille*

He who always waits upon God, is ready whensoever he calls. He is a happy man who so lives that death at all times may find him at leisure to die. *Feltham*

> There is no Death! What seems so is transition;
> This life of mortal breath
> Is but a suburb of the life elysian,
> Whose portal we call Death. *Longfellow*

Death and love are the two wings that bear the good man to heaven. *Michelangelo*

We begin to die as soon as we are born, and the end is linked to the beginning. *Manilius*

If Socrates died like a philosopher, Jesus Christ died like a God. *Rousseau*

> There is no death! the stars go down
> To rise upon some other shore,
> And bright in Heaven's jeweled crown,
> They shine for ever more. *John L. McCreery*

Not by lamentations and mournful chants ought we to celebrate the funeral of a good man, but by hymns, for in ceasing to be numbered with mortals he enters upon the heritage of a diviner life. *Plutarch*

I am dying, Egypt, dying. *Shakespeare*

> No more; and, by a sleep to say we end
> The heart-ache and the thousand natural shocks
> That flesh is heir to, 'tis a consummation
> Devoutly to be wished. *Shakespeare*

> Nothing in his life
> Became him like the leaving it. *Shakespeare*

Death lies on her, like an untimely frost
Upon the sweetest flower of all the field. *Shakespeare*

God's finger touched him, and he slept. *Tennyson*

> First our pleasures die—and then
> Our hopes, and then our fears—and when
> These are dead, the debt is due,
> Dust claims dust—and we die too. *Shelley*

Sunset and evening star,
And one clear call for me!
And may there be no moaning of the bar
When I put out to sea. *Tennyson*

Twilight and evening bell,
And after that the dark!
And may there be no sadness of farewell
When I embark. *Tennyson*

Nothing can happen more beautiful than death. *Walt Whitman*

DEBT

A pig bought on credit is forever grunting. *Spanish proverb*

Debt is the worst poverty. *M. G. Lichtwer*

Debt is a bottomless sea. *Carlyle*

> Neither a borrower nor a lender be;
> For loan oft loses both itself and friend,

And borrowing dulls the edge of husbandry.
Shakespeare

DECEPTION

Hateful to me as are the gates of hell,
Is he who, hiding one thing in his heart,
Utters another   *Homer*

No man, for any considerable period, can wear one face to himself and another to the multitude, without finally getting bewildered as to which may be true. *Hawthorne*

You can fool some of the people all of the time, and all of the people some of the time, but you cannot fool all of the people all the time. *Lincoln*

No man was ever so much deceived by another as by himself. *Greville*

One is easily fooled by that which one loves. *Moliere*

O, what a tangled web we weave, when first we practice to deceive. *Walter Scott*

DECISION

Once to every man and nation comes the moment to decide,
In the strife of Truth with Falsehood, for the good or evil side. *Lowell*

Decision of character will often give to an inferior mind command over a superior. *W. Wirt*

Here I stand; I can do no otherwise. God help me. Amen. *Luther*

Men must be decided on what they will not do, and then they are able to act with vigor in what they ought to do. *Mencius*

There's small choice in rotten apples. *Shakespeare*

DEFEAT

It is defeat that turns bone to flint; it is defeat that turns gristle to muscle; it is defeat that makes men invincible. *Henry Ward Beecher*

What is defeat? Nothing but education; nothing but the first step to something better. *Wendell Phillips*

You are never so near to victory as when defeated in a good cause. *H. W. Beecher*

Delay

Tomorrow I will live, the fool does say; today itself's too late; the wise lived yesterday. *Martial*

Every delay is hateful, but it gives wisdom. *Publilius Syrus*

Some one speaks admirably of the well-ripened fruit of sage delay. *Balzac*

Democracy

It would be folly to argue that the people cannot make political mistakes. They can and do make grave mistakes. They know it, they pay the penalty, but compared with the mistakes which have been made by every kind of autocracy they are unimportant. *Calvin Coolidge*

The love of democracy is that of equality. *Montesquieu*

While democracy must have its organization and controls, its vital breath is individual liberty. *Charles Evans Hughes*

In every village there will arise some miscreant, to establish the most grinding tyranny by calling himself the people. *Sir Robert Peel*

Democracy is the government of the people, by the people, for the people. *Lincoln*

The real democratic American idea is not that every man shall be on a level with every other, but that every one shall have liberty, without hindrance, to be what God made him. *H. W. Beecher*

I believe in Democracy because it releases the energies of every human being. *Woodrow Wilson*

Despair

All hope abandon, ye who enter here. *Dante*

What we call despair is often only the painful eagerness of unfed hope. *George Eliot*

Despair is the conclusion of fools. *Disraeli*

It is impossible for that man to despair who remembers that his Helper is omnipotent. *Jeremy Taylor*

Destiny

Every man meets his Waterloo at last. *Wendell Phillips*

Man proposes, but God disposes. *Thomas a Kempis*

> There is a divinity that shapes our ends.
> Rough-hew them how we will. *Shakespeare*

Destiny is the scapegoat which we make responsible for all our crimes and follies; a necessity which we set down for invincible when we have no wish to strive against it. *Balfour*

Devotion

All is holy where devotion kneels. *O. W. Holmes*

The inward sighs of humble penitence rise to the ear of heaven, when pealed hymns are scattered to the common air. *Joanna Baillie*

The best and sweetest flowers in paradise, God gives to his people when they are on their knees in the closet. Prayer, if not the very gate of heaven, is the key to let us into its holiness and joys. *T. Brooks*

Difficulty

The best way out of a difficulty is through it. *Anonymous*

The greatest difficulties lie where we are not looking for them. *Goethe*

It is not every calamity that is a curse, and early adversity is often a blessing. Surmounted difficulties not only teach, but hearten us in our future struggles. *Sharp*

It cannot be too often repeated that it is not helps, but obstacles, not facilities, but difficulties that make men. *W. Mathews*

Difficulties strengthen the mind, as labor does the body. *Seneca*

Disappointment

> The best-laid schemes o' mice an' men,
> Gang aft a-gley,
> And leave us nought but grief and pain,
> For promised joy. *Burns*

The disappointment of manhood succeeds to the delusion of youth. *Disraeli*

There is many a thing which the world calls disappointment, but there is no such a word in the dictionary of faith. What to others are disappointments are to believers intimations of the way of God. *John Newton*

We mount to heaven mostly on the ruins of our cherished schemes, finding our failures were successes. *A. B. Alcott*

DISCONTENT

Discontent is the want of self-reliance; it is infirmity of will. *Emerson*

Noble discontent is the path to heaven. *T. W. Higginson*

The root of all discontent is self-love. *J. F. Clarke*

DISCUSSION

Free and fair discussion will ever be found the firmest friend to truth. *G. Campbell*

It is an excellent rule to be observed in all discussions, that men should give soft words and hard arguments; that they should not so much strive to silence or vex, as to convince their opponents. *Wilkins*

He who knows only his own side of the case, knows little of that. *J. Stuart Mill*

Whosoever is afraid of submitting any question, civil or religious, to the test of free discussion, is more in love with his own opinion than with truth. *T. Watson*

Men are never so likely to settle a question rightly, as when they discuss it freely. *Macaulay*

If thou take delight in idle argumentation, thou mayest be qualified to combat with the sophists, but will never know how to live with men. *Socrates*

DISHONESTY

Dishonesty is a forsaking of permanent for temporary advantages. *Bovee*

He who purposely cheats his friend, would cheat his God. *Lavater*

DOUBT

We know accurately only when we know little; with knowledge doubt increases. *Goethe*

> To be, or not to be, that is the question:
> Whether 'tis nobler in the mind to suffer
> The slings and arrows of outrageous fortune;
> Or to take arms against a sea of troubles,
> And by opposing end them? *Shakespeare*

> Our doubts are traitors
> And make us lose the good we oft might win
> By fearing to attempt. *Shakespeare*

DUTY

To do my duty in that state of life unto which it shall please God to call me. *Book of Common Prayer*

Do the duty which lieth nearest to thee! Thy second duty will already have become clearer. *Thomas Carlyle*

> So nigh is grandeur to our dust,
> So near is God to man.
> When Duty whispers low, *Thou must,*
> The youth replies, *I can. Emerson*

Duty is the grandest of ideas, because it implies the idea of God, of the soul, of liberty, of responsibility, of immortality. *Lacordaire*

It is thy duty oftentimes to do what thou wouldst not; thy duty, too, to leave undone that thou wouldst do. *Thomas a Kempis*

The reward of one duty done is the power to fulfill another. *George Eliot*

Let us have faith that right makes might, and in that faith let us, to the end, dare to do our duty as we understand it. *Lincoln*

God always has an angel of help for those who are willing to do their duty. *T. L. Cuyler*

> Theirs not to make reply,
> Theirs not to reason why,
> Theirs but to do and die. *Tennyson*

Do thy duty; that is best; leave unto the Lord the rest.
Longfellow

    Not once or twice in our rough island story,
    The path of duty was the way to glory. *Tennyson*

When the soul resolves to perform every duty, immediately it is conscious of the presence of God. *Bacon*

Every hour comes with some little fagot of God's will fastened upon its back. *Faber*

The duty of man is plain and simple, and consists but of two points; his duty to God, which every man must feel; and his duty to his neighbor, to do as he would be done by. *Thomas Paine*

Let men laugh, if they will, when you sacrifice desire to duty. You have time and eternity to rejoice in. *Theodore Parker*

EATING

Eat, drink, and be merry, for tomorrow ye diet. *William Gilmore Beymer*

The proof of the pudding is in the eating. *Cervantes*

I want every peasant to have a chicken in his pot on Sundays. *Henry IV of France*

For a man seldom thinks with more earnestness of anything than he does of his dinner. *Samuel Johnson*

He hath eaten me out of house and home. *Shakespeare*

ECONOMY

Buy not what you want, but what you have need of; what you do not want is dear at a farthing. *Cato*

If you know how to spend less than you get, you have the philosopher's stone. *Franklin*

He who will not economize will have to agonize. *Confucius*

Economy is in itself a source of great revenue. *Seneca*

After order and liberty, economy is one of the highest essentials of a free government. . . . Economy is always a guarantee of peace. *Calvin Coolidge*

The regard one shows economy, is like that we show an old aunt, who is to leave us something at last. *Shenstone*

Beware of little expenses; a small leak will sink a great ship. *Franklin*

No man is rich whose expenditures exceed his means; and no one is poor whose incomings exceed his outgoings. *Haliburton*

Nothing is cheap which is superfluous, for what one does not need, is dear at a penny. *Plutarch*

Take care to be an economist in prosperity, there is no fear of your not being one in adversity. *Zimmerman*

Ere you consult fancy, consult your purse. *Franklin*

The back door robs the house. *Herbert*

EDUCATION

Education commences at the mother's knee, and every word spoken within the hearsay of little children tends towards the formation of character. *Hosea Ballou*

Education is the apprenticeship of life. *Willmott*

Education makes a people easy to lead, but difficult to drive; easy to govern, but impossible to enslave. *Lord Brougham*

Education does not mean teaching people to know what they do not know; it means teaching them to behave as they do not behave. *Ruskin*

"Reeling and Writhing, of course, to begin with," the Mock Turtle replied, "and the different branches of Arithmetic—Ambition, Distraction, Uglification and Derision." *Lewis Carroll*

He is to be educated not because he is to make shoes, nails, and pins, but because he is a man. *Channing*

The foundation of every state is the education of its youth. *Diogenes*

Educate men without religion, and you make them but clever devils. *Wellington*

If a man empties his purse into his head, no one can take it from him. *Franklin*

An industrious and virtuous education of children is a better inheritance for them than a great estate. *Addison*

Education is the cheap defense of nations. *Burke*

Schoolhouses are the republican line of fortifications. *Horace Mann*

That which we are we are all the while teaching, not voluntarily, but involuntarily. *Emerson*

'Tis education forms the common mind;
Just as the twig is bent the tree's inclined. *Pope*

The schoolmaster is abroad, and I trust him, armed with his primer, against the soldier in full military array. *Brougham*

Efficiency

He did nothing in particular,
And did it very well. *W. S. Gilbert*

The best carpenters make the fewest chips. *German proverb*

Effort

Things don't turn up in this world until somebody turns them up. *Garfield*

Egotism

The reason why lovers are never weary of one another is this—they are always talking of themselves. *La Rochefoucauld*
Egotism is the tongue of vanity. *Chamfort*
Do you wish men to speak well of you? Then never speak well of yourself. *Pascal*
There is not one wise man in twenty that will praise himself. *Shakespeare*

Eloquence

Eloquence is the poetry of prose. *Bryant*
Brevity is a great charm of eloquence. *Cicero*
The manner of your speaking is full as important as the matter, as more people have ears to be tickled than understandings to judge. *Chesterfield*
Those who would make us feel, must feel themselves. *Churchill*
Noise proves nothing. Often a hen who has merely laid an egg cackles as if she laid an asteroid. *Mark Twain*
Eloquence is in the assembly, not merely in the speaker. *William Pitt*
True eloquence consists in saying all that is necessary, and nothing but what is necessary. *La Rochefoucauld*

Eloquence is logic on fire. *Lyman Beecher*

There is no eloquence without a man behind it. *Emerson*

Speech is the body; thought, the soul, and suitable action the life of eloquence. *C. Simmons*

ENDURANCE

The greater the difficulty, the more glory in surmounting it. Skilful pilots gain their reputation from storms and tempests. *Epicurus*

ENEMIES

If we could read the secret history of our enemies, we should find in each man's life sorrow and suffering enough to disarm all hostility. *Longfellow*

It is much safer to reconcile an enemy than to conquer him; victory may deprive him of his poison, but reconciliation of his will. *Feltham*

If you want enemies, excel others; if friends, let others excel you. *Colton*

ENERGY

The longer I live, the more deeply am I convinced that that which makes the difference between one man and another—between the weak and powerful, the great and insignificant, is energy—invisible determination—a purpose once formed, and then death or victory. This quality will do anything that is to be done in the world; and no talents, no circumstances, no opportunities will make one a man without it. *Buxton*

Energy will do anything that can be done in the world; and no talents, no circumstances, no opportunities will make a two-legged animal a man without it. *Goethe*

The truest wisdom, in general, is resolute determinations. *Napoleon*

ENTHUSIASM

In things pertaining to enthusiasm no man is sane who does not know how to be insane on proper occasions. *Henry Ward Beecher*

Every great and commanding movement in the annals of the world is the triumph of enthusiasm. Nothing great was ever achieved without it. *Emerson*

The sense of this word among the Greeks affords the noblest definition of it; enthusiasm signifies God in us. *Madame de Stael*

Every production of genius must be the production of enthusiasm. *Disraeli*

Opposition always inflames the enthusiast, never converts him. *Schiller.*

Envy

Envy has no other quality but that of detracting from virtue. *Livy*

As a moth gnaws a garment, so doth envy consume a man. *St. John Chrysostom*

Emulation looks out for merits, that she may exalt herself by a victory; envy spies out blemishes, that she may lower another by a defeat. *Colton*

It is the practice of the multitude to bark at eminent men, as little dogs do at strangers. *Seneca*

Envy feels not its own happiness but when it may be compared with the misery of others. *Johnson*

There is no surer mark of the absence of the highest moral and intellectual qualities than a cold reception of excellence. *Bailey*

The envious praise only that which they can surpass; that which surpasses them they censure. *Colton*

Epitaph

A tomb now suffices him for whom the whole world was not sufficient. *Epitaph on Alexander the Great*

The body of Benjamin Franklin, Printer, (Like the cover of an old book, its contents torn out and stript of its lettering and gilding), lies here, food for worms; but the work shall not be lost, for it will (as he believed) appear once more in a new and more elegant edition, revised and corrected by the author. *Benjamin Franklin—Epitaph on himself, written in 1728*

Equality

We hold these truths to be self-evident: that all men are created equal; that they are endowed by their Creator with certain unalienable rights; that among these are life, liberty and the pursuit of happiness. *Jefferson*

Your levellers wish to level down as far as themselves, but they cannot bear levelling up to themselves. *Samuel Johnson*

> For the colonel's lady an' Judy O'Grady
> Are sisters under their skins. *Kipling*

Fourscore and seven years ago, our fathers brought forth on this continent a new nation, conceived in liberty, and dedicated to the proposition that all men are created equal. *Lincoln*

Let's go hand in hand, not one before another. *Shakespeare*

Equanimity

In this thing one man is superior to another, that he is better able to bear prosperity or adversity. *Philemon*

Error

To stumble twice against the same stone is a proverbial disgrace. *Cicero*

Find earth where grows no weed, and you may find a heart wherein no error grows. *Knowles*

To err is human, to forgive divine. *Pope*

A man should never be ashamed to own he has been in the wrong, which is but saying, in other words, that he is wiser today than he was yesterday. *Pope*

In all science error precedes the truth, and it is better it should go first than last. *Walpole*

Our greatest glory is not in never falling, but in rising every time we fall. *Confucius*

From the errors of others a wise man corrects his own. *Publilius Syrus*

Eternity

No man can pass into eternity, for he is already in it. *Farrar*

There is, I know not how, in the minds of men, a certain presage, as it were, of a future existence, and this takes the deepest root, and is most discoverable in the greatest geniuses and most exalted souls. *Cicero*

All great natures delight in stability; all great men find eternity affirmed in the very promise of their faculties. *Emerson*

EVENING

The curfew tolls the knell of parting day,
The lowing herd winds slowly o'er the lea,
The ploughman homeward plods his weary way,
And leaves the world to darkness and to me. *Gray*

Day hath put on his jacket, and around
His burning bosom buttoned it with stars. *Holmes*

EVIL

Evil often triumphs, but never conquers. *Joseph Roux*

It is some compensation for great evils, that they enforce great lessons. *Bovee*

The evil that men do lives after them;
The good is oft interred with their bones.
Shakespeare

Many have puzzled themselves about the origin of evil. I am content to observe that there is evil, and that there is a way to escape from it, and with this I begin and end. *John Newton*

As sure as God is good, so surely there is no such thing as necessary evil. *Southey*

Good has but one enemy, the evil; but the evil has two enemies, the good and itself. *J. von Muller*

We cannot do evil to others without doing it to ourselves. *Desmahis*

EXAGGERATION

Exaggeration is a blood relation to falsehood, and nearly as blameable. *H. Ballou*

Some men can never state an ordinary fact in ordinary terms. All their geese are swans, till you see the birds. *J. B. Owen*

Excellence

Those who attain to any excellence commonly spend life in some one single pursuit, for excellence is not often gained upon easier terms. *Johnson*
Fearless minds climb soonest unto crowns. *Shakespeare*
Too low they build who build beneath the stars. *Young*

Expectation

Nothing is so good as it seems beforehand. *George Eliot*
We love to expect, and when expectation is either disappointed or gratified, we want to be again expecting. *Johnson*
With what a heavy and retarding weight does expectation load the wing of time. *W. Mason*

Experience

Experience is the best of schoolmasters, only the schoolees are heavy. *Carlyle*
Experience is the name men give to their follies or their sorrows. *Musset*
A burnt child dreads the fire. *English proverb*
Experience is the shroud of illusions. *Finod*
I have but one lamp by which my feet are guided, and that is the lamp of experience. *Patrick Henry*
To most men experience is like the stern lights of a ship, which illumine only the tracks it has passed. *Coleridge*
Is there anyone so wise as to learn by the experience of others? *Voltaire*
He cannot be a perfect man, not being tried and tutored in the world. Experience is by industry achieved, and perfected by the swift course of time. *Shakespeare*
It is foolish to try to live on past experience. It is a very dangerous, if not a fatal habit to judge ourselves to be safe because of something that we felt or did twenty years ago. *Spurgeon*
That man is wise to some purpose who gains his wisdom at the expense and from the experience of another. *Plautus*
Experience is a jewel, and it had need be so, for it is often purchased at an infinite rate. *Shakespeare*

Each succeeding day is the scholar of that which went before it. *Publilius Syrus*

Every man's experience of today, is that he was a fool yesterday and the day before yesterday. Tomorrow he will most likely be of exactly the same opinion. *Mackay*

EYE

It is the eyes of other people that ruin us. If all but myself were blind I should neither want a fine house nor fine furniture. *Franklin*

The curious questioning eye, that plucks the heart of every mystery. *Mellen*

FACE

He had a face like a benediction. *Cervantes*

There is a garden in her face, where roses and white lilies show—a heavenly paradise wherein all pleasant fruits do grow. *R. Alison*

A countenance more in sorrow than in anger. *Shakespeare*

In thy face I see the map of honor, truth, and loyalty. *Shakespeare*

FAILURE

We mount to heaven mostly on the ruins of our cherished schemes, finding our failures were successes. *A. B. Alcott*

Failure is often God's own tool for carving some of the finest outlines in the character of his children; and, even in this life, bitter and crushing failures have often in them the germs of new and quite unimagined happiness. *T. Hodgkin*

They never fail who die in a great cause. *Byron*

FAITH

Faith is the continuation of reason. *William Adams*

All the scholastic scaffolding falls, as a ruined edifice, before one single word—faith. *Napoleon*

An outward and visible sign of an inward and spiritual grace. *Book of Common Prayer*

Faith marches at the head of the army of progress. It is found beside the most refined life, the freest government, the profoundest philosophy, the noblest poetry, the purest humanity. *T. T. Munger*

All I have seen teaches me to trust the Creator for all I have not seen. *Emerson*

Christian faith is a grand cathedral, with divinely pictured windows. Standing without, you can see no glory, nor can imagine any, but standing within every ray of light reveals a harmony of unspeakable splendors. *Hawthorne*

Let us have faith that right makes might; and in that faith, let us, to the end, dare to do our duty as we understand it. *Lincoln*

Epochs of faith, are epochs of fruitfulness; but epochs of unbelief, however glittering, are barren of all permanent good. *Goethe*

Faith is the substance of things hoped for, the evidence of things not seen. *Hebrews XI, 1*

Faith is to believe, on the word of God, what we do not see, and its reward is to see and enjoy what we believe. *Augustine*

FALSEHOOD

O, what a goodly outside falsehood hath; a goodly apple rotten at the heart! *Shakespeare*

This above all; to thine own self be true; and it must follow, as the night the day, thou canst not then be false to any man. *Shakespeare*

FAME

If you would not be forgotten as soon as you are dead, either write things worth reading or do things worth writing. *Franklin*

Fame, to the ambitious, is like salt water to the thirsty —the more one gets, the more he wants. *Ebers*

The fame of great men ought always to be estimated by the means used to acquire it. *La Rochefoucauld*

I am not covetous for gold; but if it be a sin to covet honor, I am the most offending soul alive. *Shakespeare*

I do not like the man who squanders life for fame; give me the man who living makes a name. *Martial*

As the pearl ripens in the obscurity of its shell, so ripens in the tomb all the fame that is truly precious. *Landor*

Fame is but the breath of the people, and that often unwholesome. *Rousseau*

Fame is the perfume of heroic deeds. *Socrates*

What a heavy burden is a name that has become too famous. *Voltaire*

FAMILY

The happiest moments of my life have been the few which I have passed at home in the bosom of my family. *Jefferson*

A happy family is but an earlier heaven. *Bowring*

"The last word" is the most dangerous of infernal machines, and the husband and wife should no more fight to get it than they would struggle for the possession of a lighted bombshell. *Douglas Jerrold*

FATE

We make our fortunes and we call them fate. *Disraeli*

The Moving Finger writes; and having writ,
Moves on; nor all your Piety nor Wit
Shall lure it back to cancel half a Line,
Nor all your Tears wash out a Word of it.
Omar Khayyam

FAULT

The greatest of faults, I should say, is to be conscious of none. *Carlyle*

We confess small faults, in order to insinuate that we have no great ones. *Rochefoucauld*

The wise man has his foibles as well as the fool. Those of the one are known to himself, and concealed from the world; while those of the other are known to the world, and concealed from himself. *J. Mason*

To find fault is easy; to do better may be difficult. *Plutarch*

FEAR

Fear makes us feel our humanity. *Disraeli*

Fear is the mother of foresight. *H. Taylor*

Fear always springs from ignorance. *Emerson*

No one loves the man whom he fears. *Aristotle*

FLATTERY

Imitation is the sincerest flattery. *Colton*

The art of flatterers is to take advantage of the foibles of the great, to foster their errors, and never to give advice which may annoy. *Moliere*

Men are like stone jugs—you may lug them where you like by the ears. *Samuel Johnson*

You play the spaniel, and think with wagging of your tongue to win me. *Shakespeare*

It is easy to flatter; it is harder to praise. *Jean Paul Richter*

The most skilful flattery is to let a person talk on, and be a listener. *Addison*

> O, that men's ears should be
> To counsel deaf, but not to flattery! *Shakespeare*

'Tis an old maxim in the schools, that flattery is the food of fools. Yet now and then you men of wit will condescend to take a bit. *Swift*

FLOWERS

Flowers may beckon toward us, but they speak toward heaven and God. *Henry Ward Beecher*

> The buttercups, bright-eyed and bold,
> Held up their chalices of gold
> To catch the sunshine and the dew. *Julia C. R. Dorr*

> In Flanders' fields the poppies blow
> Between the crosses, row on row,
> That mark our place; and in the sky,
> The larks, still bravely singing, fly
> Scarce heard among the guns below.
> *John McCrae*

> 'Tis the last rose of summer,
> Left blooming alone. *Moore*

I sometimes think that never blows so red
The Rose as where some buried Caesar bled;

> That every Hyacinth the Garden wears
> Dropt in her Lap from some once lovely Head.
> *Omar Khayyam*

> To me the meanest flower that blows can give
> Thoughts that do often lie too deep for tears.
> *Wordsworth*

Fool

A fool always finds one still more foolish to admire him. *Boileau*

Young men think old men are fools; but old men know young men are fools. *George Chapman*

A fool and his money are soon parted. *English proverb*

A learned fool is more foolish than an ignorant fool. *Moliere*

For fools rush in where angels fear to tread. *Pope*

Forgetfulness

There is no remembrance which time does not obliterate, nor pain which death does not terminate. *Cervantes*

And when he is out of sight, quickly also he is out of mind. *Thomas a Kempis*

> God of our father, known of old,
> Lord of our far-flung battle-line,
> Beneath whose awful Hand we hold
> Dominion over palm and pine—
> Lord God of Hosts, be with us yet,
> Lest we forget—lest we forget!
> The tumult and the shouting dies,
> The captains and the kings depart;
> Still stands thine ancient sacrifice,
> A humble and a contrite heart,
> Lord God of Hosts, be with us yet,
> Lest we forget—lest we forget. *Kipling*

Forgiveness

God pardons like a mother, who kisses the offense into everlasting forgetfulness. *Henry Ward Beecher*

We forgive so long as we love. *La Rochefoucauld*

His heart was as great as the world, but there was no room in it to hold the memory of a wrong. *Emerson*

Forgive others often, yourself never. *Syrus*

Never does the human soul appear so strong and noble as when it foregoes revenge and dares to forgive an injury. *E. H. Chapin*

Humanity is never so beautiful as when praying for forgiveness, or else forgiving another. *Richter*

The more we know, the better we forgive. Whoe'er feels deeply, feels for all that live. *Madame de Stael*

Fortune

Fortune makes him fool, whom she makes her darling. *Bacon*

It is fortune, not wisdom, that rules man's life. *Cicero*

Men are seldom blessed with good fortune and good sense at the same time. *Livy*

Freedom

The cause of freedom is the cause of God. *Samuel Bowles*

Personal liberty is the paramount essential to human dignity and human happiness. *Bulwer-Lytton*

In a free country there is much clamor, with little suffering; in a despotic state there is little complaint, with much grievance. *Carnot*

> For what avail the plough or sail,
> Or land, or life, if freedom fail? *Emerson*

I am for freedom of religion and against all maneuvers to bring about a legal ascendancy of one sect over another. *Jefferson*

Freedom is that faculty which enlarges the usefulness of all other faculties. *Kant*

... that this nation, under God, shall have a new birth of freedom.... *Lincoln*

Those who deny freedom to others deserve it not for themselves and under a just God cannot long retain it. *Lincoln*

Friends

Animals are such agreeable friends—they ask no questions, they pass no criticisms. *George Eliot*

The only way to have a friend is to be one. *Emerson*

The friends thou hast and their adoption tried, grapple them to thy soul with hooks of steel. *Shakespeare*

The light of friendship is like the light of phosphorus, seen plainest when all around is dark. *Crowell*

I am wealthy in my friends. *Shakespeare*

Life is to be fortified by many friendships. To love and to be loved is the greatest happiness of existence. *Sydney Smith*

A friend must not be injured, even in jest. *Syrus*

A friend that you have to buy won't be worth what you pay for him, no matter what that may be. *G. D. Prentice*

True friendship is a plant of slow growth, and must undergo and withstand the shocks of adversity before it is entitled to the appellation. *Washington*

Two persons cannot long be friends if they cannot forgive each other's little failings. *Bruyere*

There is no brotherhood of man without the fatherhood of God. *H. M. Field*

The crest and crowning of all good,
Life's final star, is Brotherhood. *Edwin Markham*

If God is thy father, man is thy brother. *Lamartine*

The brotherhood of man is an integral part of Christianity no less than the Fatherhood of God; and to deny the one is no less infidel than to deny the other. *Lyman Abbott*

Future

I know of no way of judging the future but by the past. *Patrick Henry*

Trust no Future, howe'er pleasant!
Let the dead Past bury its dead! *Longfellow*

I believe the future is only the past again, entered through another gate. *Pinero*

After us the deluge. *Madame de Pompadour*

'Til the sun grows cold,
And the stars are old,
And the leaves of the Judgment Book unfold.
Bayard Taylor

Generosity

Men of the noblest dispositions think themselves happiest when others share their happiness with them. *Duncan*

A man there was, and they called him mad; the more he gave, the more he had. *Bunyan*

If there be any truer measure of a man than by what he does, it must be by what he gives. *South*

I would have a man generous to his country, his neighbors, his kindred, his friends, and most of all his poor friends. Not like some who are most lavish with those who are able to give most to them. *Pliny*

It is not enough to help the feeble up, but to support him after. *Shakespeare*

Genius

There is no great genius without a mixture of madness. *Aristotle*

Genius is infinite painstaking. *Longfellow*

Genius is a promontory jutting out into the infinite. *Victor Hugo*

Genius is nothing but continued attention. *Helvetius*

Genius is but a mind of large general powers accidentally determined in a particular direction. *Johnson*

When a true genius appears in the world, you may know him by this sign, that the dunces are all in confederacy against him. *Swift*

The first and last thing required of genius is the love of truth. *Goethe*

Giving

You give but little when you give of your possessions. It is when you give of yourself that you truly give. *Kahlil Gibran*

I make presents to the mother, but think of the daughter. *Goethe*

I fear the Greeks, even when they bring gifts. *Vergil*

God

Nearer, my God, to Thee—
Nearer to Thee—
E'en though it be a cross
That raiseth me;
Still all my song shall be
Nearer, my God, to Thee,
Nearer to Thee! *Sarah Flower Adams*

Nature is too thin a screen; the glory of the omnipresent God bursts through everywhere. *Emerson*

Man proposes, and God disposes. *Ariosto*

Live near to God, and so all things will appear to you little in comparison with eternal realities. *R. M. McCheyne*

God's in His Heaven—
All's right with the world! *Browning*

To escape from evil we must be made, as far as possible, like God; and this resemblance consists in becoming just, and holy, and wise. *Plato*

God moves in a mysterious way
His wonders to perform;
He plants his footsteps in the sea
And rides upon the storm. *Cowper*

"We trust, Sir, that God is on our side." "It is more important to know that we are on God's side." *Lincoln*

A mighty fortress is our God,
A bulwark never failing,
Our helper he amid the flood
Of mortal ills prevailing. *Luther*

He mounts the storm, and walks upon the wind. *Pope*

Goodness

In nothing do men approach so nearly to the gods as in doing good to men. *Cicero*

The best portion of a good man's life is his little, nameless, unremembered acts of kindness and of love. *Wordsworth*

How far that little candle throws his beams! so shines a good deed in a naughty world. *Shakespeare*

Your actions, in passing, pass not away, for every good work is a grain of seed for eternal life. *Bernard*

Gossip

Foul whisperings are abroad. *Shakespeare*

There is only one thing in the world worse than being talked about, and that is not being talked about. *Wilde*

Government

Experience teaches us to be most on our guard to protect liberty when the government's purposes are beneficent. *Brandeis*

The best of all governments is that which teaches us to govern ourselves. *Goethe*

Government is a contrivance of human wisdom to provide for human wants. *Burke*

The punishment suffered by the wise who refuse to take part in the government, is to live under the government of bad men. *Plato*

Government is a trust, and the officers of the government are trustees; and both the trust and the trustees are created for the benefit of the people. *Henry Clay*

It is to self-government, the great principle of popular representation and administration, the system that lets in all to participate in its counsels, that we owe what we are, and what we hope to be. *Daniel Webster*

Though the people support the government the government should not support the people. *Grover Cleveland*

Republics end through luxury; monarchies through poverty. *Montesquieu*

All good government must begin in the home. It is useless to make good laws for bad people. Public sentiment is more than law. *H. R. Haweis*

Nothing will ruin the country if the people themselves will undertake its safety; and nothing can save it if they leave that safety in any hands but their own. *Daniel Webster*

GRATITUDE

He enjoys much who is thankful for little; a grateful mind is both a great and a happy mind. *Secker*

He who receives a benefit should never forget it; he who bestows should never remember it. *Charron*

He who acknowledges a kindness has it still, and he who has a grateful sense of it has requited it. *Cicero*

When I find a great deal of gratitude in a poor man, I take it for granted there would be as much generosity if he were rich. *Pope*

O Lord, who lends me life, lend me a heart replete with thankfulness. *Shakespeare*

GREATNESS

Great warriors, like great earthquakes, are principally remembered for the mischief they have done. *Bovee*

Nothing can be truly great which is not right. *Johnson*

The nearer we come to great men the more clearly we see that they are only men. They rarely seem great to their valets. *La Bruyere*

Distinction is the consequence, never the object of a great mind. *Washington Allston*

It is the prerogative of great men only to have great defects. *La Rochefoucauld*

Great men never make bad use of their superiority; they see it, and feel it, and are not less modest. The more they have, the more they know their own deficiencies. *Rousseau*

Some are born great, some achieve greatness, and some have greatness thrust upon 'em. *Shakespeare*

He who is great when he falls is great in his prostration, and is no more an object of contempt than when men tread on the ruins of sacred buildings, which men of piety venerate no less than if they stood. *Seneca*

What millions died that Caesar might be great. *Campbell*

Great is he who enjoys his earthenware as if it were plate, and not less great is the man to whom all his plate is no more than earthenware. *Seneca*

There never was yet a truly great man that was not at the same time truly virtuous. *Franklin*

He is not great, who is not greatly good. *Shakespeare*

GRIEF

Never does a man know the force that is in him till some mighty affection or grief has humanized the soul. *F. W. Robertson*

No grief is so acute but that time ameliorates it. *Cicero*

HABIT

Habit, if not resisted, soon becomes necessity. *St. Augustine*

All habits gather, by unseen degrees, as brooks make rivers, rivers run to seas. *Dryden*

Sow an act and you reap a habit. Sow a habit and you reap a character. Sow a character and you reap a destiny. *Charles Reade*

Habit is a cable. We weave a thread of it every day, and at last we cannot break it. *H. Mann*

Habits are at first cobwebs, then cables. *Spanish proverb*

The phrases that men hear or repeat continually, end by becoming convictions and ossify the organs of intelligence. *Goethe*

Habit with him was all the test of truth; "it must be right, I've done it from my youth." *Crabbe*

HAPPINESS

I have learned to seek my happiness by limiting my desires, rather than in attempting to satisfy them. *John Stuart Mill*

No man is happy who does not think himself so. *Marcus Antoninus*

Happiness grows at our own firesides, and is not to be picked in strangers' gardens. *Douglas Jerrold*

Happiness is neither within us only, or without us; it is the union of ourselves with God. *Pascal*

Men of the noblest dispositions think themselves happiest when others share their happiness with them. *Jeremy Taylor*

All who would win joy, must share it; happiness was born a twin. *Byron*

The strength and the happiness of a man consists in finding out the way in which God is going, and going in that way, too. *H. W. Beecher*

Call no man happy till you know the end of his life. Till then, at most, he can only be counted fortunate. *Herodotus*

Don't try to be happy. Happiness is a shy nymph, and if you chase her you will never catch her; but just go quietly on in the way of duty and she will come to you. *Eliphalet Nott*

The Greeks said grandly in their tragic phrase, "Let no one be called happy till his death"; to which I would add, "Let no one, till his death, be called unhappy." *E. B. Browning*

It is an inevitable law that a man cannot be happy if he does not live for something higher than his own happiness. He cannot live in or for himself. Every desire he has links him with others. *Bulwer-Lytton*

True happiness renders men kind and sensible; and that happiness is always shared with others. *Montesquieu*

Silence is the perfectest herald of joy. I were but little happy if I could say how much. *Shakespeare*

Do not speak of happiness to one less fortunate than yourself. *Plutarch*

To be happy is not the purpose of our being, but to deserve happiness. *Fichte*

To be happy you must forget yourself. Learn benevolence; it is the only cure of a morbid temper. *Bulwer-Lytton*

Philosophical happiness is to want little; civil or vulgar happiness is to want much and enjoy much. *Burke*

HARDSHIP

Ability and necessity dwell near each other. *Pythagoras*

It is not helps, but obstacles, not facilities but difficulties, that make men. *W. Mathews*

HATRED

Malice can always find a mark to shoot at, and a pretence to fire. *C. Simmons*

If I wanted to punish an enemy it should be by fastening on him the trouble of constantly hating somebody. *H. More*

I will tell you what to hate. Hate hypocrisy; hate cant; hate intolerance, oppression, injustice, Pharisaism; hate them as Christ hated them—with a deep, abiding, God-like hatred. *F. W. Robertson*

Hate no one; hate their vices, not themselves. *J. G. C. Brainard*

Hatred is active, and envy passive dislike; there is but one step from envy to hate. *Goethe*

I shall never permit myself to stoop so low as to hate any man. *Booker T. Washington*

We hate some persons because we do not know them; and we will not know them because we hate them. *Colton*

There are glances of hatred that stab, and raise no cry of murder. *George Eliot*

HEALTH

He who has health has hope, and he who has hope has everything. *Arabian proverb*

The fate of a nation has often depended on the good or bad digestion of a prime minister. *Voltaire*

HEART

Soul of fibre and heart of oak. *Cervantes*
A loving heart is the truest wisdom. *Dickens*

> Still stands thine ancient sacrifice—
> An humble and a contrite heart. *Kipling*

There is no instinct like that of the heart. *Byron*
Hearts are stronger than swords. *Wendell Phillips*
The heart has reasons that reason does not understand. *Bossuet*

The wrinkles of the heart are more indelible than those of the brow. *Deluzy*

To judge human character rightly, a man may sometimes have very small experience, provided he has a very large heart. *Bulwer-Lytton*

The hardest trial of the heart is, whether it can bear a rival's failure without triumph. *Aikin*

A noble heart, like the sun, showeth its greatest countenance in its lowest estate. *Sir P. Sidney*

The heart of a good man is the sanctuary of God in this world. *Madame Necker*

HEAVEN

Heaven will be inherited by every man who has heaven in his soul. *Henry Ward Beecher*

If I ever reach heaven I expect to find three wonders there; first, to meet some I had not thought to see there; second, to miss some I had expected to see there; and third, the greatest wonder of all, to find myself there. *John Newton*

When Christ ascended
Triumphantly from star to star
He left the gates of Heaven ajar. *Longfellow*

My gems are falling away; but it is because God is making up his jewels. *Wolfe*

Earth has no sorrow that heaven cannot heal. *Moore*

The love of heaven makes one heavenly. *Shakespeare*

Heaven must be in me before I can be in heaven. *Stanford*

It is heaven only that is given away—only God may be had for the asking. *J. R. Lowell*

I would not give one moment of heaven for all the joy and riches of the world, even if it lasted for thousands and thousands of years. *Luther*

HISTORY

There is properly no history, only biography. *Emerson*

History is a voice forever sounding across the centuries the laws of right and wrong. Opinions alter, manners change, creeds rise and fall, but the moral law is written on the tablets of eternity. *Froude*

History is indeed little more than the register of the crimes, follies, and misfortunes of mankind. *Gibbon*

We read history through our prejudices. *Wendell Phillips*

What is history but a fable agreed upon? *Napoleon*

History is neither more nor less than biography on a large scale. *Lamartine*

The historian is a prophet looking backwards. *Schlegel*

The history of the past is a mere puppet show. A little man comes out and blows a little trumpet, and goes in again. You look for something new, and lo! another little man comes out and blows another little trumpet, and goes in again. And it is all over. *Longfellow*

History is only a record of crimes and misfortunes. *Voltaire*

History needs distance, perspective. Facts and events which are too well attested cease, in some sort, to be malleable. *Joubert*

Not to know what has been transacted in former times is to be always a child. If no use is made of the labors of past ages, the world must remain always in the infancy of knowledge. *Cicero*

HOLINESS

It must be a prospect pleasing to God to see his creatures forever drawing nearer to him by greater degrees of resemblance. *Addison*

Our holy lives must win a new world's crown. *Shakespeare*

Not all the pomp and pageantry of worlds reflect such glory on the eye supreme, as the meek virtues of the holy man. *R. Montgomery*

The essence of true holiness consists in conformity to the nature and will of God. *Lucas*

The serene, silent beauty of a holy life is the most powerful influence in the world, next to the might of the Spirit of God. *Pascal*

HOME

For a man's house is his castle. *Sir Edward Coke*
Without hearts there is no home. *Byron*

> Weep no more, my lady;
> Oh, weep no more today!
> We will sing one song for the old Kentucky home,
> For the old Kentucky home, far away. *Foster*

The first indication of domestic happiness is the love of one's home. *Montlosier*

He is happiest, be he king or peasant who finds peace in his home. *Goethe*

A cottage, if God be there, will hold as much happiness as might stock a palace. *J. Hamilton*

'Mid pleasures and palaces though we may roam,
Be it ever so humble, there's no place like Home.
J. Howard Payne

HONESTY

An honest man's the noblest work of God. *Pope*

Make yourself an honest man, and then you may be sure there is one rascal less in the world. *Carlyle*

Ay, sir; to be honest, as this world goes, is to be one man picked out of ten thousand. *Shakespeare*

I hope I shall always possess firmness and virtue enough to maintain what I consider the most enviable of all titles, the character of an honest man. *Washington*

HONOR

Honor lies in honest toil. *Grover Cleveland*

For Brutus is an honourable man;
So are they all, all honourable men. *Shakespeare*

The nation's honor is dearer than the nation's comfort; yes, than the nation's life itself. *Woodrow Wilson*

HOPE

Abandon hope, all ye who enter here. *Dante*

Hope springs eternal in the human breast; man never is, but always to be blest. *Pope*

Hope for the best, but prepare for the worst. *English proverb*

The miserable hath no other medicine but only hope. *Shakespeare*

True hope is swift, and flies with swallow's wings; kings it makes gods, and meaner creatures kings. *Shakespeare*

The mighty hopes that make us men. *Tennyson*

Where there is no hope, there can be no endeavor. *Johnson*

HUMANITY

Our humanity were a poor thing but for the divinity that stirs within us. *Bacon*

I love my country better than my family; but I love humanity better than my country. *Fenelon*

After all there is but one race—humanity. *George Moore*

I am not an Athenian, nor a Greek, but a citizen of the world. *Socrates*

The age of chivalry has gone; the age of humanity has come. *Charles Sumner*

HUMILITY

Humility is the solid foundation of all the virtues. *Confucius*

Humility that low sweet root, from which all heavenly virtues shoot. *Moore*

> God hath sworn to lift on high
> Who sinks himself by true humility. *Keble*

They that know God will be humble; they that know themselves cannot be proud. *Flavel*

I believe the first test of a truly great man is his humility. *John Ruskin*

Humility is the genuine proof of Christian virtue. Without it we keep all our defects; and they are only crusted over by pride, which conceals them from others, and often from ourselves. *La Rochefoucauld*

God walks with the humble; he reveals himself to the lowly; he gives understanding to the little ones; he discloses his meaning to pure minds, but hides his grace from the curious and the proud. *Thomas a Kempis*

Humility and love are the essence of true religion; the humble formed to adore; the loving to associate with eternal love. *Lavater*

HYPOCRISY

The devil can cite Scripture for his purpose. An evil soul, producing holy witness, is like a villain with a smiling cheek; a goodly apple rotten at the heart: Oh, what a goodly outside falsehood hath! *Shakespeare*

Hypocrites do the devil's drudgery in Christ's livery. *M. Henry*

False face must hide what the false heart doth know. *Shakespeare*

No man can, for any considerable time, wear one face to himself, and another to the multitude, without finally getting bewildered as to which is the true one. *Hawthorne*

IDEALS

Ideals are the world's masters. *J. G. Holland*

A man's ideal, like his horizon, is constantly receding from him as he advances toward it. *W. G. T. Shedd*

IDEAS

Ideas control the world. *Garfield*

In these days we fight for ideas, and newspapers are our fortresses. *H. Heine*

Ideas make their way in silence like the waters that, filtering behind the rocks of the Alps, loosen them from the mountains on which they rest. *D'Aubigne*

IDLENESS

Idleness is the holiday of fools. *Chesterfield*

In idleness there is perpetual despair. *Carlyle*

Some people have a perfect genius for doing nothing, and doing it assiduously. *Haliburton*

Not only is he idle who is doing nothing, but he that might be better employed. *Socrates*

Idleness is the burial of a living man. *Jeremy Taylor*

IGNORANCE

Where ignorance is bliss,
'Tis folly to be wise. *Gray*

Nothing is so indicative of deepest culture as a tender consideration of the ignorant. *Emerson*

Ignorance is the mother of fear. *Henry Home*

To be ignorant of one's ignorance is the malady of ignorance. *A. B. Alcott*

The more we study, the more we discover our ignorance. *Shelley*

To be proud of learning is the greatest ignorance. *Jeremy Taylor*

If thou art wise thou knowest thine own ignorance; and thou art ignorant if thou knowest not thyself. *Luther*

Nothing is so good for an ignorant man as silence; and if he was sensible of this he would not be ignorant. *Saadi*

Ignorance is the night of the mind, but a night without moon or star. *Confucius*

There are times when ignorance is bliss, indeed. *Dickens*

IMAGINATION

Imagination rules the world. *Napoleon*

The soul without imagination is what an observatory would be without a telescope. *H. W. Beecher*

Imagination disposes of everything; it creates beauty, justice, and happiness, which are everything in this world. *Pascal*

IMITATION

We imitate only what we believe and admire. *Willmott*

He who imitates evil always goes beyond the example that is set; he who imitates what is good always falls short. *Guicciardini*

Imitation causes us to leave natural ways to enter into artificial ones; it therefore makes slaves. *Vinet*

IMMORTALITY

I have been dying for twenty years, now I am going to live. *James Drummond Burns*

Those who hope for no other life are dead even for this. *Goethe*

Immortality is the glorious discovery of Christianity. *William Ellery Channing*

For the great hereafter I trust in the infinite love of God as expressed in the life and death of our Lord and Saviour Jesus Christ. *J. G. Holland*

No one could ever meet death for his country without the hope of immortality. *Cicero*

Those who live in the Lord never see each other for the last time. *German motto*

Oh, may I join the choir invisible
Of those immortal dead who live again. *George Eliot*

The spirit of man, which God inspired, cannot together perish with this corporeal clod. *Milton*

Life is the childhood of our immortality. *Goethe*

Whatsoever that be within us that feels, thinks, desires

and animates, is something celestial, divine, and, consequently, imperishable. *Aristotle*

The nearer I approach the end, the plainer I hear around me the immortal symphonies of the worlds which invite me. It is marvelous; yet simple. *Victor Hugo*

The monuments of the nations are all protests against nothingness after death; so are statues and inscriptions; so is history. *Lew Wallace*

> For tho' from out our bourne of time an' place
> The flood may bear me far,
> I hope to see my Pilot face to face
> When I have crost the bar. *Tennyson*

One short sleep past, we wake eternally, and death shall be no more. *Donne*

INDUSTRY

It is better to wear out than to rust out. *Cumberland*

In every rank, both great and small, it is industry that supports us all. *Gay*

If you have great talents, industry will improve them; if but moderate abilities, industry will supply their deficiencies. *S. Smiles*

There is always hope in a man who actually and earnestly works. In idleness alone is there perpetual despair. *Carlyle*

Industry keeps the body healthy, the mind clear, the heart whole, and the purse full. *C. Simmons*

INGRATITUDE

How sharper than a serpent's tooth it is to have a thankless child. *Shakespeare*

One ungrateful man does an injury to all who stand in need of aid. *Publilius Syrus*

Blow, blow, thou winter wind, thou art not so unkind as man's ingratitude. Freeze, freeze, thou bitter sky, thou dost not bite so nigh, as benefits forget. *Shakespeare*

INJUSTICE

He who commits injustice is ever made more wretched than he who suffers it. *Plato*

No one will dare maintain that it is better to do injustice than to bear it. *Aristotle*

INTELLIGENCE

God has placed no limits to the exercise of the intellect he has given us, on this side of the grave. *Bacon*

While the world lasts, the sun will gild the mountain-tops before it shines upon the plain. *Bulwer-Lytton*

The men of action are, after all, only the unconscious instruments of the men of thought. *Heine*

If a man empties his purse into his head, no one can take it from him. *Franklin*

JOY

The most profound joy has more of gravity than of gaiety in it. *Montaigne*

He who can conceal his joys is greater than he who can hide his griefs. *Lavater*

Joy never feasts so high as when the first course is of misery. *Suckling*

There is not a joy the world can give like that it takes away. *Byron*

JUDGMENT

One man's word is no man's word; we should quietly hear both sides. *Goethe*

Judgment is forced upon us by experience. *Johnson*

We judge ourselves by what we feel capable of doing, while others judge us by what we have already done. *Longfellow*

It is with our judgments as with our watches: no two go just alike, yet each believes his own. *Pope*

O judgment! thou art fled to brutish beasts,
And men have lost their reason! *Shakespeare*

Everyone complains of the badness of his memory, but nobody of his judgment. *La Rochefoucauld*

In judging of others a man laboreth in vain, often erreth, and easily sinneth; but in judging and examining himself, he always laboreth fruitfully. *Thomas a Kempis*

JUSTICE

God's mill grinds slow, but sure. *George Herbert*

Man is unjust, but God is just; and finally justice triumphs. *Longfellow*

The sword of the law should never fall but on those whose guilt is so apparent as to be pronounced by their friends as well as foes. *Jefferson*

Be just and fear not; let all the ends thou aimest at be thy country's, thy God's, and truth's. *Shakespeare*

Whenever a separation is made between liberty and justice, neither, in my opinion, is safe. *Burke*

All are not just because they do no wrong; but he who will not wrong me when he may, he is truly just. *Cumberland*

Justice is to give to every man his own. *Aristotle*

KINDNESS

Kindness is the golden chain by which society is bound together. *Goethe*

The best portion of a good man's life is his little, nameless, unremembered acts of kindness and of love. *Wordsworth*

Kindness in ourselves is the honey that blunts the sting of unkindness in another. *Landor*

Ask thyself, daily, to how many ill-minded persons thou hast shown a kind disposition. *Marcus Antoninus*

I had rather never receive a kindness, than never bestow one. Not to return a benefit is the greater sin, but not to confer it, is the earlier. *Seneca*

KNOWLEDGE

For knowledge, too, is itself a power. *Bacon*

The first step to knowledge is to know that we are ignorant. *Cecil*

To be conscious that you are ignorant is a great step to knowledge. *Disraeli*

The end of all learning is to know God, and out of that knowledge to love and imitate him. *Milton*

Our knowledge is the amassed thought and experience of innumerable minds. *Emerson*

Reading maketh a full man; conference, a ready man; histories make men wise; poets, witty; the mathematics, subtle; natural philosophy, deep; moral philosophy, grave; logic and rhetoric, able to contend. *Bacon*

We know what we are, but know not what we may be. *Shakespeare*

Man is not born to solve the problem of the universe, but to find out what he has to do; and to restrain himself within the limits of his comprehension. *Goethe*

And still they gazed, and still the wonder grew,
That one small head should carry all it knew.
Goldsmith

All wish to be learned, but no one is willing to pay the price. *Juvenal*

A little learning is a dangerous thing;
Drink deep, or taste not the Pierian spring;
Their shallow draughts intoxicate the brain,
And drinking largely sobers us again. *Pope*

LABOR

He who prays and labors lifts his heart to God with his hands. *St. Bernard*

Without labor nothing prospers. *Sophocles*

Labor is life. From the inmost heart of the worker rises his God-given force—the sacred celestial life-essence breathed into him by Almighty God. *Thomas Carlyle*

Blessed is the man that has found his work. One monster there is in the world, the idle man. *Carlyle*

The labor union is an elemental response to the human instinct for group action in dealing with group problems. *William Green*

Genius begins great works; labor alone finishes them. *Joubert*

If you want knowledge, you must toil for it; if food, you must toil for it; and if pleasure, you must toil for it: toil is the law. *Ruskin*

There are many ways of being frivolous, only one way of being intellectually great; that is honest labor. *Sydney Smith*

Labor was the first price, the original purchase money that was paid for all things. *Adam Smith*

LANGUAGE

Language as well as the faculty of speech, was the immediate gift of God. *Noah Webster*

Language is the dress of thought. *Johnson*

Language most shows a man; speak that I may see thee; it springs out of the most retired and inmost part of us. *Ben Jonson*

One great use of words is to hide our thoughts. *Voltaire*

The language denotes the man; a coarse or refined character finds its expression naturally in a coarse or refined phraseology. *Bovee*

Thinking cannot be clear till it has had expression. We must write, or speak, or act our thoughts, or they will remain in half torpid form. Our feelings must have expression, or they will be as clouds, which, till they descend in rain, will never bring up fruit or flower. So it is with all the inward feelings; expression gives them development. Thought is the blossom; language the opening bud; action the fruit behind it. *H. W. Beecher*

Language is a solemn thing: it grows out of life—out of its agonies and ecstasies, its wants and its weariness. Every language is a temple in which the soul of those who speak it is enshrined. *O. W. Holmes*

LAUGHTER

A laugh is worth a hundred groans in any market. *Lamb*

I like the laughter that opens the lips and the heart, that shows at the same time pearls and the soul. *Victor Hugo*

Man is the only creature endowed with the power of laughter; is he not also the only one that deserves to be laughed at? *Greville*

Beware of him who hates the laugh of a child. *Lavater*

That laughter costs too much which is purchased by the sacrifice of decency. *Quintilian*

Men show their character in nothing more clearly than by what they think laughable. *Goethe*

A laugh, to be joyous, must flow from a joyous heart, for without kindness there can be no true joy. *Carlyle*

A good laugh is sunshine in a house. *Thackeray*

LAW

There is but one law for all; namely, that law which governs all law,—the law of our Creator, the law of humanity, justice, equity; the law of nature and of nations. *Burke*

A countryman between two lawyers is like a fish between two cats. *Franklin*

If the law is upheld only by government officials, then all law is at an end. *Herbert Hoover*

Law is the embodiment of the moral sentiment of the people. *Blackstone*

There is no man so good, who, were he to submit all his thoughts and actions to the laws, would not deserve hanging ten times in his life. *Montaigne*

God is a law to men of sense; but pleasure is a law to the fool. *Plato*

Where law ends, there tyranny begins. *William Pitt*

Laws are silent in the midst of arms. *Cicero*

LIAR, LIES

A liar is not believed even though he tell the truth. *Cicero*

All that one gains by falsehood is, not to be believed when he speaks the truth. *Aristotle*

A good memory is needed once we have lied. *Corneille*

He who tells a lie is not sensible how great a task he undertakes; for he must be forced to invent twenty more to maintain one. *Pope*

> Who dares think one thing, and another tell,
> My heart detests him as the gates of hell. *Homer*

The liar's punishment is not in the least that he is not believed, but that he cannot believe anyone else. *George Bernard Shaw*

LIBERTY

The people never give up their liberties but under some delusion. *Burke*

Liberty is to the collective body, what health is to every individual body. Without health no pleasure can be tasted by man; without liberty, no happiness can be enjoyed by society. *Bolingbroke*

Eternal vigilance is the price of liberty. *John Philpot Curran*

What is life? It is not to stalk about, and draw fresh air, or gaze upon the sun; it is to be free. *Addison*

Those who would give up essential liberty to purchase a little temporary safety deserve neither liberty nor safety. *Franklin*

True liberty consists in the privilege of enjoying our own rights, not in the destruction of the rights of others. *Pinckard*

Give me liberty, or give me death. *Patrick Henry*

The God who gave us life, gave us liberty at the same time. *Jefferson*

Give me the liberty to know, to think, to believe, and to utter freely according to conscience, above all other liberties. *Milton*

Liberty is the only thing you cannot have unless you are willing to give it to others. *William Allen White*

LIBRARIES

Next to acquiring good friends, the best acquisition is that of good books. *Colton*

The student has his Rome, his Florence, his whole glowing Italy, within the four walls of his library. He has in his books the ruins of an antique world and the glories of a modern one. *Longfellow*

LIFE

All are but parts of one stupendous whole,
Whose body Nature is, and God the soul. *Pope*

One life; a little gleam of time between two eternities; no second chance for us forever more. *Carlyle*

The world embarrasses me, and I cannot dream
That this watch exists and has no watchmaker.
Voltaire

Remember that life is neither pain nor pleasure; it is serious business, to be entered upon with courage and in a spirit of selfsacrifice. *De Tocqueville*

Every man's life is a fairy-tale written by God's fingers. *Hans Christian Anderson*

We live no more of our time here than we live well. *Carlyle*

Life is a long lesson in humility. *Barrie*

Life is no idle dream, but a solemn reality, based on and encompassed by eternity. Find out your work, and stand to it; the night cometh when no man can work. *Carlyle*

For life in general, there is but one decree: youth is a blunder, manhood a struggle, old age a regret. *Disraeli*

It is a truth to be remembered, that this life, which is mortal, is given to us that we may prepare for the life which is immortal. *De Sales*

Dost thou love life? Then do not squander time, for that is the stuff life is made of. *Franklin*

A useless life is only an early death. *Goethe*

> Tell me not, in mournful numbers,
> Life is but an empty dream! *Longfellow*

Christian life consists in faith and charity. *Luther*
The white flower of a blameless life. *Tennyson*

> Our lives are albums written through
> With good or ill, with false or true
> And as the blessed angels turn
> The pages of our years,
> God grant they read the good with smiles,
> And blot the ill with tears! *Whittier*

LIGHT

> Lead, kindly light, amid the encircling gloom,
> Lead Thou me on!
> The night is dark, and I am far from home—
> Lead Thou me on!
> Keep Thou my feet; I do not ask to see
> The distant scene,—one step enough for me. *John Henry Newman*

LISTENING

A good listener is not only popular everywhere, but after a while he knows something. *Wilson Mizner*

LOVE

Man's love is of man's life a thing apart,
'Tis woman's whole existence. *Byron*

The heart of him who truly loves is a paradise on earth; he has God in himself, for God is love. *Lamennais*

Heaven has no rage like love to hatred turned. *Congreve*

We are shaped and fashioned by what we love. *Goethe*

How wise are they that are but fools in love! *Joshua Cooke*

Love is never lost. If not reciprocated it will flow back and soften and purify the heart. *Washington Irving*

We are all born for love.... It is the principle of existence and its only end. *Disraeli*

'Tis better to have loved and lost, than never to have loved at all. *Tennyson*

All mankind love a lover. *Emerson*

If you would be loved, love and be lovable. *Franklin*

Girls we love for what they are;
Young men for what they promise to be. *Goethe*

Pale hands I loved beside the Shalimar,
Where are they now? Who lies beneath your spell?
Whom do you lead on Rapture's roadway, far,
Before you agonize them in farewell? *Lawrence Hope*

But there's nothing half so sweet in life
As love's young dream. *Moore*

The only victory over love is flight. *Napoleon*
Everybody in love is blind. *Propertius*

As one who cons at evening o'er an album all alone,
And muses on the faces of the friends that he has known,
So I turn the leaves of Fancy, till in shadowy design
I find the smiling features of an old sweetheart of mine.
James Whitcomb Riley

The hours I spent with thee, dear heart,
Are as a string of pearls to me;
I count them over, every one apart,
My rosary, my rosary. *Robert Cameron Rogers*

SIXTEEN HUNDRED QUOTATIONS FROM LITERATURE 229

Ay me! for aught that I ever could read,
Could ever hear by tale or history,
The course of true love never did run smooth.
Shakespeare

Give me my Romeo; and, when he shall die,
Take him, and cut him out in little stars,
And he will make the face of heaven so fine,
And all the world will be in love with night,
And pay no worship to the garish sun.
Shakespeare

I love thee, I love but thee,
With a love that shall not die
Till the sun grows cold,
And the stars are old,
And the leaves of the Judgment Book unfold!
Bayard Taylor

"I'm sorry that I spell'd the word;
I hate to go above you,
Because"—the brown eyes lower fell,—
"Because, you see, I love you!" *Whittier*

LUCK

A pound of pluck is worth a ton of luck. *James A. Garfield*

MAN

Let each man think himself an act of God.
His mind a thought, his life a breath of God. *Bailey*

The test of every religious, political, or education system is the man that it forms. *Amiel*

Man's inhumanity to man
Makes countless thousands mourn! *Burns*

Man himself is the crowning wonder of creation; the study of his nature the noblest study the world affords. *Gladstone*

Men!
Thou pendulum betwixt a smile and tear. *Byron*

The man who is deserving the name is the one whose thoughts and exertions are for others rather than for himself. *Walter Scott*

We are the miracle of miracles, the great inscrutable mystery of God. *Carlyle*

The chief constituents of what we call manhood, are moral rather than intellectual. *J. S. Kieffer*

Every man is a volume, if you know how to read him. *William Ellery Channing*

Bounded in his nature, infinite in his desires, man is a fallen god who has a recollection of heaven. *Lamartine*

Man is a piece of the universe made alive. *Emerson*

The way of a superior man is three-fold: virtuous, he is free from anxieties; wise, he is free from perplexities; bold, he is free from fear. *Confucius*

>   Man wants but little here below,
>   Nor wants that little long. *Goldsmith*

God give us men. A time like this demands
Strong minds, great hearts, true faith and ready hands!
Men whom the lust of office does not kill,
Men whom the spoils of office cannot buy,
Men who possess opinions and a will,
Men who love honor, men who cannot lie.
                              J. G. Holland

>   Know then thyself, presume not God to scan;
>   The proper study of mankind is man. *Pope*

>   He was a man, take him for all in all,
>   I shall not look upon his like again. *Shakespeare*

His life was gentle, and the elements
So mix'd in him that Nature might stand up,
And say to all the world, This was a man!
                              Shakespeare

>   When faith is lost, when honor dies,
>   The man is dead! *Whittier*

MARRIAGE

To have and to hold from this day forward, for better, for worse, for richer, for poorer, in sickness, and in health, to love and to cherish, till death us do part. *Book of Common Prayer*

The happiness of married life depends upon making small sacrifices with readiness and cheerfulness. *Selden*

A deaf husband and a blind wife are always a happy couple. *Danish proverb*

The love of some men for their wives is like that of Alfieri for his horse. "My attachment for him," said he, "went so far as to destroy my peace every time that he had the least ailment; but my love for him did not prevent me from fretting and chafing him whenever he did not wish to go my way." *Bovee*

Keep thy eyes wide open before marriage; and half shut afterward. *Thomas Fuller*

If you would have the nuptial union last, let virtue be the bond that ties it fast. *Rowe*

Matrimony,—the high sea for which no compass has yet been invented. *Heine*

Marriage is something you have to give your whole mind to. *Ibsen*

> Something old, something new,
> Something borrowed, something blue.
> *Old English rhyme*

Marriages are made in heaven. *Tennyson*

MEDICINE

The physician heals, Nature makes well. *Aristotle*
An apple a day keeps the doctor away. *English proverb*
God heals and the doctor takes the fee. *Franklin*

But nothing is more estimable than a physician who, having studied nature from his youth, knows the properties of the human body, the diseases which assail it, the remedies which will benefit it, exercises his art with caution, and pays equal attention to the rich and the poor. *Voltaire*

MELANCHOLY

> There's not a string attuned to mirth
> But has its chord in melancholy. *Hood*

Melancholy is the pleasure of being sad. *Victor Hugo*

Memory

Time whereof the memory of man runneth not to the contrary. *Blackstone*

> To live in hearts we leave behind,
> Is not to die. *Campbell*

Vanity plays lurid tricks with our memory. *Joseph Conrad*

O memory, thou bitter sweet,—both a joy and a scourge! *Madame de Stael*

Mercy

Among the attributes of God, although they are all equal, mercy shines with even more brilliancy than justice. *Cervantes*

Mercy to him that shows it, is the rule. *Cowper*

How would you be, if he, who is the top of judgment, should but judge you as you are? O, think on that, and mercy then will breathe within your lips, like man new made. *Shakespeare*

> The quality of mercy is not strain'd,
> It droppeth as the gentle rain from heaven
> Upon the place beneath: it is twice blest;
> It blesseth him that gives and him that takes;
> 'Tis mightiest in the mightiest; it becomes
> The throned monarch better than his crown;
> His sceptre shows the force of temporal power,
> The attribute to awe and majesty,
> Wherein doth sit the dread and fear of kings;
> But mercy is above this sceptred sway;
> It is entroned in the hearts of kings,
> It is an attribute to God himself;
> And earthly power doth then show likest God's
> When mercy seasons justice. *Shakespeare*

Mind

Whatever that be which thinks, understands, wills, and acts, it is something celestial and divine. *Cicero*

The march of the human mind is slow. *Burke*

If we work upon marble, it will perish; if we work upon brass, time will efface it; if we rear temples, they will crumble into dust, but if we work upon immortal minds and instill into them just principles, we are then engraving that upon tablets which no time will efface, but will brighten and brighten to all eternity. *Daniel Webster*

MISFORTUNE

Little minds are tamed and subdued by misfortune; but great minds rise above it. *Washington Irving*

When I was happy I thought I knew men, but it was fated that I should know them only in misfortune. *Napoleon*

We have all of us sufficient fortitude to bear the misfortunes of others. *La Rochefoucauld*

The greatest misfortune of all is, not to be able to bear misfortune. *Bias*

Misfortune makes of certain souls a vast desert through which rings the voice of God. *Balzac*

MOB

The mob is man voluntarily descending to the nature of the beast. *Emerson*

It has been very truly said that the mob has many heads, but no brains. *Rivarol*

MODESTY

The modest person seldom fails to gain the good will of those he converses with, because nobody envies a man who does not appear to be pleased with himself. *Steele*

Modesty is the citadel of beauty and virtue. *Demades*

MONEY

Money is a good servant but a bad master. *Bacon*

All love has something of blindness in it, but the love of money especially. *South*

A fool and his money are soon parted. *George Buchanan*

By doing good with his money, a man, as it were, stamps the image of God upon it, and makes it pass current for the merchandise of heaven. *Rutledge*

Ah, take the cash, and let the Credit go,
Nor heed the rumble of a distant Drum!
Omar Khayyam

Make all you can, save all you can, give all you can.
J. Wesley

Money is not required to buy one necessity of the soul.
Thoreau

To possess money is very well; it may be a most valuable servant; to be possessed by it, is to be possessed by a devil, and one of the meanest and worst kind of devils.
Tryon Edwards

MORNING

Sweet is the breath of morn, her rising sweet,
With charm of earliest birds. *Milton*

The morning steals upon the night, melting the darkness.
Shakespeare

The grey-ey'd morn smiles on the frowning night,
Chequering the eastern clouds with streaks of light.
Shakespeare

The silent hours steal on, and flaky darkness breaks within the east. *Shakespeare*

Lose an hour in the morning, and you will be all day hunting for it. *Whately*

The morning, pouring everywhere, its golden glory on the air. *Longfellow*

MOTHER

A mother is a mother still,
The holiest thing alive. *Coleridge*

I think it must somewhere be written, that the virtues of mothers shall be visited on their children, as well as the sins of the fathers. *Dickens*

Men are what their mothers made them. *Emerson*

The future destiny of the child is always the work of the mother. *Napoleon*

If I were hanged on the highest hill,
Mother o' mine, O mother o' mine!

> I know whose love would follow me still,
> Mother o' mine, O mother o' mine! *Kipling*

A man never sees all that his mother has been to him till it's too late to let her know that he sees it. *W. D. Howells*

All that I am or hope to be, I owe to my angel mother. *Lincoln*

> For the hand that rocks the cradle
> Is the hand that rules the world. *William Ross Wallace*

MUSIC

All of heaven we have below. *Addison*
Music is well said to be the speech of angels. *Carlyle*
Music is the universal language of mankind. *Longfellow*

> The man that hath no music in himself,
> Nor is not moved with concord of sweet sounds,
> Is fit for treasons, stratagems and spoils.
>
> *Shakespeare*

NATURE

> Earth's crammed with Heaven
> And every common bush afire with God.
>
> *E. B. Browning*

Nature is but a name for an effect whose cause is God. *Cowper*

> To him who in the love of Nature holds
> Communion with her visible forms, she speaks
> A various language. *Bryant*

Looks through nature up to nature's God. *Pope*
Nature is a volume of which God is the author. *Harvey*
In contemplation of created things, by steps we may ascend to God. *Milton*
Nature, like a kind and smiling mother, lends herself to our dreams and cherishes our fancies. *Victor Hugo*
Epicureanism is human nature drunk, cynicism is human nature mad, and stoicism is human nature in despair. *S. J. Wilson*
When I would recreate myself, I seek the darkest wood, the thickest and most interminable, and to the citizen,

most dismal swamp. I enter a swamp as a sacred place—a *sanctum sanctorum*. There is the strength, the marrow of Nature. *Thoreau*

> Nature never did betray
> The heart that loved her. *Wordsworth*

NECESSITY

Necessity is often the spur to genius. *Balzac*

Necessity is the plea for every infringement of human freedom. It is the argument of tyrants; it is the creed of slaves. *William Pitt*

Necessity makes even the timid brave. *Sallust*

NEIGHBOR

When your neighbor's house is afire, your own property is at stake. *Horace*

The crop always seems better in our neighbor's field, and our neighbor's cow gives more milk. *Ovid*

In the field of world policy I would dedicate this nation to the policy of the good neighbor. *F. D. Roosevelt*

NEWSPAPER

Newspapers are the world's mirrors. *James Ellis*

In the long, fierce struggle for freedom of opinion, the press, like the Church, counted its martyrs by thousands. *James A. Garfield*

Were it left to me to decide whether we should have a government without newspapers or newspapers without government, I should not hesitate a moment to prefer the latter. *Jefferson*

Four hostile newspapers are more to be feared than a thousand bayonets. *Napoleon*

NIGHT

> The Night has a thousand eyes,
> The Day but one;
> Yet the light of the bright world dies
> With the dying sun. *F. W. Bourdillon*

Night's black mantle covers all alike. *Du Bartas*

And the night shall be filled with music
And the cares, that infest the day,
Shall fold their tents, like the Arabs,
And as silently steal away. *Longfellow*

The night is dark, and I am far from home. *John Henry Newman*

OLD AGE

Youthful follies growing on old age, are like the few young shoots on the bare top of an old stump of an oak. *John Foster*

To know how to grow old is the master-work of wisdom, and one of the most difficult chapters in the great art of living. *Amiel*

OPINION

The greater part of men have no opinion, still fewer an opinion of their own, well reflected and founded upon reason. *Seume*

What I admire in Columbus is not his having discovered a world, but his having gone to search for it on the faith of an opinion. *Turgot*

I do not regret having braved public opinion, when I knew it was wrong and was sure it would be merciless. *Horace Greeley*

Wind puffs up empty bladders; opinion, fools. *Socrates*

Fly no opinion because it is new, but strictly search, and after careful view, reject it if false, embrace it if 'tis true. *Lucretius*

OPPORTUNITY

There is an hour in each man's life appointed.
To make his happiness, if then he seize it.
Beaumont and Fletcher

Who makes quick use of the moment, is a genius of prudence. *Lavater*

Plough deep while sluggards sleep. *Benjamin Franklin*

You will never "find" time for anything. If you want time you must make it. *Charles Buxton*

There is a tide in the affairs of men,
Which, taken at the flood, leads on to fortune.
Shakespeare

Many do with opportunities as children do at the seashore; they fill their little hands with sand, and then let the grains fall through, one by one, till all are gone. *T. Jones*

A word spoken in season, at the right moment, is the matter of ages. *Carlyle*

OPTIMISM

Keep your face to the sunshine and you cannot see the shadow. *Helen Keller*

Two men look out through the same bars;
One sees the mud, and one the stars.
Frederick Langbridge

ORATORY

Oratory is the power to talk people out of their sober and natural opinions. *Chatfield*

It is the first rule in oratory that a man must appear such as he would persuade others to be; and that can be accomplished only by the force of his life. *Swift*

I am not fond of uttering platitudes
In stained-glass attitudes. *W. S. Gilbert*

Every man should study conciseness in speaking; it is a sign of ignorance not to know that long speeches, though they may please the speaker, are the torture of the hearer. *Feltham*

What the orators want in depth, they give you in length. *Montesquieu*

In oratory, the greatest art is to conceal art. *Swift*

An orator or author is never successful till he has learned to make his words smaller than his ideas. *Emerson*

PARENTS

Parents wonder why the streams are bitter, when they themselves have poisoned the fountain. *Locke*

We speak of educating our children. Do we know that our children also educate us? *Mrs. Sigourney*

Passion

He only employs his passion who can make use of his reason. *Cicero*

When passion rules, how rare the hours that fall to virtue's share. *Walter Scott*

Our headstrong passions shut the door of our souls against God. *Confucius*

Past

So sad, so fresh, the days that are no more. *Tennyson*

The past is the sepulchre of our dead emotions. *Bovee*

Things without remedy, should be without regard; what is done, is done. *Shakespeare*

Patience

He that can have patience can have what he will. *Franklin*

Patience waiting is often the highest way of doing God's will. *Collier*

All things come round to him who will but wait. *Longfellow*

How poor are they who have not patience! What wound did ever heal but by degrees? *Shakespeare*

And make us rather bear those ills we have
Than fly to others that we know not of? *Shakespeare*

Trust to God to weave your thread into the great web, though the pattern shows it not yet. *G. Macdonald*

Patriotism

The noblest motive is the public good. *Virgil*

Be just and fear not; let all the ends thou aimest at, be thy country's, thy God's, and truth's. *Shakespeare*

I do love my country's good with a respect more tender, more holy and profound than mine own life. *Shakespeare*

Peace

I prefer the most unfair peace to the most righteous war. *Cicero*

Peace rules the day, where reason rules the mind. *William Collins*

> Peace hath her victories,
> No less renowned than war. *Milton*

If they want peace, nations should avoid the pin-pricks that precede cannonshots. *Napoleon*

> The war-drum throbb'd no longer, and the battle-flags were furl'd
> In the parliament of man, the federation of the world.
> *Tennyson*

There is such a thing as a man being too proud to fight. There is such a thing as a nation being so right that it does not need to convince others by force that it is right. *Woodrow Wilson*

It must be a peace without victory. Only a peace between equals can last: only a peace, the very principle of which is equality, and a common participation in a common benefit. *Woodrow Wilson*

PERFECTION

There are many lovely women, but no perfect ones. *Victor Hugo*

Bachelor's wives and old maid's children are always perfect. *Chamfort*

Trifles make perfection, and perfection is no trifle. *Michelangelo*

Perfection is attained by slow degrees; it requires the hand of time. *Voltaire*

Faultily faultless, icily regular, splendidly null, dead perfection; no more. *Tennyson*

This is the very perfection of a man, to find out his own imperfection. *Saint Augustine*

PERSEVERANCE

Much rain wears the marble. *Shakespeare*

The virtue lies in the struggle, not in the prize. *Milnes*

Perseverance and audacity generally win. *Madame Deluzy*

Never despair; but if you do, work on in despair. *Burke*

PHILOSOPHY

A little philosophy inclineth man's mind to atheism; but depth in philosophy bringeth men's minds about to religion. *Bacon*

> There are more things in heaven and earth, Horatio,
> Than are dreamt of in your philosophy.
>
> *Shakespeare*

> There was never yet philosopher
> That could endure the toothache patiently.
>
> *Shakespeare*

When he to whom one speaks does not understand, and he who speaks himself does not understand, this is metaphysics. *Voltaire*

PLEASURE

Fly the pleasure that bites tomorrow. *Herbert*

A life of pleasure makes even the strongest mind frivolous at last. *Bulwer-Lytton*

He buys honey too dear who licks it from thorns. *Old proverb*

Most pleasures, like flowers, when gathered, die. *Young*

POET

A great poet is the most precious jewel of a nation. *Beethoven*

No man was ever yet a great poet, without at the same time being a profound philosopher. *Coleridge*

All men are poets at heart. *Emerson*

All that is best in the great poets of all countries is not what is national in them, but what is universal. *Longfellow*

Every man is a poet when he is in love. *Plato*

Poetry is truth dwelling in beauty. *Gilfillan*

POLITENESS

Self-command is the main elegance. *Emerson*

Politeness is as natural to delicate natures as perfume is to flowers. *De Finod*

Politeness has been well defined as benevolence in small things. *Macaulay*

POLITICS

A majority is always better than the best repartee. *Disraeli*

Real political issues cannot be manufactured by the leaders of parties, and cannot be evaded by them. They declare themselves, and come out of the depths of that deep which we call public opinion. *Garfield*

It is a *condition* which confronts us—not a theory. *Grover Cleveland*

In politics, merit is rewarded by the possessor being raised, like a target, to a position to be fired at. *Bovee*

I always voted at my party's call,
And I never thought of thinking for myself at all.
W. S. Gilbert

Nothing is politically right which is morally wrong. *Daniel O'Connell*

Every time I fill a vacant office I make ten malcontents and one ingrate. *Louis XIV*

Something is rotten in the state of Denmark. *Shakespeare*

POVERTY

Over the hill to the poor-house I'm trudgin' my weary way. *Will Carleton*

Poverty is not dishonorable in itself, but only when it comes from idleness, intemperance, extravagance, and folly. *Plutarch*

He is now fast rising from affluence to poverty. *Mark Twain*

Poor and content is rich, and rich enough; but riches endless is as poor as winter to him that ever fears he shall be poor. *Shakespeare*

The greatest man in history was the poorest. *Emerson*

Few save the poor feel for the poor. *L. E. Landon*

As poor as a church mouse. *English phrase*

POWER

Power will intoxicate the best hearts, as wine the strongest heads. No man is wise enough, nor good enough to be trusted with unlimited power. *Colton*

I have never been able to conceive how any rational

being could propose happiness to himself from the exercise of power over others. *Jefferson*

Wherever I found a living creature, there I found the will to power. *Nietzsche*

Unlimited power corrupts the possessor. *William Pitt*

Lust of power is the most flagrant of all the passions. *Tacitus*

PRAISE

I praise loudly; I blame softly. *Catherine II of Russia*

It is a great happiness to be praised of them who are most praiseworthy. *Sir P. Sidney*

The sweetest of all sounds is praise. *Xenophon*

One good deed, dying tongueless, slaughters a thousand waiting upon that. Our praises are our wages. *Shakespeare*

One of the most essential preparations for eternity is delight in praising God; a higher acquirement I do think, than even delight and devotedness in prayer. *Chalmers*

As the Greek said, many men know how to flatter; few know how to praise. *Wendell Phillips*

PRAYER

I pray the prayer the Easterners do,
May the peace of Allah abide with you. *Anonymous*

Prayer is not overcoming God's reluctance; it is laying hold of His highest willingness. *Trench*

A prayer, in its simplest definition, is merely a wish turned heavenward. *Phillips Brooks*

He prayeth best who loveth best. *Coleridge*

They never sought in vain that sought the Lord aright! *Burns*

Let our prayers, like the ancient sacrifices, ascend morning and evening. Let our days begin and end with God. *Channing*

At church, with meek and unaffected grace,
His looks adorn'd the venerable place;
Truth from his lips prevailed with double sway,
And fools, who came to scoff, remain'd to pray.
Goldsmith

Trouble and perplexity drive me to prayer, and prayer drives away perplexity and trouble. *Fenelon*

Prayer is the voice of faith. *Horne*

God warms his hands at man's heart when he prays. *Masefield*

Pray as if everything depended on God, and work as if everything depended upon man. *Cardinal Francis J Spellman*

PREACHING

I would have every minister of the gospel address his audience with the zeal of a friend, with the generous energy of a father, and with the exuberant affection of a mother. *Fenelon*

The test of a preacher is that his congregation goes away saying, not What a lovely sermon, but, I will do something! *St. Francis de Sales*

Some plague the people with too long sermons; for the faculty of listening is a tender thing, and soon becomes weary and satiated. *Luther*

The Christian ministry is the worst of all trades, but the best of all professions. *Newton*

PREJUDICE

A fox should not be of the jury at a goose's trial. *Thomas Fuller*

He who knows only his own side of the case knows little of that. *John Stuart Mill*

He who never leaves his country is full of prejudices. *Goldoni*

All looks yellow to the jaundiced eye. *Pope*

Prejudice is the child of ignorance. *Hazlitt*

Opinions grounded on prejudice are always sustained with the greatest violence. *Jeffrey*

Prejudice and self-sufficiency, naturally proceed from inexperience of the world, and ignorance of mankind. *Addison*

When we destroy an old prejudice we have need of a new virtue. *Madame de Stael*

PRESS

Congress shall make no law abridging the freedom of speech or of the press. *Constitution of the United States.*

Our liberty depends on the freedom of the press, and that cannot be limited without being lost. *Jefferson*

Freedom of conscience, of education, of speech, of assembly are among the very fundamentals of democracy and all of them would be nullified should freedom of the press ever be successfully challenged. *F. D. Roosevelt*

Every burned book enlightens the world. *Emerson*

If there had been a censorship of the press in Rome we should have had today neither Horace nor Juvenal, nor the philosophical writings of Cicero. *Voltaire*

PRIDE

Pride that dines on vanity, sups on contempt. *Franklin*

Pride is increased by ignorance; those assume the most who know the least. *Gay*

> A flash of the lightning, a break of the wave,
> Man passes from life to his rest in the grave.
> *William Knox*

Pride is a vice, which pride itself inclines every man to find in others, and to overlook in himself. *Johnson*

> In pride, in reas'ning pride, our error lies;
> All quit their sphere and rush into the skies.
> Pride still is aiming at the bless'd abodes,
> Men would be angels, angels would be gods. *Pope*

We rise in glory as we sink in pride. *Young*

The infinitely little have a pride infinitely great. *Voltaire*

PROCRASTINATION

By the street of "By and By" one arrives at the house of "Never." *Cervantes*

The man who procrastinates struggles with ruin. *Hesiod*

There is, by God's grace, an immeasurable distance between late and too late. *Madame Swetchine*

PROGRESS

Westward the star of empire takes its way. *John Quincy Adams*

"Can any good come out of Nazareth?" This is always the question of the wiseacres and knowing ones. But the good, the new, comes from exactly that quarter whence it is not looked for, and is always something different from what is expected. Everything new is received with contempt, for it begins in obscurity. It becomes a power unobserved. *Fuerbach*

Progress—the onward stride of God. *Victor Hugo*

New occasions teach new duties, time makes ancient good uncouth;
They must upward still and onward, who would keep abreast of truth. *Lowell*

PROPERTY

Property is at once the consequence and the basis of the state. *Bakunin*

Property is desirable, is a positive good in the world. Let not him who is houseless pull down the house of another, but let him work diligently and build one for himself, thus by example assuring that his own shall be safe from violence when built. *Lincoln*

PROPHECY

Of all the horrid, hideous notes of woe,
Sadder than owl-songs or the midnight blast;
Is that portentous phrase, "I told you so." *Byron*

I shall always consider the best guesser the best prophet. *Cicero*

PROSPERITY

Prosperity is the touchstone of virtue; for it is less difficult to bear misfortunes, than to remain uncorrupted by pleasure. *Tacitus*

It is the bright day that brings forth the adder, and that craves wary walking. *Shakespeare*

Nothing is harder to direct than a man in prosperity;

nothing more easily managed than one in adversity. *Plutarch*

PROVIDENCE

There's a divinity that shapes our ends, rough hew them how we will. *Shakespeare*

> He that doth the ravens feed,
> Yea, providently caters for the sparrow,
> Be comfort to my age! *Shakespeare*

The longer I live, the more faith I have in Providence, and the less faith in my interpretation of Providence. *J. Day*

I firmly believe in Divine Providence. Without belief in Providence I think I should go crazy. Without God the world would be a maze without a clue. *Woodrow Wilson*

I once asked a hermit in Italy how he could venture to live alone, in a single cottage, on the top of a mountain, a mile from any habitation? He replied, that Providence was his next-door neighbor. *Sterne*

The providence that watches over the affairs of men, works out of their mistakes, at times, a healthier issue than could have been accomplished by their own wisest forethought. *Froude*

PUBLIC

The public is wiser than the wisest critic. *Bancroft*

The public wishes itself to be managed like a woman; one must say nothing to it except what it likes to hear. *Goethe*

QUIET

What sweet delight a quiet life affords. *Drummond*

I have often said that all the misfortunes of men spring from their not knowing how to live quietly at home, in their own rooms. *Pascal*

RAIN

Nature, like man, sometimes weeps for gladness. *Disraeli*

Be still, sad heart, and cease repining;
Behind the clouds is the sun still shining;
Thy fate is the common fate of all,
Into each life some rain must fall,
Some days must be dark and dreary. *Longfellow*

READING

No entertainment is so cheap as reading, nor any pleasure so lasting. *Lady M. W. Montague*

If the riches of the Indies, or the crowns of all the kingdoms of Europe were laid at my feet in exchange for my love of reading, I would spurn them all. *Fenelon*

Happy is he who has laid up in his youth, and held fast in all fortune, a genuine and passionate love for reading. *Rufus Choate*

Resolve to edge in a little reading every day, if it is but a single sentence. If you gain fifteen minutes a day, it will make itself felt at the end of the year. *H. Mann*

By reading a man does, as it were, antedate his life, and make himself contemporary with past ages. *Jeremy Collier*

Every reader if he has a strong mind, reads himself into the book, and amalgamates his thoughts with those of the author. *Goethe*

When I take up a book I have read before, I know what to expect; and the satisfaction is not lessened by being anticipated. I shake hands with and look the old tried and valued friends in the face, compare notes, and chat the hour away. *Hazlitt*

If we encountered a man of rare intellect we should ask him what books he read. *Emerson*

The first time I read an excellent work, it is to me just as if I had gained a new friend; and when I read over a book I have perused before, it resembles the meeting with an old one. *Goldsmith*

REASON

He who will not reason, is a bigot; he who cannot is a fool; and he who dares not, is a slave. *William Drummond*

Reason is the glory of human nature, and one of the chief eminences whereby we are raised above the beasts, in this lower world. *Watts*

The feast of reason and the flow of soul. *Pope*

There are few things reason can discover with so much certainty and ease as its own insufficiency. *Jeremy Collier*

I have no other but a woman's reason.
I think him so because I think him so. *Shakespeare*

Reason cannot show itself more reasonable, than to cease reasoning on things above reason. *Sir P. Sidney*

Never reason from what you do not know. If you do, you will soon believe what is utterly against reason. *Ramsay*

It is useless to attempt to reason a man out of a thing he has never reasoned into. *Swift*

Strong reasons make strong actions. *Shakespeare*

Wouldst thou subject all things to thyself? Subject thyself to thy reason. *Seneca*

An idle reason lessens the weight of the good ones you gave before. *Swift*

The heart has reasons that reason does not understand. *Bossuet*

RECREATION

The bow cannot possibly always stand bent, nor can human nature or human frailty subsist without some lawful recreation. *Cervantes*

Make thy recreation servant to thy business, lest thou become a slave to thy recreation. *Quarles*

REFORM

We are reformers in Spring and Summer; in Autumn and Winter we stand by the old; reformers in the morning, conservers at night. *Emerson*

It is easier to enrich ourselves with a thousand virtues, than to correct ourselves of a single fault. *Bruyere*

Reform must come from within, not from without. You cannot legislate for virtue. *James Cardinal Gibbons*

The great fundamental principle of the Reformation was the individual responsibility of the human soul to its Maker and Judge. *T. W. Chambers*

Conscious remorse and anguish must be felt, to curb desire, to break the stubborn will, and work a second nature in the soul. *Rowe*

RELIGION

Men will wrangle for religion; write for it; fight for it; die for it; anything but—live for it. *Colton*

Religion, in its purity, is not so much a pursuit as a temper; or rather it is a temper, leading to the pursuit of all that is high and holy. Its foundation is faith; its action, works; its temper, holiness; its aim, obedience to God in improvement of self and benevolence to men. *Tryon Edwards*

If men are so wicked with religion, what would they be without it? *Franklin*

Philosophy can do nothing which religion cannot do better than she; and religion can do a great many other things which philosophy cannot do at all. *Rousseau*

Religion is nothing else but love to God and man. *William Penn*

Religion would not have enemies, if it were not an enemy to their vices. *Massillon*

He that hath no cross deserves no crown. *Quarles*

There are few signs in a soul's state more alarming than that of religious indifference; that is, the spirit of thinking all religions equally true, the real meaning of which is, that all religions are equally false. *F. W. Robertson*

What I want is, not to possess religion, but to have a religion that shall possess me. *Charles Kingsley*

The call to religion is not a call to be better than your fellows, but to be better than yourself. *H. W. Beecher*

Unless we place our religion and our treasure in the same thing religion will always be sacrificed. *Epictetus*

No sciences are better attested than the religion of the Bible. *Sir Isaac Newton*

When I was young, I was sure of many things; now there are only two things of which I am sure: one is, that I am a miserable sinner; and the other, that Christ is an all-sufficient Saviour. He is well taught who learns these two lessons. *John Newton*

REPENTANCE

Repentance, to be of any avail, must work a change of heart and conduct. *T. L. Cuyler*

Before God can deliver us we must undeceive ourselves. *Saint Augustine*

You cannot repent too soon, because you do not know how soon it may be too late. *Fuller*

It is never too late with us, so long as we are aware of our faults and bear them impatiently. *Jacobi*

REPUBLIC

Republics come to an end by luxurious habits; monarchies by poverty. *Montesquieu*

Republicanism is not the phantom of a deluded imagination. On the contrary, under no form of government are laws better supported, liberty and property better secured, or happiness more effectually dispensed to mankind. *Washington*

REPUTATION

Reputation is what men and women think of us; character is what God and angels know of us. *Paine*

The purest treasure mortal times afford is spotless reputation; that away, men are but gilded loam or painted clay. *Shakespeare*

He that tears away a man's good name tears his flesh from his bones, and by letting him live gives him only a cruel opportunity of feeling his misery, of burying his better part and surviving himself. *South*

REST

Rest is the sweet sauce of labor. *Plutarch*

Rest is valuable only so far as it is a contrast. Pursued as an end, it becomes a most pitiable condition. *D. Swing*

RESURRECTION

Earth to earth, ashes to ashes, dust to dust, in sure and certain hope of the resurrection. *Book of Common Prayer*

> The last loud trumpet's wondrous sound,
> Shall thro' the rending tombs rebound,
> And wake the nations under ground.
>
> *Wentworth Dillon*

REVENGE

Revenge is the abject pleasure of an abject mind. *Juvenal*

The best manner of avenging ourselves is by not resembling him who has injured us. *Jane Porter*

RHETORIC

Rhetoric is nothing but reason well dressed, and argument put in order. *Jeremy Collier*

The best rules of rhetoric are, to speak intelligently; speak from the heart; have something to say; say it; and stop when you've done. *Tryon Edwards*

Rhetoric without logic is like a tree with leaves and blossoms, but no roots; yet more are taken with rhetoric than logic, because they are caught with fine expressions when they understand not reason. *Selden*

RICHES

The pride of dying rich raises the loudest laugh in hell. *John Foster*

Agur said, "Give me neither poverty nor riches"; and this will ever be the prayer of the wise. Our incomes should be like our shoes: if too small, they will gall and pinch us, but if too large, they will cause us to stumble and to trip. But wealth, after all, is a relative thing, since he that has little, and wants less, is richer than he that has much, but wants more. True contentment depends not upon what we have; a tub was large enough for Diogenes, but a world was too little for Alexander. *Colton*

To have what we want is riches, but to be able to do without is power. *G. Macdonald*

One cause, which is not always observed, of the insufficiency of riches, is that they very seldom make their owner rich. *Johnson*

He is richest who is content with the least, for content is the wealth of nature. *Socrates*

Some of God's noblest sons, I think, will be selected from those that know how to take wealth, with all its temptations, and maintain godliness therewith. It is hard to be a saint standing in a golden niche. *H. W. Beecher*

Nothing is so hard for those who abound in riches as to conceive how others can be in want. *Swift*

RIDICULE

Ridicule may be the evidence of wit or bitterness and may gratify a little mind, or an ungenerous temper, but it is no test of reason or truth. *Tryon Edwards*

Ridicule is a weak weapon when levelled at strong minds, but common men are cowards and dread an empty laugh. *Tupper*

RIGHT

Sir, I would rather be right than be President. *Henry Clay*

Let us have faith that right makes might, and in that faith, let us to the end, dare to do our duty, as we understand it. *Lincoln*

He will hew to the line of right, let the chips fly where they may. *Roscoe Conkling*

Nothing but the right can ever be expedient, since that can never be true expediency which would sacrifice a greater good to a less. *Whately*

There is no right without a parallel duty, no liberty without the supremacy of the law, no high destiny without earnest perseverance, no greatness without self-denial. *Lieber*

All men are endowed by their Creator with certain unalienable rights; among these are life, liberty, and the pursuit of happiness. *Jefferson*

RUIN

While in the progress of their long decay,
Thrones sink to dust, and nations pass away.
Earl of Carlisle

The ruins of himself! now worn away
With age, yet still majestic in decay. *Homer*

SABBATH

He that remembers not to keep the Christian Sabbath at the beginning of the week, will be in danger of forgetting, before the end of the week, that he is a Christian. *E. Turner*

The green oasis, the little grassy meadow in the wilderness, where, after the week-day's journey, the pilgrim halts for refreshment and repose. *C. Reade*

Sunday is like a stile between the fields of toil, where we can kneel and pray, or sit and meditate. *Longfellow*

SADNESS

Take my word for it, the saddest thing under the sky is a soul incapable of sadness. *Countess de Gasparin*

The deep undertone of the world is sadness—a solemn bass, occurring at measured intervals and heard through all other tones. Ultimately, all the strains of this world's music resolve themselves into that tone; and I believe that, rightly felt, the cross, and the cross alone, interprets the mournful mystery of life the sorrow of the Highest—the Lord of Life,—the result of error and sin, but ultimately remedial, purifying and exalting. *F. W. Robertson*

SCANDAL

Great numbers of moderately good people think it fine to talk scandal; they regard it as a sort of evidence of their own goodness. *F. W. Faber*

In scandal, as in robbery, the receiver is always as bad as the thief. *Chesterfield*

A cruel story runs on wheels, and every hand oils the wheels as they run. *George Eliot*

SCIENCE

Steam is no stronger now than it was a hundred years ago, but it is put to better use. *Emerson*

False interpretation of the Bible has often clashed with science, as false science has with true interpretation; but true science is the natural ally of religion, for both are from God. *Tryon Edwards*

Science and art belong to the whole world, and before them vanish the barriers of nationality. *Goethe*

Science—in other words, knowledge—is not the enemy of religion; for, if so, then religion would mean ignorance; but it is often the antagonist of school-divinity. *O. W. Holmes*

I will frankly tell you that my experience in prolonged scientific investigations convinces me that a belief in God—a God who is behind and within the chaos of vanishing points of human knowledge—adds a wonderful stimulus to the man who attempts to penetrate into the regions of the unknown. *Agassiz*

SELF-DENIAL

There never did, and never will exist anything permanently noble and excellent in character which is a stranger to the exercise of resolute self-denial. *Walter Scott*

Every personal consideration that we allow, costs us heavenly state. We sell the thrones of angels for a short and turbulent pleasure. *Emerson*

In vain do they talk of happiness who never subdued an impulse in obedience to a principle. He who never sacrificed a present to a future good, or a personal to a general one, can speak of happiness only as the blind speak of color. *H. Mann*

The first lesson in Christ's school is self-denial. *M. Henry*

SELFISHNESS

That man who lives for self alone
Lives for the meanest mortal known. *Joaquin Miller*

The essence of true nobility is neglect of self. Let the thought of self pass in, and the beauty of a great action is gone like the bloom from a soiled flower. *J. A. Froude*

> Despite those titles, power, and pelf,
> The wretch, concentrated all in self,
> Living, shall forfeit fair renown,
> And, doubly dying, shall go down
> To the vile dust from whence he sprung,
> Unwept, unhonour'd and unsung. *Scott*

So long as we are full of self we are shocked at the faults of others. Let us think often of our own sin, and we shall be lenient to the sins of others. *Fenelon*

Milton has carefully marked, in his Satan, the intense selfishness which would rather reign in hell than serve in heaven. *Coleridge*

As a man goes down in self, he goes up in God. *G. B. Cheever*

SELF-RELIANCE

Our remedies oft in ourselves do lie, which we ascribe to Heaven. *Shakespeare*

"Give me a standing place," said Archimedes, "and I will move the world"—Goethe has changed the postulate into the precept: "Make good thy standing place, and move the world." *S. Smiles*

Men seem neither to understand their riches nor their strength. Of the former they believe greater things than they should; of the latter, less. *Bacon*

SERVICE

They also serve who only stand and wait. *Milton*
Servant of God, well done. *Milton*

They serve God well,
Who serve his creatures. *Caroline Norton*

He profits most who serves best. *Arthur F. Sheldon*

SILENCE

Silence gives consent. *Pope Boniface VIII*

He can never speak well, who knows not how to hold his peace. *Plutarch*

Silence is more eloquent than words. *Carlyle*

A man's profundity may keep him from opening on a first interview, and his caution on a second; but I should suspect his emptiness, if he carried on his reserve to a third. *Colton*

Silence is the unbearable repartee. *Chesterton*

If the prudence of reserve and decorum dictates silence in some circumstances, in others prudence of a higher order may justify us in speaking our thoughts. *Burke*

It is a great misfortune neither to have enough wit to talk well nor enough judgment to be silent. *La Bruyere*

Silence, when nothing need be said, is the eloquence of discretion. *Bovee*

Blessed are they who have nothing to say, and who cannot be persuaded to say it. *Lowell*

Silence is the perfectest herald of joy; I were but little happy if I could say how much. *Shakespeare*

Smooth runs the water where the brook is deep. *Shakespeare*

Speech is often barren; but silence also does not necessarily brood over a full nest. Your still fowl, blinking at you without remark, may all the while be sitting on one addled nest-egg, and when it takes to cackling, will have nothing to announce but that addled delusion. *George Eliot*

As we must render an account of every idle word, so we must of our idle silence. *Ambrose*

SIMPLICITY

Nothing is more simple than greatness; indeed, to be simple is to be great. *Emerson*

Simplicity of character is the natural result of profound thought. *Hazlitt*

The fewer our wants, the nearer we resemble the gods. *Socrates*

SIN

It is not only what we do, but also what we do not do, for which we are accountable. *Moliere*

If I were sure God would pardon me, and men would not know my sin, yet I should be ashamed to sin, because of its essential baseness. *Plato*

There is no fool equal to the sinner, who every moment ventures his soul. *Tillotson*

SLANDER

The worthiest people are the most injured by slander, as it is the best fruit which the birds have been pecking at. *Swift*

Done to death by slanderous tongues. *Shakespeare*

Sleep

Soft closer of our eyes!
Low murmur of tender lullabies! *Keats*

Sleep, that knits up the ravell'd sleave of care; the death of each day's life, sore labor's bath; balm of hurt minds; great nature's second course; chief nourisher in life's feast. *Shakespeare*

To sleep! perchance to dream; ay, there's the rub;
For in that sleep of death what dreams may come,
When we have shuffled off this mortal coil,
Must give us pause. *Shakespeare*

Sleep, thou repose of all things; thou gentlest of the duties; thou peace of the mind, from which care flies; who doth soothe the hearts of men wearied with the toils of the day, and refittest them for labor. *Ovid*

Soldier

But in a larger sense we cannot dedicate, we cannot consecrate, we cannot hallow this ground. The brave men, living and dead, who struggled here, have consecrated it far above our poor power to add or detract. *Lincoln*

The muffled drum's sad roll has beat
The soldier's last tattoo;
No more on Life's parade shall meet
The brave and fallen few.
On Fame's eternal camping-ground
Their silent tents are spread,
And Glory guards, with solemn round
The bivouac of the dead. *Theodore O'Hara*

Solitude

In solitude, when we are least alone. *Byron*

A wise man is never less alone than when he is alone. *Swift*

Alone, alone, all, all alone,
Alone on a wide, wide sea. *Coleridge*

No doubt solitude is wholesome, but so is abstinence after a surfeit. The true life of man is in society. *Simms*

I never found the companion that was so companionable as solitude. *Thoreau*

Solitude is the audience chamber of God. *L. E. Landon*

Solitude bears the same relation to the mind that sleep does to the body. It affords it the necessary opportunities for repose and recovery. *Simms*

SORROW

On the sands of life sorrow treads heavily, and leaves a print time cannot wash away. *H. Neele*

Wherever souls are being tried and ripened, in whatever commonplace and homely way, there God is hewing out the pillars for His temple. *Phillips Brooks*

We tell our triumphs to the crowd, but our own hearts are the sole confidants of our sorrows. *Bulwer-Lytton*

SOUL

Either we have an immortal soul, or we have not. If we have not, we are beasts; the first and wisest of beasts it may be; but still beasts. We only differ in degree, and not in kind; just as the elephant differs from the slug. But by the concession of the materialists, we are not of the same kind as beasts; and this also we say from our own consciousness. Therefore, methinks, it must be the possession of a soul within us that makes the difference. *Coleridge*

Heaven-born, the soul a heavenward course must hold; beyond the world she soars; the wise man, I affirm, can find no rest in that which perishes, nor will he lend his heart to aught that doth on time depend. *Michelangelo*

I am fully convinced that the soul is indestructible, and that its activity will continue through eternity. It is like the sun, which, to our eyes, seems to set in night; but it has in reality only gone to diffuse its light elsewhere. *Goethe*

SPEECH

Speech is power: speech is to persuade, to convert, to compel. *Emerson*

Such as thy words are, such will thine affections be esteemed; and such as thine affections, will be thy deeds; and such as thy deeds will be thy life. *Socrates*

Rhetoric is the art of ruling the minds of men. *Plato*
Think all you speak, but speak not all you think. Thoughts are your own; your words are so no more. *Delany*

STATESMANSHIP

A thousand years scarce serve to form a state;
An hour may lay it in the dust. *Byron*

The worth of a state, in the long run, is the worth of the individuals composing it. *J. Stuart Mill*

States are as the men are; they grow out of human characters. *Plato*

What morality requires, true statesmanship should accept. *Burke*

STUPIDITY

We are growing serious, and, let me tell you, that's a very next step to being dull. *Addison*

Against stupidity the very gods
Themselves contend in vain. *Schiller*

SUCCESS

Nothing can seem foul to those that win. *Shakespeare*

All the proud virtue of this vaunting world fawns on success and power, however acquired. *Thomson*

Success has a great tendency to conceal and throw a veil over the evil deeds of men. *Demosthenes*

Not what men do worthily, but what they do successfully, is what history makes haste to record. *H. W. Beecher*

SYMPATHY

Shame on those hearts of stone, that cannot melt in soft adoption of another's sorrow! *A. Hill*

Let us cherish sympathy. It prepares the mind for receiving the impressions of virtue; and without it there can be no true politeness. Nothing is more odious than that insensibility which wraps a man up in himself and his own concerns, and prevents his being moved with either the joys or the sorrows of another. *Beattie*

TACT

Tact comes as much from goodness of heart as from fineness of taste. *Endymion*

Tact is one of the first mental virtues, the absence of which is often fatal to the best of talents; it supplies the place of many talents. *Simms*

TALKING

Never hold any one by the button, or the hand, in order to be heard out; for if people are unwilling to hear you, you had better hold your tongue than them. *Chesterfield*

When I think of talking, it is of course with a woman. For talking at its best being an inspiration, it wants a corresponding divine quality of receptiveness, and where will you find this but in a woman? *O. W. Holmes*

There is the same difference between the tongues of some, as between the hour and the minute hand; one goes ten times as fast, and the other signifies ten times as much. *Sydney Smith*

It is a sad thing when men have neither the wit to speak well, nor judgment to hold their tongues. *Bruyere*

TAXES

Taxes are the sinews of the state. *Cicero*

Taxing is an easy business. Any projector can contrive new impositions; any bungler can add to the old; but is it altogether wise to have no other bounds to your impositions than the patience of those who are to bear them? *Burke*

Kings ought to shear, not skin their sheep. *Herrick*

TEACHING

You cannot teach a man anything; you can only help him to find it within himself. *Galileo*

The true aim of every one who aspires to be a teacher should be, not to impart his own opinions, but to kindle minds. *F. W. Robertson*

I am not a teacher: only a fellow-traveller of whom you asked the way. I pointed ahead—ahead of myself as well as of you. *George Bernard Shaw*

The one exclusive sign of a thorough knowledge is the power of teaching. *Aristotle*

The best teacher is the one who suggests rather than dogmatizes, and inspires his listener with the wish to teach himself. *Bulwer*

TEARS

Tears are the safety-valves of the heart when too much pressure is laid on it. *Albert Smith*

Tears are sometimes the happiest smiles of love. *Stendhal*

O, banish the tears of children! Continual rains upon the blossoms are hurtful. *Richter*

The graceful tear that streams for other's woes. *A. Kenside*

TEMPTATION

It is one thing to be tempted, another thing to fall. *Shakespeare*

If there were no evil in ourselves there could be no temptation from without, for nothing evil could seem pleasant. *F. M. Crawford*

Better shun the bait than struggle in the snare. *Dryden*

THANKFULNESS

The worship most acceptable to God, comes from a thankful and cheerful heart. *Plutarch*

God's goodness hath been great to thee. Let never day nor night unhallowed pass but still remember what the Lord hath done. *Shakespeare*

THEORIES

To despise theory is to have the excessively vain pretension to do without knowing what one does, and to speak without knowing what one says. *Fontenelle*

THOUGHT

Thoughts are but dreams till their effects be tried. *Shakespeare*

I think, therefore I am. *Descartes*

The greatest events of an age are its best thoughts. Thought finds its way into action. *Boice*

There is nothing either good or bad, but thinking makes it so. *Shakespeare*

Those who have finished by making all others think with them, have usually been those who began by daring to think for themselves. *Colton*

They are never alone that are accompanied with noble thoughts. *Sir Philip Sidney*

To have thought far too little, we shall find in the review of life, among our capital faults. *J. Foster*

A man might frame, and let loose a star, to roll in its orbit, and yet not have done so memorable a thing before God, as he who lets go a golden-orbed thought to roll through the generation of time. *H. W. Beecher*

TIME

I recommend you to take care of the minutes, for the hours will take care of themselves. *Chesterfield*

Time is the chrysalis of eternity. *Richter*

> Gather ye rose-buds while ye may,
> Old Time is still aflying,
> And this same flower that smiles today,
> Tomorrow will be dying. *Herrick*

Youth is not rich in time, it may be poor; part with it as with money, sparing; pay no moment, but in purchase of its worth; and what it's worth, ask death-beds; they can tell. *Young*

These are the times that try men's souls. *Thomas Paine*

Time hurries on with a resistless, unremitting stream, yet treads more soft than e'er did midnight thief that slides his hand under the miser's pillow, and carries off his prize. *Blair*

The time is out of joint. *Shakespeare*

Those who know the value of time use it in preparation for eternity. *Dugnet*

Time hath often cured the wound which reason failed to heal. *Seneca*

There is not a single moment in life that we can afford to lose. *Goulburn*

We sleep, but the loom of life never stops, and the pattern which was weaving when the sun went down is weaving when it comes up in the morning. *H. W. Beecher*

Travel

Those who visit foreign nations, but associate only with their own countrymen, change their climate, but not their customs. They see new meridians, but the same men; and with heads as empty as their pockets, return home with travelled bodies, but untravelled minds. *Colton*

The travelled mind is the catholic mind, educated out of exclusiveness and egotism. *A. B. Alcott*

Trifles

He who esteems trifles for themselves is a trifler; he who esteems them for the conclusions to be drawn from them or the advantage to which they can be put, is a philosopher. *Bulwer-Lytton*

Johnson well says, "He who waits to do a great deal of good at once will never do anything." Life is made up of little things. It is very rarely that an occasion is offered for doing a great deal at once. True greatness consists in being great in little things. *C. Simmons*

Those who give too much attention to trifling things become generally incapable of great ones. *La Rochefoucauld*

A grain of sand leads to the fall of a mountain when the moment has come for the mountain to fall. *Ernest Renan*

The creation of a thousand forests is in one acorn. *Emerson*

Trouble

If all men were to bring their miseries together in one place, most would be glad to take each his own home again rather than take a portion out of the common stock. *Solon*

Troubles are often the tools by which God fashions us for better things. *H. W. Beecher*

In all troublous events we may find comfort, though it be only in the negative admission that things might have been worse. *Barr*

Truth

'Tis strange—but true; for truth is always strange,
Stranger than fiction. *Byron*

One of the sublimest things in the world is plain truth. *Bulwer-Lytton*

We know the truth, not only by the reason, but also by the heart. *Pascal*

If a thousand old beliefs were ruined in our march to truth we must still march on. *Stopford A. Brooke*

To thine own self be true,
And it must follow, as the night the day,
Thou canst not then be false to any man. *Shakespeare*

Truth is not only violated by falsehood; it may be equally outraged by silence. *Amien*

Truth is by its very nature intolerant, exclusive, for every truth is the denial of its opposing error. *Luthardt*

The first and last thing which is required of genius is the love of truth. *Goethe*

Peace if possible, but truth at any rate. *Luther*

Usefulness

There is but one virtue—the eternal sacrifice of self. *George Sand*

Have I done anything for society? I have then done more for myself. Let that question and truth be always present to thy mind, and work without cessation. *Simms*

Amid life's quests there seems but worthy one, to do men good. *Bailey*

Valor

Dare to do your duty always; this is the height of true valor. *C. Simmons*

The mean of true valor lies between the extremes of cowardice and rashness. *Cervantes*

When valor preys on reason, it eats the sword it fights with. *Shakespeare*

Vanity

Take away from mankind their vanity and their ambition, and there would be but few claiming to be heroes or patriots. *Seneca*

It is our own vanity that makes the vanity of others intolerable to us. *La Rochefoucauld*

Vanity is the quicksand of reason. *George Sand*

She neglects her heart who studies her glass. *Lavater*

Vice

Vice can deceive under the shadow and guise of virtue. *Juvenal*

There is no vice so simple but assumes some mark of virtue on his outward parts. *Shakespeare*

A few vices are sufficient to darken many virtues. *Plutarch*

Virtue

All bow to virtue, and then walk away. *De Finod*

To be able under all circumstances to practise five things constitutes perfect virtue; these five are gravity, generosity of soul, sincerity, earnestness, and kindness. *Confucius*

We rarely like the virtues we have not. *Shakespeare*

It would not be easy, even for an unbeliever, to find a better translation of the rule of virtue from the abstract into the concrete, than to endeavor so to live that Christ would approve our life. *John Stuart Mill*

Vision

Abou Ben Adhem (may his tribe increase!)
Awoke one night from a deep dream of peace,
And saw, within the moonlight in his room,
Making it rich, and like a lily in bloom,
An angel, writing in a book of gold;
Exceeding peace had made Ben Adhem bold,
And to the presence in the room he said—
"What writest thou?" The Vision raised its head,
And, with a look made all of sweet accord,
Answered, "The names of those who love the Lord."
Leigh Hunt

VOICE

How wonderful is the human voice! It is indeed the organ of the soul. The intellect of man sits enthroned, visibly, on his forehead and in his eye, and the heart of man is written on his countenance, but the soul reveals itself in the voice only. *Longfellow*

Her voice was ever soft, gentle, and low, an excellent thing in woman. *Shakespeare*

The tones of human voices are mightier than strings or brass to move the soul. *Klopstock*

Thy voice is celestial melody. *Longfellow*

WAR

War is the science of destruction. *John S. C. Abbott*

When wars do come, they fall upon the many, the producing class, who are the sufferers. *U. S. Grant*

What millions died—that Caesar might be great! *Campbell*

Men who have nice notions of religion have no business to be soldiers. *Wellington*

By the rude bridge that arched the flood,
Their flag to April's breeze unfurl'd;
Here once the embattl'd farmers stood,
And fired the shot heard round the world. *Emerson*

The greatest curse that can be entailed on mankind is a state of war. All the atrocious crimes committed in years of peace, all that is spent in peace by the secret corruptions, or by the thoughtless extravagance of nations, are mere trifles compared with the gigantic evils which stalk over this world in a state of war. God is forgotten in war; every principle of Christianity is trampled upon. *Sydney Smith*

Mine eyes have seen the glory of the coming of the Lord:
He is trampling out the vintage where the grapes of wrath are stored:
He hath loosed the fateful lightning of his terrible swift sword:
His truth is marching on. *Julia Ward Howe*

War is nothing less than a temporary repeal of the principles of virtue. It is a system out of which almost all the virtues are excluded, and in which nearly all the vices are included. *Robert Hall*

War is as much a punishment to the punisher as to the sufferer. *Jefferson*

The chief evil of war is more evil. War is the concentration of all human crimes. Here is its distinguishing, accursed brand. Under its standard gather violence, malignity, rage, fraud, perfidy, rapacity, and lust. If it only slew man, it would do little. It turns man into a beast of prey. *Channing*

There is no such thing as an inevitable war. If war comes it will be from failure of human wisdom. *Bonar Law*

The next dreadful thing to a battle lost is a battle won. *Wellington*

War is the greatest plague that can afflict humanity; it destroys religion, it destroys states, it destroys families. *Martin Luther*

Even in a righteous cause force is a fearful thing; God only helps when man can help no more. *Schiller*

> Take up our quarrel with the foe!
> To you from failing hands we throw
> The torch; be yours to hold it high.
> If ye break faith with us who die
> We shall not sleep, though poppies grow
> In Flanders' fields. *John McCrae*

Mad wars destroy in one year the works of many years of peace. *Franklin*

> And this I hate—not men, nor flag nor race,
> But only War with its wild, grinning face.
> *Joseph Dana Miller*

These are the times that try men's souls. The summer soldier and the sunshine patriot will, in this crisis, shrink from the service of their country, but he that stands it now deserves the love and thanks of man and woman. Tyranny, like Hell, is not easily conquered; yet we have this consolation with us, that the harder the conflict the more glorious the triumph. What we obtain too cheaply we esteem too lightly; it is dearness only that gives everything its value. Heaven knows how to put a proper price upon its goods; and it would be strange indeed if so celestial an article as freedom should not be highly rated. *Thomas Paine*

WEALTH

Surplus wealth is a sacred trust which its possessor is bound to administer in his lifetime for the good of the community. *Andrew Carnegie*

There are not a few who believe in no God but Mammon, no devil but the absence of gold, no damnation but being poor, and no hell but an empty purse; and not a few of their descendants are living still. *South*

The wealth of nations is men, not silk and cotton and gold. *Richard Honey*

He is richest who is content with the least, for content is the wealth of nature. *Socrates*

Life is short. The sooner that a man begins to enjoy his wealth the better. *Samuel Johnson*

Wealth is not his that has it, but his that enjoys it. *Franklin*

All wealth is the product of labor. *Locke*

Money and time are the heaviest burdens of life, and the unhappiest of all mortals are those who have more of either than they know how to use. *Johnson*

If thou art rich thou art poor; for like an ass, whose back with ingots bows, thou bearest thy heavy riches but a journey, and death unloads thee. *Shakespeare*

It is only when the rich are sick that they fully feel the impotence of wealth. *Colton*

It requires a great deal of boldness and a great deal of caution to make a great fortune; and when you have got it, it requires ten times as much wit to keep it. *Rothschild*

WIFE

All other goods by fortune's hand are given:
A wife is the peculiar gift of Heav'n. *Pope*

Sole partner, and sole part of all my joys, dearer thyself than all. *Milton*

A faithful wife becomes the truest and tenderest friend, the balm of comfort, and the source of joy; through every various turn of life the same. *Savage*

No man knows what the wife of his bosom is—what a ministering angel she is, until he has gone with her through the fiery trials of this world. *Washington Irving*

The highest gift and favor of God is a pious, kind, godly, and domestic wife, with whom thou mayest live peaceably, and to whom thou mayest intrust all thy possessions, yea, thy body and thy life. *Luther*

WILL

Barkis is willin'! *Dickens*

Great souls have wills; feeble ones have only wishes. *Chinese proverb*

He who is firm in will molds the world to himself. *Goethe*

Do God's will as if it were thy will, and he will accomplish thy will as if it were his own. *Rabbi Gamaliel*

People do not lack strength; they lack will. *Victor Hugo*

WISDOM

Wisdom is only found in truth. *Goethe*

There is one person that is wiser than anybody, and that is everybody. *Tallyrand*

The heart is wiser than the intellect. *J. G. Holland*

Very few men are wise by their own counsel, or learned by their own teaching; for he that was only taught by himself had a fool to his master. *Ben Jonson*

As for me, all I know is that I know nothing. *Socrates*

The doorstep to the temple of wisdom is a knowledge of our own ignorance. *Spurgeon*

The wise man is but a clever infant, spelling letters from a hieroglyphical prophetic book, the lexicon of which lies in eternity. *Carlyle*

No man can be wise on an empty stomach. *George Eliot*

The wisest man is generally he who thinks himself the least so. *Boileau*

In seeking wisdom thou art wise; in imagining that thou hast attained it thou art a fool. *Rabbi Ben-Azai*

WIT

Sharp wits, like sharp knives, do often cut their owner's fingers. *Arrowsmith*

Wit is brushwood; judgment, timber; the one gives the greatest flame, and the other yields the most durable heat; and both meeting make the best fire. *Overlung*

Wit is the salt of conversation, not the food. *Hazlitt*

Where judgment has wit to express it, there is the best orator. *Penn*

He who has provoked the shaft of wit, cannot complain that he smarts from it. *Johnson*

WOMAN

Man has his will,—but woman has her way. *Holmes*

Next to God we are indebted to women, first for life itself, and then for making it worth having. *Bovee*

Suffer women once to arrive at an equality with you, and they will from that moment become your superiors. *Cato the Censor*

Kindness in women, not their beauteous looks, shall win my love. *Shakespeare*

There is no worse evil than a bad woman; and nothing has ever been produced better than a good one. *Euripides*

The deepest tenderness a woman can show to a man, is to help him to do his duty. *Mulock*

  The colonel's lady and Judy O'Grady
  Are sisters under their skins. *Kipling*

Women are the poetry of the world in the same sense as the stars are the poetry of heaven. Clear, light-giving, harmonious, they are the terrestrial planets that rule the destinies of mankind. *Hargrave*

For the female of the species is more deadly than the male. *Kipling*

O woman! in ordinary cases so mere a mortal, how in the great and rare events of life dost thou swell into the angel! *Bulwer-Lytton*

A rag and a bone and a hank of hair. *Kipling*

Earth has nothing more tender than a woman's heart when it is the abode of piety. *Luther*

There are no ugly women; there are only women who do not know how to look pretty. *La Bruyere*

Purity of heart is the noblest inheritance, and love the fairest ornament of women. *M. Claudius*

> Grace was in all her steps, heaven in her eye,
> In every gesture dignity and love. *Milton*

Honor women! they entwine and weave heavenly roses in our earthly life. *Schiller*

> O Woman! in our hours of ease,
> Uncertain, coy, and hard to please,
> And variable as the shade
> By the light quivering aspen made;
> When pain and anguish wring the brow,
> A ministering angel thou! *Scott*

I am glad that I am not a man, for then I should have to marry a woman. *Madame de Stael*

> She was a Phantom of delight
> When first she gleamed upon my sight;
> A lovely Apparition sent
> To be a moment's ornament. *Wordsworth*

WORDS

Words that weep, and tears that speak. *Cowley*

What you keep by you, you may change and mend; but words, once spoken, can never be recalled. *Roscommon*

A very great part of the mischiefs that vex this world arises from words. *Burke*

Words are both better and worse than thoughts; they express them, and add to them; they give them power for good or evil; they start them on an endless flight, for instruction and comfort and blessing, or for injury and sorrow and ruin. *Tryon Edwards*

Fair words butter no parsnips. *John Clarke*

No man has a prosperity so high or firm, but that two or three words can dishearten it; and there is no calamity which right words will not begin to redress. *Emerson*

Words are the most powerful drug used by mankind. *Kipling*

Seest thou a man that is hasty in his words? there is more hope of a fool than of him. *Solomon*

We should have a great many fewer disputes in the world if words were taken for what they are, the signs of our ideas only, and not for things themselves. *Locke*

Men suppose their reason has command over their words; still it happens that words in return exercise authority on reason. *Bacon*

The word impossible is not in my dictionary. *Napoleon*

Words are things; and a small drop of ink, falling like dew upon a thought, produces that which makes thousands, perhaps millions, think. *Byron*

One of our defects as a nation is a tendency to use what have been called "weasel words." When a weasel sucks eggs the meat is sucked out of the egg. If you use a "weasel word" after another there is nothing left of the other. *Theodore Roosevelt*

Syllables govern the world. *Coke*

> My words fly up, my thoughts remain below:
> Words without thoughts never to heaven go.
>
> *Shakespeare*

> But yesterday the word of Caesar might
> Have stood against the world; now lies he there,
> And none so poor to do him reverence.
>
> *Shakespeare*

He utters empty words, he utters sound without mind. *Virgil*

You [Pindar] who possessed the talent of speaking much without saying anything. *Voltaire*

> For of all sad words of tongue or pen,
> The saddest are these: "It might have been!"
>
> *Whittier*

WORK

Better to wear out than to rust out. *Bishop Cumberland*

The modern majesty consists in work. What a man can do is his greatest ornament, and he always consults his dignity by doing it. *Carlyle*

The workers are the saviors of society, the redeemers of the race. *Eugene V. Debs*

The law of nature is, that a certain quantity of work is necessary to produce a certain quantity of good of any kind whatever. If you want knowledge, you must toil for it; if food, you must toil for it; and if pleasure, you must toil for it. *Ruskin*

I never did anything worth doing by accident, nor did any of my inventions come by accident; they came by work. *Edison*

Work is as much a necessity to man as eating and sleeping. Even those who do nothing that can be called work still imagine they are doing something. The world has not a man who is an idler in his own eyes. *W. Humboldt*

A ploughman on his legs is higher than a gentleman on his knees. *Franklin*

I like work; it fascinates me. I can sit and look at it for hours. I love to keep it by me: the idea of getting rid of it nearly breaks my heart. *Jerome K. Jerome*

> No man is born into the world whose work
> Is not born with him; there is always work,
> And tools to work withal, for those who will;
> And blessed are the horny hands of toil! *Lowell*

WORLD

Believe everything you hear said of the world; nothing is too impossibly bad. *Balzac*

That one vast thought of God which we call the world. *Bulwer-Lytton*

Socrates, indeed, when he was asked of what country he called himself, said, "Of the world"; for he considered himself an inhabitant and a citizen of the whole world. *Cicero*

All the world's ends, arrangements, changes, disappointments, hopes, and fears, are without meaning, if not seen and estimated by eternity! *Tryon Edwards*

Come, follow me, and leave the world to its babblings. *Dante*

The unrest of this weary world is its unvoiced cry after God. *Munger*

Glorious indeed is the world of God around us, but more glorious the world of God within us. There lies the Land of Song; there lies the poet's native land. *Longfellow*

The world is God's workshop for making men. *H. W. Beecher*

> This world is all a fleeting show,
> For man's illusion given;
> The smiles of joy, the tears of woe,
> Deceitful shine, deceitful flow,—
> There's nothing true but Heaven. *Moore*

> So many worlds, so much to do,
> So little done, such things to be. *Tennyson*

WORSHIP

We should worship as though the Deity were present. If my mind is not engaged in my worship, it is as though I worshipped not. *Confucius*

A church-going people are apt to be a law-abiding people. *E. A. Park*

WRONG

Truth forever on the scaffold, wrong forever on the throne. *Lowell*

The remedy for wrongs is to forget them. *Syrus*

YOUTH

Young men are fitter to invent than to judge; fitter for execution than for counsel; and fitter for new projects than for settled business. *Bacon*

Tell me what are the prevailing sentiments that occupy the minds of your young men, and I will tell you what is to be the character of the next generation. *Burke*

> In the lexicon of youth, which fate reserves
> For a bright manhood, there is no such word
> As fail. *Bulwer-Lytton*

Reckless youth makes rueful age. *Moore*

I remember my youth and the feeling that will never come back any more—the feeling that I could last forever, outlast the sea, the earth, and all men. *Joseph Conrad*

The greatest part of mankind employ their first years to make their last miserable. *Bruyere*

Keep true to the dreams of thy youth. *Schiller*

> When all the world is young, lad,
> And all the trees are green;

> And every goose a swan, lad,
> And every lass a queen;
> Then hey, for boot and horse, lad,
> And round the world away;
> Young blood must have its course, lad,
> And every dog his day. *Charles Kingsley*

The golden age never leaves the world; it exists still, and shall exist, till love, health, and poetry, are no more—but only for the young. *Bulwer-Lytton*

> How beautiful is youth; how bright it gleams
> With its illusions, aspirations, dreams!
> Book of Beginnings, Story without End,
> Each maid a heroine, and each man a friend!
>
>   *Longfellow*

My salad days, when I was green in judgment. *Shakespeare*

ZEAL

Zeal is very blind, or badly regulated, when it encroaches upon the rights of others. *Quesnel*

Zeal without knowledge is like expedition to a man in the dark. *John Newton*

Chapter XIII

SIX HUNDRED BIBLICAL QUOTATIONS

ABILITY

If ye have faith as a grain of mustard seed . . . nothing shall be impossible unto you. *Matthew 17:20*

With men this is impossible; but with God all things are possible. *Matthew 19:26*

The spirit indeed is willing, but the flesh is weak. *Matthew 26:41*

All things are possible to him that believeth. *Mark 9:23*

I can do all things through Christ which strengtheneth me. *Philippians 4:13*

ABSENT

The Lord watch between me and thee, when we are absent one from another. *Genesis 31:49*

Absent in body, but present in spirit. *I Corinthians 5:3*

Whilst we are at home in the body, we are absent from the Lord. *II Corinthians 5:6*

ACHIEVEMENT

God saw every thing that he had made, and behold, it was very good. *Genesis 1:31*

The desire accomplished is sweet to the soul. *Proverbs 13:19*

The Lord will do great things. *Joel 2:21*

I have glorified thee on the earth: I have finished the work which thou gavest me to do. *John 17:4*

ADULTERY

Thou shalt not commit adultery. *Exodus 20:14*

Whoso committeth adultery with a woman lacketh understanding: he that doeth it destroyeth his own soul. *Proverbs 6:32*

Whosoever looketh on a woman to lust after her hath committed adultery with her already in his heart. *Matthew 5:28*

Out of the heart proceed evil thoughts, adulteries, fornications. *Matthew 15:19*

I made a covenant with mine eyes; why then should I think upon a maid? *Job 31:1*

AFFLICTION

In my distress I called upon the Lord, and cried to my God: and he did hear my voice out of his temple. *II Samuel 22:7*

He delivereth the poor in his affliction, and openeth their ears in oppression. *Job 36:15*

Yea, though I walk through the valley of the shadow of death, I will fear no evil: for thou art with me; thy rod and thy staff they comfort me. *Psalms 23:4*

Many are the afflictions of the righteous: but the Lord delivereth him out of them all. *Psalms 34:19*

My flesh and my heart faileth: but God is the strength of my heart, and my portion for ever. *Psalms 73:26*

Like as a father pitieth his children, so the Lord pitieth them that fear him. For he knoweth our frame; he remembereth that we are dust. *Psalms 103:13, 14*

Trouble and anguish have taken hold on me; yet thy commandments are my delights. *Psalms 119:143*

The Lord upholdeth all that fall, and raiseth up all those that be bowed down. *Psalms 145:14*

If thou faint in the day of adversity, thy strength is small. *Proverbs 24:10*

Thou hast been a strength to the poor, a strength to the needy in his distress, a refuge from the storm, a shadow from the heat. *Isaiah 25:4*

Blessed are they that mourn: for they shall be comforted. . . . Blessed are they which are persecuted for righteousness' sake: for theirs is the kingdom of heaven. Blessed are ye, when men shall revile you, and persecute you, and shall say all manner of evil against you falsely, for my sake. Rejoice, and be exceeding glad: for great is your reward in heaven: for so persecuted they the prophets which were before you. *Matthew 5:4, 10-12*

Come unto me, all ye that labour and are heavy laden, and I will give you rest. *Matthew 11:28*

O my Father, if it be possible, let this cup pass from me: nevertheless, not as I will, but as thou wilt. *Matthew 25:39*

These things I have spoken unto you, that in me ye might have peace. In the world ye shall have tribulation; but be of good cheer, I have overcome the world. *John 16:33*

We must through much tribulation enter into the kingdom of God. *Acts 14:22*

Cast thy burden upon the Lord, and he shall sustain thee; he shall never suffer the righteous to be moved. *Psalms 55:22*

We know that all things work together for good to them that love God, to them who are the called according to his purpose. *Romans 8:28*

Bear ye one another's burdens, and so fulfil the law of Christ. *Galations 6:2*

The Lord is my helper, and I will not fear what man shall do unto me. *Hebrews 13:6*

Is any among you afflicted? let him pray. *James 5:13*

Have mercy upon me, O Lord, for I am in trouble. *Psalms 31:9*

Call upon me in the day of trouble: I will deliver thee, and thou shalt glorify me. *Psalms 50:15*

AGE

Thou shalt rise up before the hoary head, and honour the face of the old man. *Leviticus 19:32*

With the ancient is wisdom; and in length of days understanding. *Job 12:2*

Days should speak, and multitude of years should teach wisdom. *Job 32:7*

I have been young, and now am old; yet have I not seen the righteous forsaken. *Psalms 37:25*

Mine age is as nothing before thee. *Psalms 39:5*

We spend our years as a tale is told *Psalms 90:9*

So teach us to number our days, that we may apply our hearts unto wisdom. *Psalms 90:12*

The hoary head is a crown of glory, if it be found in the way of righteousness. *Proverbs 16:31*

Old things are passed away; behold, all things are become new. *II Corinthians 5:17*

Rebuke not an elder, but intreat him as a father. *I Timothy 5:1*

Aged men be sober, grave, temperate, sound in faith, in charity, in patience. *Titus 2:2*

AMBITION

Let us make us a name. *Genesis 11:4*

He that is greedy of gain troubleth his own house. *Proverbs 15:27*

How can ye believe, which receive honour one of another, and seek not the honour that cometh from God only? *John 5:44*

Better is it to be of an humble spirit with the lowly, than to divide the spoil with the proud. *Proverbs 16:19*

Labour not to be rich. . . . Wilt thou set thine eyes upon that which is not? for riches certainly make themselves wings; they fly away as an eagle toward heaven. *Proverbs 23:4, 5*

Better it is that it be said unto thee, Come up hither; than that thou shouldest be put lower in the presence of the prince whom thine eyes have seen. *Proverbs 25:7*

Seekest thou great things for thyself? seek them not. *Jeremiah 45:5*

Though thou exalt thyself as the eagle, and though thou set thy nest among the stars, thence will I bring thee down, saith the Lord. *Obadiah 4*

What is a man profited, if he shall gain the whole world, and lose his own soul? *Matthew 16:26*

The last shall be first, and the first last. *Matthew 20:16*

He that is greatest among you shall be your servant. And whosoever shall exalt himself shall be abased; and he that shall humble himself shall be exalted. *Matthew 23:11, 12*

Labour not for the meat which perisheth, but for that meat which endureth unto everlasting life. *John 6:27*

Covet earnestly the best gifts. *1 Corinthians 12:31*

Set your affection on things above, not on things on the earth. *Colossians 3:2*

ANGER

Cease from anger, and forsake wrath: fret not thyself in any wise to do evil. *Psalms 37:8*

He that is soon angry dealeth foolishly. *Proverbs 14:17*

A soft answer turneth away wrath: but grievous words stir up anger. *Proverbs 15:1*

He that is slow to anger is better than the mighty; and he that ruleth his spirit than he that taketh a city. *Proverbs 16:32*

He that is slow to wrath is of great understanding. *Proverbs 14:29*

Be ye angry, and sin not: let not the sun go down upon your wrath. *Ephesians 4:6*

Let all bitterness, and wrath, and anger, and clamour, and evil speaking, be put away from you, with all malice. *Ephesians 4:31*

Be not hasty in thy spirit to be angry: for anger resteth in the bosom of fools. *Ecclesiastes 7:9*

BEAUTY

Worship the Lord in the beauty of holiness. *I Chronicles 16:29*

Beauty is a fading flower. *Isaiah 28:1*

Consider the lilies of the field, how they grow; they toil not, neither do they spin: And yet I say unto you, That even Solomon in all his glory was not arrayed like one of these. *Matthew 6:28, 29*

Whatsoever things are lovely . . . think on these things. *Philippians 4:8*

BENEDICTION

The Lord bless thee, and keep thee. The Lord make his face shine upon thee, and be gracious unto thee: The Lord lift up his countenance upon thee, and give the peace. *Numbers 6:24-26*

The grace of the Lord Jesus Christ, and the love of God, and the communion of the Holy Ghost, be with you all. *II Corinthians 13:14*

Now the God of peace, that brought again from the dead our Lord Jesus, that great shepherd of the sheep, through the blood of the everlasting covenant, Make you perfect in every good work to do his will, working in you that which is well-pleasing in his sight, through Jesus Christ; to whom be glory for ever and ever. Amen. *Hebrews 13:20, 21*

BLESSED

Blessed are all they that put their trust in him. *Psalms 2:12*

Blessed is the man that maketh the Lord his trust. *Psalms 40:4*

Blessed is he that considereth the poor: the Lord will deliver him in time of trouble. *Psalms 41:1*

Blessed is the man that feareth the Lord, that delighteth greatly in his commandments. *Psalms 112:1*

Blessed are the poor in spirit: for theirs is the kingdom of heaven. Blessed are they that mourn: for they shall be comforted. Blessed are the meek: for they shall inherit the earth. Blessed are they which do hunger and thirst after righteousness: for they shall be filled. Blessed are the merciful: for they shall obtain mercy. Blessed are the pure in heart: for they shall see God. Blessed are the peace-makers: for they shall be called the children of God. Blessed are they which are persecuted for righteousness' sake: for theirs is the kingdom of heaven. Blessed are ye, when men shall revile you, and persecute you, and shall say all manner of evil against you falsely, for my sake. *Matthew 5:3-10*

Blessed are they that hear the word of God, and keep it. *Luke 11:28*

Blessed are they that keep judgment, and he that doeth righteousness at all times. *Psalms 106:3*

BURDEN

Cast thy burden upon the Lord, and he shall sustain thee: he shall never suffer the righteous to be moved. *Psalms 55:22*

Come unto me, all ye that labour, and are heavy laden, and I will give you rest. Take my yoke upon you. . . . My yoke is easy, and my burden is light. *Matthew 11:28, 29, 30*

Humble yourselves therefore under the mighty hand of God . . . casting all your care upon him; for he careth for you. *1 Peter 5:6, 7*

BUSINESS

They that go down to the sea in ships, that do business in great waters. *Psalms 107:23*

Seest thou a man diligent in his business? He shall stand before kings. *Proverbs 22:29*

He that hath received the five talents went and traded with the same, and made them other five talents. *Matthew 25:16*

Make not my Father's house an house of merchandise. *John 2:16*

Thy merchants were the great men of the earth. *Revelation 18:23*

CHARITY

Knowledge puffeth up, but charity edifieth. *I Corinthians 8:1*

Though I speak with the tongues of men and of angels, and have not charity, I am become as sounding brass, or a tinkling cymbal. And though I have the gift of prophecy, and understand all mysteries, and all knowledge; and though I have all faith, so that I could remove mountains, and have not charity, I am nothing. And though I bestow all my goods to feed the poor, and though I give my body to be burned, and have not charity, it profiteth me nothing. Charity suffereth long, and is kind; charity envieth not; charity vaunteth not itself, is not puffed up, Doth not behave itself unseemly, seeketh not her own, is not easily provoked, thinketh no evil; Rejoiceth not in iniquity, but rejoiceth in the truth; Beareth all things, believeth all things, hopeth all things, endureth all things. *I Corinthians 13:1-7*

And now abideth faith, hope, charity, these three; but the greatest of these is charity. *I Corinthians 13:13*

Be ye kind one to another, tender-hearted, forgiving one another, even as God for Christ's sake hath forgiven you. *Ephesians 4:32*

Speak evil of no man. *Titus 3:2*

CHILDREN

As arrows are in the hand of a mighty man; so are children of the youth. Happy is the man that hath his quiver full of them. *Psalms 127:4, 5*

A wise son maketh a glad father: but a foolish son is the heaviness of his mother. *Proverbs 10:1*

Train up a child in the way he should go: and when he is old, he will not depart from it. *Proverbs 22:6*

Remember now thy Creator in the days of thy youth, while the evil days come not, nor the years draw nigh, when thou shalt say, I have no pleasure in them. *Ecclesiastes 12:1*

Except ye be converted, and become as little children, ye shall not enter into the kingdom of heaven. *Matthew 18:3*

Suffer little children, and forbid them not, to come unto me: for of such is the kingdom of heaven. *Matthew 19:14*

When I was a child, I spake as a child, I understood as a child, I thought as a child: but when I became a man, I put away childish things. *I Corinthians 13:11*

CHOICE

Choose you this day whom ye will serve. *Joshua 24:15*

How long halt ye between two opinions? if the Lord be God, follow him; but if Baal, then follow him. *I Kings 18:21*

A good name is rather to be chosen than great riches, and loving favour than silver and gold. *Proverbs 22:1*

CHRIST

Behold, a virgin shall conceive, and bear a son, and shall call his name Immanuel. *Isaiah 7:14*

Thou shalt call his name Jesus: for he shall save his people from their sins. *Matthew 1:21*

This is my beloved Son, in whom I am well pleased. *Matthew 17:5*

The Son of man came not to be ministered unto, but to minister, and to give his life a ransom for many. *Matthew 20:28*

One is your Master, even Christ; and all ye are brethren. *Matthew 23:8*

The Son of man hath power on earth to forgive sins. *Mark 2:10*

Let not your heart be troubled: ye believe in God, believe also in me. *John 14:1*

I am the door: by me if any man enter in, he shall be saved. *John 10:9*

I am the way, the truth, and the life. *John 14:6*

God was in Christ, reconciling the world unto himself. *II Corinthians 5:19*

Jesus Christ, the same yesterday, and today, and for ever. *Hebrews 13:8*

CHURCH

Mine house shall be called a house of prayer for all people. *Isaiah 56:7*

Upon this rock I will build my church; and the gates of hell shall not prevail against it. *Matthew 16:18*

There is neither Jew nor Greek, there is neither bond nor free, there is neither male nor female; for ye are all one in Christ Jesus. *Galatians 3:28*

COMFORT

Naked came I out of my mother's womb, and naked shall I return thither: the Lord gave, and the Lord hath taken away; blessed be the name of the Lord. *Job 1:21*

My flesh and my heart faileth: but God is the strength of my heart, and my portion for ever. *Psalms 73:26*

Let, I pray thee, thy merciful kindness be for my comfort. *Psalms 119:76*

In the day when I cried thou answeredst me, and strengthenedst me with strength in my soul. *Psalms 138:3*

Comfort ye, comfort ye my people, saith your God. *Isaiah 40:1*

Is there no balm in Gilead? *Jeremiah 8:22*

Blessed are they that mourn: for they shall be comforted. *Matthew 5:4*

I will never leave thee, nor forsake thee. *Hebrews 13:5*

CONCEIT

The way of a fool is right in his own eyes: but he that hearkeneth unto counsel is wise. *Proverbs 12:15*

Seest thou a man wise in his own conceit? there is more hope of a fool than of him. *Proverbs 26:12*

The rich man is wise in his own conceit; but the poor that hath understanding searcheth him out. *Proverbs 28:11*

Let not the wise man glory in his wisdom, neither let the mighty man glory in his might, let not the rich man glory in his riches. *Jeremiah 9:23*

If any man think that he knoweth any thing he knoweth nothing yet as he ought to know. *I Corinthians 8:2*

COURAGE

Be strong and of good courage. *Deuteronomy 31:6*

Wait on the Lord: be of good courage, and he shall strengthen thine heart. *Psalms 27:14*

Be of good courage, and he shall strengthen your heart, all ye that hope in the Lord. *Psalms 31:24*

Death

Dust thou art, and unto dust shalt thou return. *Genesis 3:19*

The Lord gave, and the Lord hath taken away; blessed be the name of the Lord. *Job 1:21*

All flesh shall perish together, and man shall turn again unto dust. *Job 34:15*

God will redeem my soul from the power of the grave: for he shall receive me. *Psalms 49:15*

Then shall the dust return to the earth as it was: and the spirit shall return unto God who gave it. *Ecclesiastes 12:7*

This corruptible must put on incorruption, and this mortal must put on immortality. *I Corinthians 15:53*

O death, where is thy sting? O grave, where is thy victory? *I Corinthians 15:55*

We know that if our earthly house of this tabernacle were dissolved, we have a building of God, an house not made with hands, eternal in the heavens. *II Corinthians 5:1*

We brought nothing into this world, and it is certain we can carry nothing out. *I Timothy 6:7*

God shall wipe away all tears from their eyes; and there shall be no more death, neither sorrow, nor crying, neither shall there be any more pain: for the former things are passed away. *Revelation 21:4*

Discouraged

Fear not, neither be discouraged. *Deuteronomy 1:21*

My God, my God, why hast thou forsaken me? *Psalms 22:1*

We are perplexed, but not in despair. *II Corinthians 4:8*

Duty

Fear God, and keep his commandments: for this is the whole duty of man. *Ecclesiastes 12:13*

What doth the Lord require of thee, but to do justly, and to love mercy, and to walk humbly with thy God? *Micah 6:8*

Render therefore unto Caesar the things which be Caesar's, and unto God the things which be God's. *Luke 20:25*

We then that are strong ought to bear the infirmities of the weak, and not to please ourselves. *Romans 15:1*

Faith

It is better to trust in the Lord than to put confidence in man. *Psalms 118:8*

Trust in the Lord with all thine heart; and lean not unto thine own understanding. *Proverbs 3:5*

If ye have faith as a grain of mustard seed . . . nothing shall be impossible unto you. *Matthew 17:20*

All things, whatsoever ye shall ask in prayer, believing, ye shall receive. *Matthew 21:2*

The just shall live by faith. *Romans 1:17; Galatians 3:11*

We walk by faith, not by sight. *II Corinthians 5:7*

Fight the good fight of faith. *I Timothy 6:12*

I have fought a good fight, I have finished my course, I have kept the faith. *II Timothy 4:7*

Faith is the substance of things hoped for, the evidence of things not seen. *Hebrews 11:1*

Shew me thy faith without thy works, and I will shew thee my faith by my works. *James 2:18*

Faith without works is dead. *James 220*

Fear

Yea, though I walk through the valley of the shadow of death, I will fear no evil: for thou art with me; thy rod and thy staff they comfort me. *Psalms 23:4*

I sought the Lord, and he heard me, and delivered me from all my fears. *Psalms 34:4*

Behold, God is my salvation: I will trust, and not be afraid. *Isaiah 12:2*

Fear thou not; for I am with thee. *Isaiah 41:10*

Take no thought for your life, what ye shall eat, or what ye shall drink; nor yet for your body, what ye shall put on. Is not the life more than meat, and the body than raiment? *Matthew 6:25*

Which of you by taking thought can add one cubit unto his stature? *Matthew 6:27*

Take therefore no thought for the morrow: for the morrow shall take thought for the things of itself. Sufficient unto the day is the evil thereof. *Matthew 6:34*

Peace I leave with you, my peace I give unto you: not as the world giveth, give I unto you. Let not your heart be troubled, neither let it be afraid. *John 14:27*

God hath not given us the spirit of fear; but of power, and of love, and of a sound mind. *II Timothy 1:7*

Fool

The fear of the Lord is the beginning of knowledge: but fools despise wisdom and instruction. *Proverbs 1:7*

The way of a fool is right in his own eyes: but he that hearkeneth unto counsel is wise. *Proverbs 12:15*

Answer not a fool according to his folly, lest thou also be like unto him. *Proverbs 26:4*

Forgiveness

If thine enemy be hungry, give him bread to eat; and if he be thirsty, give him water to drink. *Proverbs 25:21*

Resist not evil: but whosoever shall smite thee on thy right cheek, turn to him the other also. *Matthew 5:39*

Love your enemies, bless them that curse you, do good to them that hate you, and pray for them which despitefully use you, and persecute you. *Matthew 5:44*

Forgive us our debts, as we forgive our debtors. *Matthew 6:12*

If ye forgive men their trespasses, your heavenly Father will also forgive you. *Matthew 6:14*

Judge not, that ye be not judged. *Matthew 7:1*

Why beholdest thou the mote that is in thy brother's eye, but considerest not the beam that is in thine own eye? *Matthew 7:3*

When ye stand praying, forgive, if ye have aught against any: that your Father also which is in heaven may forgive you your trespasses. *Mark 11:25*

Bless them which persecute you: bless, and curse not. *Romans 12:14*

Recompense to no man evil for evil. *Romans 12:17*

GIVING

If thine enemy be hungry, give him bread to eat; and if he be thirsty, give him water to drink. *Proverbs 25:21*

Give to him that asketh thee, and from him that would borrow of thee turn not thou away. *Matthew 5:42*

Freely ye have received; freely give. *Matthew 10:8*

Whosoever shall give you a cup of water to drink in my name . . . shall not lose his reward. *Mark 9:41*

He that hath two coats, let him impart to him that hath none; and he that hath meat, let him do likewise. *Luke 3:11*

Give, and it shall be given unto you; good measure, pressed down, and shaken together, and running over. *Luke 6:38*

Give alms of such things as ye have. *Luke 11:41*

It is more blessed to give than to receive. *Acts 20:35*

Though I bestow all my goods to feed the poor, and though I give my body to be burned, and have not charity, it profiteth me nothing. *I Corinthians 13:3*

God loveth a cheerful giver. *II Corinthians 9:7*

Whoso hath this world's good, and seeth his brother have need, and shutteth up his bowels of compassion from him, how dwelleth the love of God in him? *John 3:17*

GLORY

He is thy life, and the length of thy days. *Deuteronomy 30:20*

The eternal God is thy refuge, and underneath are the everlasting arms. *Deuteronomy 33:27*

In whose hand is the soul of every living thing, and the breath of all mankind. *Job 12:10*

The heavens declare the glory of God; and the firmament sheweth his handy work. *Psalms 19:1*

The fool hath said in his heart, There is no God. *Psalms 14:1*

The Lord is my shepherd; I shall not want. *Psalms 23:1*

Thou art my father, my God, and the rock of my salvation. *Psalms 89:26*

Holy, holy, holy, is the Lord of hosts: the whole earth is full of his glory. *Isaiah 6:3*

I am the first, and I am the last; and beside me there is no God. *Isaiah 44:6*

Our Father which art in heaven, Hallowed be thy name. *Matthew 6:9*

There is but one God, the Father, of whom are all things. *I Corinthians 8:6*

God is love. *I John 4:8*

Holy, holy, holy, Lord God Almighty, which was, and is, and is to come. *Revelation 4:8*

GREED

Thou shalt not covet thy neighbour's house, thou shalt not covet thy neighbour's wife, nor his manservant, nor his maidservant, nor his ox, nor his ass, nor any thing that is thy neighbor's. *Exodus 20:17*

Give me neither poverty nor riches; feed me with food convenient for me: Lest I be full, and deny thee, and say, Who is the Lord? *Proverbs 30:8, 9*

Yea, they are greedy dogs which can never have enough, and they are shepherds that cannot understand: they all look to their own way, every one for his gain, from his quarter. *Isaiah 56:11*

From the least of them even unto the greatest of them every one is given to covetousness. *Jeremiah 6:13*

As the partridge sitteth on eggs, and hatcheth them not; so he that getteth riches, and not by right, shall leave them in the midst of his days, and at his end shall be a fool. *Jeremiah 17:11*

O thou that dwellest upon many waters, abundant in treasures, thine end is come, and the measure of thy covetousness. *Jeremiah 51:13*

What is a man profited, if he shall gain the whole world, and lose his own soul? *Matthew 16:26*

Take heed, and beware of covetousness: for a man's life consisteth not in the abundance of the things which he possesseth. *Luke 12:15*

Set your affection on things above, not on things on the earth. *Colossians 3:2*

HARVEST

They have sown the wind, and they shall reap the whirlwind. *Hosea 8:7*

Ye shall know them by their fruits. Do men gather grapes of thorns, or figs of thistles? *Matthew 7:16*

Every good tree bringeth forth good fruit; but a corrupt tree bringeth forth evil fruit. *Matthew 7:17*

The harvest truly is plenteous, but the labourers are few. *Matthew 9:37*

The harvest is the end of the world; and the reapers are the angels. *Matthew 13:39*

Whatsoever a man soweth, that shall he also reap. *Galatians 6:7*

HATRED

Thou shalt not hate thy brother in thine heart. *Leviticus 19:17*

Whosoever doeth not righteousness is not of God, neither he that loveth not his brother. *I John 3:10*

Love your enemies, bless them that curse you, do good to them that hate you, and pray for them which despitefully use you, and persecute you. *Matthew 5:44*

He that hateth me hateth my Father also. *John 15:23*

He that hateth his brother is in darkness, and walketh in darkness, and knoweth not whither he goeth, because that darkness hath blinded his eyes. *I John 2:11*

If a man say I love God, and hateth his brother, he is a liar: for he that loveth not his brother whom he hath seen, how can he love God whom he hath not seen? *I John 4:20*

HEART

The Lord searcheth all hearts and understandeth all the imaginations of his thoughts. *I Chronicles 28:9*

Create in me a clean heart, O God; and renew a right spirit within me. *Psalms 51:10*

Who can say, I have made my heart clean, I am pure from my sin? *Proverbs 20:9*

Blessed are the pure in heart: for they shall see God. *Matthew 5:8*

HEAVEN

The Lord is in his holy temple, the Lord's throne is in heaven. *Psalms 11:4*

I will dwell in the house of the Lord for ever. *Psalms 23:6*

Blessed are the poor in spirit: for theirs is the kingdom of heaven. *Matthew 5:3*

Lay up for yourselves treasures in heaven, where neither moth nor rust doth corrupt, and where thieves do not break through nor steal. *Matthew 6:20*

In my Father's house are many mansions. *John 14:2*

We know that if our earthly house of this tabernacle were dissolved, we have a building of God, and house not made with hands, eternal in the heavens. *II Corinthians 5:1*

HOPE

Be of good courage, and he shall strengthen your heart, all ye that hope in the Lord. *Psalms 31:24*

The eye of the Lord is upon them that fear him, upon them that hope in his mercy. *Psalms 33:18*

It is good that a man should both hope and quietly wait for the salvation of the Lord. *Lamentations 3:26*

HUMILITY

What doth the Lord require of thee, but to ... walk humbly with thy God? *Micah 6:8*

Whosoever shall exalt himself shall be abased; and he that shall humble himself shall be exalted. *Matthew 23:12*

God forbid that I should glory, save in the cross of our Lord Jesus Christ. *Galatians 6:14*

Humble yourselves in the sight of the Lord, and he shall lift you up. *James 4:10*

All flesh is grass, and all the glory of man as the flower of grass. *1 Peter 1:24*

IDLENESS

Go to the ant, thou sluggard; consider her ways, and be wise. *Proverbs 6:6*

The sluggard will not plow by reason of the cold; therefore shall he beg in harvest, and have nothing. *Proverbs 20:4*

Love not sleep, lest thou come to poverty. *Proverbs 20:13*

IGNORANCE

The wisdom of this world is foolishness with God. *1 Corinthians 3:19*

Now we see through a glass, darkly; but then face to face: now I know in part; but then shall I know even as also I am known. *1 Corinthians 13:12*

IMMORTALITY

God will redeem my soul from the power of the grave: for he shall receive me. *Psalms 49:15*

Fear not them which kill the body, but are not able to kill the soul. *Matthew 10:28*

This is the will of him that sent me, that every one which seeth the Son, and believeth on him, may have everlasting life. *John 6:40*

I am the living bread which came down from heaven; if any man eat of this bread, he shall live for ever. *John 6:51*

I am the resurrection, and the life: he that believeth in me, though he were dead, yet shall he live. And whosoever, liveth and believeth in me shall never die. *John 11:25, 26*

Fight the good fight of faith, lay hold on eternal life. *1 Timothy 6:12*

For God so loved the world, that he gave his only begotten Son, that whosoever believeth in him should not perish, but have everlasting life. *John 3:16*

IRREVERENCE

Thou shalt not take the name of the Lord thy God in vain. *Exodus 20:7*

They shall not profane the holy things. *Leviticus 22:15*

Whosoever curseth his God shall bear his sin. *Leviticus 24:15*

Out of the same mouth proceedeth blessing and cursing. My brethren, these things ought not so to be. *James 3:10*

JOY

The joy of the Lord is your strength. *Nehemiah 8:10*

Serve the Lord with gladness: come before his presence with singing. *Psalms 104:34*

Happy is that people, whose God is the Lord. *Psalms 144:15*

They that sow in tears shall reap in joy. *Psalms 126:5*

The fruit of the Spirit is love, joy, peace. *Galatians 5:22*

JUDGMENT

Teach me good judgment. *Psalms 119:66*

He that justifieth the wicked, and he that condemneth the just, even they both are abomination to the Lord. *Proverbs 17:15*

Many seek the ruler's favour; but every man's judgment cometh from the Lord. *Proverbs 29:26*

The Lord will help me; who is he that shall condemn me? *Isaiah 50:9*

Judge not, that he be not judged. *Matthew 7:1*

With what judgment ye judge, ye shall be judged: and with what measure ye mete, shall be measured to you again . . . Why beholdest thou the mote that is in thy brother's eye, but considerest not the beam that is in thine own eye? *Matthew 7:2, 3*

First cast out the beam out of thine own eye; and then shalt thou see clearly to cast out the mote out of thy brother's eye. *Matthew 7:5*

He that is without sin among you, let him first cast a stone. *John 8:7*

Woman, where are those thine accusers? hath no man condemned thee? *John 8:10*

Speak evil of no man. *Titus 3:2*

Speak not evil one of another. *James 4:11*

KINDNESS

Thou shalt not see thy brother's ox or his sheep go astray, and hide thyself from them: thou shalt in any case bring them again unto thy brother. *Deuteronomy 22:1*

As ye would that men should do to you, do ye also to them likewise. *Luke 6:31*

Charity suffereth long, and is kind. *1 Corinthians 13:4*

If a man be overtaken in a fault, ye which are spiritual, restore such an one in the spirit of meekness; considering thyself, lest thou also be tempted. *Galatians 6:1*

As we have therefore opportunity, let us do good unto all men. *Galatians 6:10*

Speak evil of no man. *Titus 3:2*

Let brotherly love continue. *Hebrews 13:1*

KNOWLEDGE

The fear of the Lord is the beginning of knowledge. *Proverbs 1:7*

If thou criest after knowledge, and liftest up thy voice for understanding; If thou seekest her as silver and searchest for her as for hid treasures; Then shalt thou understand the fear of the Lord, and find the knowledge of God. *Proverbs 2:3-5*

Knowledge puffeth up, but charity edifieth. *1 Corinthians 8:1*

If any man think that he knoweth anything, he knoweth nothing yet as he ought to know. *1 Corinthians 8:2*

Now we see through a glass, darkly; but then face to face: now I know in part; but then shall I know even as also I am known. *1 Corinthians 13:12*

I count all things but loss for the excellency of the knowledge of Christ Jesus my Lord. *Philippians 3:8*

LAW

He that keepeth the law, happy is he. *Proverbs 29:18*

The law was given by Moses, but grace and truth came by Jesus Christ. *John 1:17*

This is the love of God, that we keep his commandments. *1 John 5:3*

The just shall live by faith. And the law is not of faith. *Galatians 3:11, 12*

LIBERTY

Proclaim liberty throughout all the land unto all the inhabitants thereof. *Leviticus 25:10*

Ye shall know the truth, and the truth shall make you free. *John 8:32*

Stand fast therefore in the liberty wherewith Christ hath made us free. *Galatians 5:1*

Use not liberty for an occasion to the flesh. *Galatians 5:13*

LIFE

All that a man hath will he give for his life. *Job 2:4*

Man that is born of woman is of few days, and full of trouble. *Job 14:1*

We spend our years as a tale that is told. *Psalms 90:9*

He that loveth his life shall lose it. *John 12:25*

LIGHT

The Lord is my light and my salvation. *Psalms 27:1*

Thy word is a lamp unto my feet, and a light unto my path. *Psalms 119:105*

The Lord shall be thine everlasting light. *Isaiah 60:20*

The light of the body is the eye: therefore when thine eye is single, thy whole body also is full of light: but when thine eye is evil, thy body also is full of darkness. *Luke 11:34*

Every one that doeth evil hateth the light, neither cometh to the light, lest his deeds should be reproved. *John 3:20*

Ye are all the children of light, and the children of the day: we are not of the night, nor of darkness. *I Thessalonians 5:5*

LOVE

Thou shalt love thy neighbour as thyself. *Leviticus 19:18*

Thou shalt love the Lord thy God with all thine heart, and with all thy soul, and with all thy might. *Deuteronomy 6:5*

A friend loveth at all times, and a brother is born for adversity. *Proverbs 17:17*

If ye love them which love you, what thank have ye? for sinners also love those that love them. *Luke 6:32*

Whoso keepeth his word, in him verily is the love of God perfected. *I John 2:5*

A new commandment I give unto you, That ye love one another; as I have loved you, that ye also love one another. By this shall all men know that ye are my disciples, if ye have love one to another. *John 13:34, 35*

Greater love hath no man than this, that a man lay down his life for his friends. *John 15:13*

He that loveth not his brother abideth in death. *1 John 3:14*

Every one that loveth is born of God. *1 John 4:7*

If God so loved us, we ought also to love one another. . . . If we love one another, God dwelleth in us, and his love is perfected in us. *1 John 4:11, 12*

God is love. *1 John 4:16*

If a man say, I love God, and hateth his brother, he is a liar: for he that loveth not his brother whom he hath seen, how can he love God whom he hath not seen? *1 John 4:20*

LUST

Whosoever looketh on a woman to lust after her hath committed adultery with her already in his heart. *Matthew 5:28*

All that is in the world, the lust of the flesh, and the lust of the eyes, and the pride of life, is not of the Father, but is of the world. *1 John 2:16*

The world passeth away, and the lust thereof: but he that doeth the will of God abideth for ever. *1 John 2:17*

MAN

God created man in his own image. *Genesis 1:27*

The Lord formed man of the dust of the ground. *Genesis 2:7*

Man that is born of woman is of few days, and full of trouble. He cometh forth like a flower, and is cut down: he fleeth also as a shadow, and continueth not. *Job 14:1, 2*

O Lord, thou art our Father; we are the clay, and thou our potter; and we all are the works of thy hand. *Isaiah 64:8*

When I was a child, I spake as a child, I understood as a child, I thought as a child: but when I became a man, I put away childish things. *1 Corinthians 13:11*

Thou madest him to have dominion over the works of thy hands; thou hast put all things under his feet. *Psalms 8:6*

Marriage

The Lord God said, It is not good that the man should be alone: I will make him an help meet for him. *Genesis 2:18*

Therefore shall a man leave his father and his mother, and shall cleave unto his wife: and they shall be one flesh. *Genesis 2:23*

Unto the woman he said . . . thy desire shall be to thy husband, and he shall rule over thee. *Genesis 3:16*

A virtuous woman is a crown to her husband. *Proverbs 12:4*

Husbands, love your wives, even as Christ also loved the church, and gave himself for it. *Ephesians 5:25*

Meekness

The meek shall inherit the earth. *Psalms 37:11*

The Lord lifteth up the meek: he casteth the wicked down to the ground. *Psalms 147:6*

He that is slow to wrath is of great understanding. *Proverbs 14:29*

A soft answer turneth away wrath. *Proverbs 15:1*

Seek ye the Lord, all ye meek of the earth, which have wrought his judgment: seek righteousness, seek meekness. *Zephaniah 2:3*

Blessed are the meek: for they shall inherit the earth. *Matthew 5:5*

Whosoever shall smite thee on thy right cheek, turn to him the other also. *Matthew 5:39*

Take my yoke upon you, and learn of me; for I am meek and lowly in heart; and ye shall find rest unto your souls. *Matthew 11:29*

Mercy

Surely goodness and mercy shall follow me all the days of my life. *Psalms 23:6*

He that hath mercy on the poor, happy is he. *Proverbs 14:21*

He that oppresseth the poor reproacheth his Maker: but he that honoureth him hath mercy on the poor. *Proverbs 14:31*

He that covereth his sins shall not prosper: but whoso confesseth and forsaketh them shall have mercy. *Proverbs 28:13*

Keep mercy and judgment, and wait on thy God continually. *Hosea 12:6*

The mercy of the Lord is from everlasting to everlasting upon them that fear him. *Psalms 103:17*

OBEY

All that the Lord hath said will we do, and be obedient. *Exodus 24:7*

Blessed is the man that feareth the Lord, that delighteth greatly in his commandments. *Psalms 112:1*

Why call ye me, Lord, Lord, and do not the things which I say? *Luke 6:46*

Thy will be done, as in heaven, so in earth. *Luke 11:2*

If a man keep my saying, he shall never see death. *John 8:51*

If ye love me, keep my commandments. *John 14:15*

If ye keep my commandments, ye shall abide in my love. *John 15:10*

We ought to obey God rather than men. *Acts 5:29*

OPPORTUNITY

The Lord called yet again, Samuel. *I Samuel 3:6*

God speaketh once, yea twice, yet man perceiveth it not. *Job 33:14*

The harvest is past, the summer is ended, and we are not saved. *Jeremiah 8:20*

Now it is high time to awake out of sleep: for now is our salvation nearer than when we believed. *Romans 13:11*

Behold, now is the accepted time; behold, now is the day of salvation. *II Corinthians 6:2*

As we have therefore opportunity, let us do good unto all men. *Galatians 6:10*

PARENTS

Honour thy father and thy mother. *Exodus 10:12*

My son, hear the instruction of thy father, and forsake not the law of thy mother. *Proverbs 1:8*

Whom the Lord loveth he correcteth; even as a father the son in whom he delighteth. *Proverbs 3:12*

A foolish son is the heaviness of his mother. *Proverbs 10:1*

A good man leaveth an inheritance to his children's children. *Proverbs 13:22*

He that wasteth his father, and chaseth away his mother, is a son that causeth shame, and bringeth reproach. *Proverbs 19:26*

Who curseth his father or his mother, his lamp shall be put out in obscure darkness. *Proverbs 20:20*

He that loveth father or mother more than me is not worthy of me. *Matthew 10:37*

If a son shall ask bread of any of you that is a father, will ye give him a stone? *Luke 11:11*

Children, obey your parents in the Lord: for this is right. *Ephesians 6:1*

PATIENCE

Rest in the Lord, and wait patiently for him. *Psalms 37:7*

Those that wait upon the Lord, they shall inherit the earth. *Psalms 37:9*

The patient in spirit is better than the proud in spirit. *Ecclesiastes 7:8*

It is good that a man should both hope and quietly wait for the salvation of the Lord. *Lamentations 3:26*

By patient continuance in well doing seek for glory and honour and immortality. *Romans 2:7*

Charity suffereth long, and is kind . . . is not easily provoked . . . Beareth all things, believeth all things, hopeth all things, endureth all things. *I Corinthians 13:4, 5, 7*

Let us not be weary in well doing: for in due season we shall reap, if we faint not. *Galatians 6:9*

Be patient toward all men. *I Thessalonians 5:14*

The Lord direct your hearts into the love of God, and into the patient waiting for Christ. *II Thessalonians 3:5*

Let us run with patience the race that is set before us. *Hebrews 12:1*

PEACE

Let there be no strife, I pray thee, between me and thee ... for we be brethren. *Genesis 13:8*

The meek shall inherit the earth; and shall delight themselves in the abundance of peace. *Psalms 37:11*

Behold, how good and how pleasant it is for brethren to dwell together in unity. *Psalms 133:1*

A soft answer turneth away wrath. *Proverbs 15:1*

He that is slow to anger is better than the mighty; and he that ruleth his spirit than he that taketh a city. *Proverbs 16:32*

Glory to God in the highest, and on earth peace, good will toward men. *Luke 2:14*

God is not the author of confusion, but of peace. *1 Corinthians 14:33*

PERFECTION

Be thou perfect. *Genesis 17:1*

Let your heart therefore be perfect with the Lord our God, to walk in his statutes, and to keep his commandments. *1 Kings 8:61*

Be ye therefore perfect, even as your Father which is in heaven is perfect. *Matthew 5:48*

PESSIMISM

All is vanity. *Ecclesiastes 1:2*

What profit hath a man of all his labour which he taketh under the sun? *Ecclesiastes 1:3*

In much wisdom is much grief; and he that increaseth knowledge increaseth sorrow. *Ecclesiastes 1:18*

What profit hath he that hath laboured for the wind? *Ecclesiastes 5:16*

It is better to go to the house of mourning, than to the house of feasting. *Ecclesiastes 7:2*

There is not a just man upon earth, that doeth good, and sinneth not. *Ecclesiastes 7:20*

POVERTY

The needy shall not always be forgotten: the expectation of the poor shall not perish for ever. *Psalms 9:18*

A little that a righteous man hath is better than the riches of many wicked. *Psalms 37:16*

Defend the poor and fatherless: do justice to the afflicted and needy. *Psalms 82:3*

He that hath mercy on the poor, happy is he. *Proverbs 14:21*

Better is a little with the fear of the Lord, than great treasure and trouble therewith. *Proverbs 15:16*

The rich and poor meet together: the Lord is the maker of them all. *Proverbs 22:2*

The rich ruleth over the poor, and the borrower is servant to the lender. *Proverbs 22:7*

The drunkard and the glutton shall come to poverty, and drowsiness shall clothe a man with rags. *Proverbs 23:21*

The rich man is wise in his own conceit; but the poor that hath understanding searcheth him out. *Proverbs 28:11*

Better is an handful with quietness, than both the hands full with travail and vexation of spirit. *Ecclesiastes 4:6*

Praise

I will bless the Lord at all times: his praise shall continually be in my mouth. *Psalms 34:1*

Because thy loving-kindness is better than life, my lips shall praise thee. *Psalms 63:3*

I will praise thee, O Lord my God, with all my heart: and I will glorify thy name for evermore. *Psalms 86:12*

Prayer

As for me, I will call upon God; and the Lord shall save me. Evening, and morning, and at noon, will I pray, and cry aloud: and he shall hear my voice. *Psalms 55:16, 17*

The Lord is nigh unto all them that call upon him, to all that call upon him in truth. *Psalms 145:18*

Seek ye the Lord while he may be found, call ye upon him while he is near. *Isaiah 55:6*

Let us lift up our heart with our hands unto God in the heavens. *Lamentations 3:41*

Our Father which art in heaven, Hallowed be thy name, Thy kingdom come. Thy will be done in earth, as it is heaven. Give us this day our daily bread. And forgive us our debts, as we forgive our debtors. And lead us not into temptation, but deliver us from evil: For thine is the kingdom, and the power, and the glory, for ever. *Matthew 6:9-13*

Ask, and it shall be given you; seek, and ye shall find; knock, and it shall be opened unto you. *Matthew 7:7*

All things, whatsoever ye shall ask in prayer, believing, ye shall receive. *Matthew 21:22*

When ye stand praying, forgive if ye have aught against any: that your Father also which is in heaven may forgive you your trespasses. *Mark 11:25*

Whatsoever ye shall ask the Father in my name, he will give it you.... Ask, and ye shall receive, that your joy may be full. *John 16:23, 24*

Pride

Him that hath an high look and a proud heart will not I suffer. *Psalms 101:5*

He that despiseth his neighbour sinneth. *Proverbs 14:21*

Every one that is proud in heart is an abomination to the Lord. *Proverbs 16:5*

Pride goeth before destruction, and an haughty spirit before a fall. Better it is to be of an humble spirit with the lowly, than to divide the spoil with the proud. *Proverbs 16:18, 19*

Before destruction the heart of man is haughty, and before honour is humility. *Proverbs 18:12*

Let not the wise man glory in his wisdom, neither let the mighty man glory in his might, let not the rich man glory in his riches: But let him that glorieth glory in this, that he understandeth and knoweth me, that I am the Lord which exercise loving-kindness, judgment, and righteousness, in the earth: for in these things I delight, saith the Lord. *Jeremiah 9:23, 24*

Whosoever will be great among you, let him be your minister; And whosoever will be chief among you, let him be your servant. *Matthew 20:26, 27*

Whosoever shall exalt himself shall be abased; and he that shall humble himself shall be exalted. *Matthew 23:12*

He hath put down the mighty from their seats, and exalted them of low degree. *Luke 1:52*

Mind not high things, but condescend to men of low estate. Be not wise in your own conceits. *Romans 12:16*

Knowledge puffeth up, but charity edifieth. *I Corinthians 8:1*

Let him that thinketh he standeth take heed lest he fall. *I Corinthians 10:12*

Charity vaunteth not itself, is not puffed up. *I Corinthians 13:4*

God forbid that I should glory, save in the cross of our Lord Jesus Christ. *Galatians 6:14*

God resisteth the proud, but giveth grace unto the humble. *James 4:6*

PROVIDENCE

The Lord is my shepherd; I shall not want. *Psalms 23:1*

Oh how great is thy goodness, which thou hast laid up for them that fear thee. *Psalms 31:19*

They that seek the Lord shall not want any good thing. *Psalms 34:10*

He maketh his sun to rise on the evil and on the good, and sendeth rain on the just and on the unjust. *Matthew 5:45*

Behold the fowls of the air: for they sow not, neither do they reap, nor gather into barns; yet your heavenly Father feedeth them. Are ye not much better than they? *Matthew 6:26*

Take no thought of your life, what ye shall eat. *Luke 12:22*

Eye hath not seen, nor ear heard, neither have entered into the heart of man, the things which God hath prepared for them that love him. *I Corinthians 2:9*

PRUDENCE

A wise man feareth, and departeth from evil: but the fool rageth, and is confident. *Proverbs 14:16*

Answer not a fool according to his folly, lest thou also be like unto him. *Proverbs 26:4*

Give not that which is holy unto the dogs, neither cast ye your pearls before swine, lest they trample them under their feet, and turn again and rend you. *Matthew 7:6*

Which of you, intending to build a tower, sitteth not down first, and counteth the cost, whether he have sufficient to finish it? *Luke 14:28*

Let every man be swift to hear, slow to speak, slow to wrath. *James 1:19*

Redemption

All we like sheep have gone astray; we have turned every one to his own way; and the Lord hath laid on him the iniquity of us all. *Isaiah 53:6*

The Son of man came not to be ministered unto, but to minister, and to give his life for a ransom for many. *Matthew 20:28*

This is my blood of the new testament, which is shed for many for the remission of sins. *Matthew 26:26*

I am the good shepherd: the good shepherd giveth his life for the sheep. *John 10:10*

There is one God, and one mediator between God and men, the man Christ Jesus; Who gave himself a ransom for all. *I Timothy 2:5, 6*

Regeneration

Create in me a clean heart, O God; and renew a right spirit within me. *Psalms 51:10*

Except a man be born again, he cannot see the Kingdom of God. *John 3:3*

Except a man be born of water and of the Spirit, he cannot enter into the kingdom of God. *John 3:5*

Ye shall know the truth, and the truth shall make you free. *John 8:32*

I am come that they might have life, and that they might have it more abundantly. *John 10:10*

I live; yet not I, but Christ liveth in me. *Galatians 2:20*

Whosoever believeth that Jesus is the Christ is born of God. *I John 5:1*

Religion

Fear God, and keep his commandments: for this is the whole duty of man. *Ecclesiastes 12:13*

What doth the Lord require of thee, but to do justly, and to love mercy, and to walk humbly with thy God? *Micah 6:8*

Love is the fulfilling of the law. *Romans 13:10*

Remission

There is forgiveness with thee. *Psalms 130:4*

Though your sins be as scarlet, they shall be as white as snow, though they be red like crimson, they shall be as wool. *Isaiah 1:18*

Forgive us our debts, as we forgive our debtors. *Matthew 6:12*

This is my blood of the new testament, which is shed for many for the remission of sins. *Matthew 26:28*

Repent, and be baptized every one of you in the name of Jesus Christ for the remission of sins. *Acts 2:38*

Even as Christ forgave you, so also do ye. *Colossians 3:13*

If we confess our sins, he is faithful and just to forgive us our sins, and to cleanse us from all unrighteousness. *I John 1:9*

Remorse

The sacrifices of God are a broken spirit: a broken and a contrite heart, O God, thou wilt not despise. *Psalms 51:17*

Lord, be merciful unto me: heal my soul; for I have sinned against thee. *Psalms 41:4*

There shall be weeping and gnashing of teeth, when ye shall see Abraham, and Isaac, and Jacob, and all the prophets, in the kingdom of God, and you yourselves thrust out. *Luke 13:28*

I have sinned against heaven, and before thee, And am no more worthy to be called thy son. *Luke 15:18, 19*

Peter went out, and wept bitterly. *Luke 22:62*

REPENTANCE

The Lord your God is gracious and merciful, and will not turn away his face from you, if ye return unto him. *II Chronicles 30:9*

Lord, be merciful unto me: heal my soul; for I have sinned against thee. *Psalms 41:4*

Repent: for the kingdom of heaven is at hand. *Matthew 4:17*

I came not to call the righteous, but sinners to repentance. *Mark 2:17*

God be merciful to me a sinner. *Luke 18:13*

RESOLUTION

As for me and my house, we will serve the Lord. *Joshua 24:15*

How long halt ye between two opinions? if the Lord be God, follow him: but if Baal, then follow him. *I Kings 18:21*

I determined not to know any thing among you, save Jesus Christ, and him crucified. *I Corinthians 2:2*

Watch ye, stand fast in the faith, quit you like men, be strong. *I Corinthians 16:13*

Stand fast, and hold the traditions which ye have been taught. *II Thessalonians 2:15*

RESPONSIBILITY

Am I my brother's keeper? *Genesis 4:9*

Every one shall die for his own iniquity. *Jeremiah 31:30*

Every one of us shall give account of himself to God. *Romans 14:12*

REVERENCE

The place whereon thou standest is holy ground. *Exodus 3:5*

Ye shall keep my sabbaths, and reverence my sanctuary. *Leviticus 19:30*

His salvation is nigh them that fear him. *Psalms 85:9*

What doth the Lord thy God require of thee, but to fear the Lord thy God, to walk in all his ways, and to love him, and to serve the Lord thy God with all thy heart and with all thy soul. *Deuteronomy 10:12*

The fear of the Lord is the beginning of wisdom. *Psalms 111: 10*

The Lord is in his holy temple: let all the earth keep silence before him. *Habakkuk 2:20*

At the name of Jesus every knee should bow. *Philippians 2:10*

Reward

The righteous shall inherit the earth. *Psalms 37:29*

The Lord preserveth all them that love him. *Psalms 145:20*

Shall not he render to every man according to his works? *Proverbs 24:12*

Cast thy bread upon the waters: for thou shalt find it after many days. *Ecclesiastes 11:1*

Blessed are the poor in spirit: for theirs is the kingdom of heaven. Blessed are they that mourn: for they shall be comforted. Blessed are the meek: for they shall inherit the earth. Blessed are they which do hunger and thirst after righteousness: for they shall be filled. Blessed are the merciful: for they shall obtain mercy. Blessed are the pure in heart: for they shall see God. Blessed are the peacemakers: for they shall be called the children of God. Blessed are they which are persecuted for righteousness' sake: for theirs is the kingdom of heaven. *Matthew 5:3-12*

He shall reward every man according to his works. *Matthew 16:27*

Well done, thou good and faithful servant: thou hast been faithful over a few things, I will make thee ruler over many things: enter thou into the joy of the Lord. *Matthew 25:21*

Come, ye blessed of my Father, inherit the kingdom prepared for you from the foundation of the world: For I was an hungered, and ye gave me meat: I was thirsty, and ye gave me drink: I was a stranger, and ye took me in. *Matthew 25:34, 35*

Whosoever shall give you a cup of water to drink in my name . . . verily I say unto you, he shall not lose his reward. *Mark 9:41*

Go thy way, sell whatsoever thou hast, and give to the poor, and thou shalt have treasure in heaven. *Mark 10:21*

Blessed are ye, when men shall hate you . . . for the Son of man's sake. Rejoice ye in that day, and leap for joy: for, behold, your reward is great in heaven. *Luke 6:22, 23*

Love ye your enemies, and do good, and lend, hoping for nothing again; and your reward shall be great. *Luke 6:35*

Whatsoever a man soweth, that shall he also reap. *Galatians 6:7*

Sacrifice

The sacrifices of God are a broken heart. *Psalms 51:17*

He that loseth his life for my sake shall find it. *Matthew 10:39*

He that loveth his life shall lose it. *John 12:25*

Greater love hath no man than this, that a man lay down his life for his friends. *John 15:13*

Though I give my body to be burned, and have not charity, it profiteth me nothing. *I Corinthians 13:3*

God forbid that I should glory, save in the cross of our Lord Jesus Christ, by whom the world is crucified unto me, and I unto the word. *Galatians 6:14*

Salvation

And it shall come to pass, that whosoever shall call on the name of the Lord shall be delivered. *Joel 2:32*

Seek ye me, and ye shall live. *Amos 5:4*

Except ye be converted, and become as little children, ye shall not enter into the kingdom of God. *Matthew 18:3*

The Son of man is come to seek and to save that which was lost. *Luke 19:10*

He that believeth on me hath everlasting life. *John 6:47*

I am the resurrection and the life: he that believeth in me, though he were dead, yet shall he live. *John 11:25*

These are written, that ye might believe that Jesus is the Christ, the Son of God; and that believing ye might have life through his name. *John 20:31*

Believe on the Lord Jesus Christ, and thou shalt be saved, and thy house. *Acts 14:31*

If thou shalt confess with thy mouth the Lord Jesus, and shalt believe in thine heart that God hath raised him from the dead, thou shalt be saved. *Romans 10:9*

Christ Jesus came into the world to save sinners; of whom I am chief. *I Timothy 1:15*

SELF-RIGHTEOUSNESS

There is a way which seemeth right unto a man, but the end thereof are the ways of death. *Proverbs 14:12*

Most men will proclaim every one his own goodness: but a faithful man who can find? *Proverbs 20:6*

Whoso boasteth himself of a false gift is like clouds and wind without rain. *Proverbs 25:14*

He that trusteth in his own heart is a fool: but whoso walketh wisely, he shall be delivered. *Proverbs 28:26*

There is a generation that are pure in their own eyes, and yet is not washed from their filthiness. *Proverbs 30:12*

God, I thank thee, that I am not as other men are. *Luke 18:9*

Let him that thinketh he standeth take heed lest he fall. *I Corinthians 10:12*

SIN

Be sure your sin will find you out. *Numbers 32:23*

As he thinketh in his heart, so is he. *Proverbs 23:7*

All we like sheep have gone astray; we have turned every one to his own way. *Isaiah 53:6*

Forgive us our sins. *Luke 11:4*

If we say that we have no sin, we deceive ourselves, and the truth is not in us. *I John 1:8*

SINCERITY

Serve the Lord with all your heart. *I Samuel 12:20*

Why call ye me, Lord, Lord, and do not the things which I say? *Luke 6:46*

Grace be with all them that love our Lord Jesus Christ in sincerity. *Ephesians 6:24*

SORROW

Mine eye poureth out tears unto God. *Job 16:20*

The Lord hath heard the voice of my weeping. *Psalms 6:8*

Blessed are they that mourn: for they shall be comforted. *Matthew 5:4*

Blessed are ye that weep now: for ye shall laugh. *Luke 6:21*

Jesus wept. *John 11:35*

Weep ye not for the dead, neither bemoan him: but weep sore for him that goeth away. *Jeremiah 22:10*

STRENGTH

Be strong, and quit yourselves like men. *I Samuel 4:9*

How are the mighty fallen! *II Samuel 1:19*

The race is not to the swift, or the battle to the strong. *Ecclesiastes 9:11*

The Lord God is my strength. *Habakkuk 3:19*

I can do all things through Christ which strengtheneth me. *Philippians 4:13*

SUFFERING

Ye shall be hated of all men for my name's sake: but he that endureth to the end shall be saved. *Matthew 10:22*

Are ye able to drink of the cup that I shall drink of, and to be baptized with the baptism that I am baptized with? *Matthew 20:22*

Being reviled, we bless; being persecuted, we suffer it. *I Corinthians 4:12*

If any man suffer as a Christian, let him not be ashamed; but let him glorify God on this behalf. *I Peter 4:16*

TEMPTATION

Watch and pray, that ye enter not into temptation. *Matthew 26:41*

Lead us not into temptation; but deliver us from evil. *Luke 11:14*

Be not overcome of evil, but overcome evil with good. *Romans 12:21*

THANKSGIVING

O Lord my God, I will give thanks unto thee for ever. *Psalms 30:12*

O give thanks unto the Lord, for he is good, for his mercy endureth for ever. *Psalms 107:1*

Thanks be to God, which giveth us the victory through our Lord Jesus Christ. *I Corinthians 15:57*

We give thanks to God and the Father of our Lord

Jesus Christ. *Colossians 1:3*
In every thing give thanks. *I Thessalonians 5:18*

TOLERANCE

Judge not, that ye be not judged. *Matthew 7:1*
Why beholdest thou the mote that is in thy brother's eye, but considerest not the beam that is in thine own eye? *Matthew 7:3*
First cast out the beam out of thine own eye; and then shalt thou see clearly to cast out the mote out of thy brother's eye. *Matthew 7:5*
Be patient toward all men. *I Thessalonians 5:14*
Speak evil of no man. *Titus 3:2*

TRUTH

Grace and truth came by Jesus Christ. *John 1:17*
If ye continue in my word, then are ye my disciples indeed; And ye shall know the truth, and the truth shall make you free. *John 8:31, 32*
He that saith, I know him, and keepeth not his commandments, is a liar, and the truth is not in him. *I John 2:4*

WANT

The Lord is my shepherd; I shall not want. *Psalms 23:1*
He that giveth to the poor shall not lack. *Proverbs 28:27*
Your Father knoweth what things ye have need of, before ye ask him. *Matthew 6:8*

WEALTH

Thou shalt remember the Lord thy God; for it is he that giveth thee power to get wealth. *Deuteronomy 8:18*
Labour not to be rich. *Proverbs 23:4*
Let not the rich man glory in his riches. *Jeremiah 9:23*
Where your treasure is, there will your heart be also. *Matthew 6:21*
It is easier for a camel to go through the eye of a needle, than for a rich man to enter into the kingdom of God. *Matthew 19:24*

Ye cannot serve God and mammon. *Luke 16:13*

WISDOM

Give instruction to a wise man, and he will be yet wiser; teach a just man, and he will increase in learning. *Proverbs 9:9*

The fear of the Lord is the beginning of wisdom: and the knowledge of the holy is understanding. *Proverbs 9:10*

Wisdom is better than strength. *Ecclesiastes 9:16*

Wise men lay up knowledge: but the mouth of the foolish is near destruction. *Proverbs 10:14*

WORK

He that tilleth his land shall be satisfied with bread. *Proverbs 12:11*

In all labour there is profit. *Proverbs 14:23*

Seest thou a man diligent in his business? he shall stand before kings; he shall not stand before mean men. *Proverbs 22:29*

Be thou diligent to know the state of thy flocks, and look well to thy herds. *Proverbs 27:23*

The sleep of a labouring man is sweet. *Ecclesiastes 5:12*

Whatsoever thy hand findeth to do, do it with thy might. *Ecclesiastes 9:10*

The labourer is worthy of his hire. *Luke 10:7*

Not slothful in business; fervent in spirit; serving the Lord. *Romans 12:11*

WORSHIP

O come, let us worship and bow down: let us kneel before the Lord our maker. *Psalms 95:6*

I was glad when they said unto me, Let us go into the house of the Lord. *Psalms 122:1*

The lord is in his holy temple: let all the earth keep silence before him. *Habakkuk 2:20*

At the name of Jesus every knee should bow. *Philippians 2:10*

All nations shall come and worship before thee. *Revelations 15:4*

Chapter XIV

FACTS, FICTION, AND FABLES

He Won the Audience

YALE UNIVERSITY was to debate at Lewiston many years ago. Some newspaper writer in New Haven tried to be funny with a story that probably the local boys would have to take dog sleds when they got to Portland in order to arrive at Lewiston. A clever Bates campus newspaper editor saw a golden opportunity to arouse interest for the debate and he reprinted the story with comments with the result that the hall was packed for the debate. When the decision was announced for Bates, a freshman who had been carried away with the build-up for the debate, shouted loudly enough to be heard on the platform, "I guess that will let 'em know we aren't hicks."

Immediately one of the Yale debaters stepped to the front of the platform and expressed the regret of himself and his colleagues that any such references should have been made in a town paper which was in no way connected with Yale University; that he himself was a native of the hills of Kentucky and would be the last to call another a "hick"; that Yale had learned by bitter experience to respect Bates debating teams for their excellence and that this occasion was no exception. His remarks were greeted with tremendous applause. He had *lost* the *debate*, but he had *won* the *audience*. Eight years after that debate, that young man, whose name was Hutchins, became president of the University of Chicago. *From an address by Lionel Crocker, chairman, Department of Speech, Denison University, before the Indiana State Teacher College High School Invitation Speech Tournament, Terre Haute, Indiana. Mr. Crocker quoted this story as told by Brooks Quimby of Bates College*

Speech

Of all things that have happened to man in his upward climb, of all the advances he has made, the one which stands out above all the rest is the development of speech. Speech is essential to the exchange of ideas on any topic at all levels and by all means of communication. Indeed the basic characteristic of an educated man is that he be literate and articulate in verbal discourse. Here is one of the keys to the major needs of education at all levels and in all departments. Anything the world over that interferes with the free flow of intelligence or information is inimical to the intent of education. . . . Nothing so imprisons a man as words. *Lawrence M. Gould, president of Carleton College*

Appreciation of What You Have

An unemployed worker stopped by a farm during the last depression and asked for some food. The farmer said, "Yes, I'll give you some food, but you will have to work for it." This farmer was very old-fashioned.

After the man had been fed, the farmer said, "Can you paint the fence?" The man said, "No, that's out of my line." The farmer said, "Well, can you hoe the field?" "Oh, no," the man said, "I don't know anything about farming." "Well," the farmer said, "can you do a little carpentry in the barn?" He said, "Oh, no, that's also out of my line." So the farmer said, "Just what can you do?" The man said, "I'm an unemployed advertising writer." So the farmer said, "That's excellent. I want to sell this farm. Will you write a piece of copy for the Sunday newspapers?"

The man sat down at the desk and he came forth with a beautiful advertisement describing the pastoral scene at this magnificent farm, with its flowing brook and the old home in a colonial setting. The farmer looked the copy over and said, "Man, I would be a fool to sell this farm."

In spite of the arrogance of pressure groups, in spite of the meanness of special propagandists and detractors, you and I live in the greatest economic and cultural civilization on the globe today. We have immensely valuable psychological and spiritual assets to conserve. We would be fools to let this thing go. *From an address by Merryle Stanley Rukeyser, journalist, at the Third Annual Meeting of the Western States Meat Packers Associations, San Francisco*

The Power of Thinking

We must learn the tremendous power of thinking—of ideas. Marcus Aurelius says that your life is what your thoughts make it. Ralph Waldo Emerson says that a man is what he thinks about all day long.

We are doing some so-called thinking in this country, and our minds are gradually being infiltrated by certain ideas which I believe are dangerous to the perpetuity of the American free enterprise system of the American way of life. One of those ideas which seems to be gaining currency in America today is that security and freedom are synonymous. One of the greatest business organizations in this country actually issued a statement saying that, "Of course, it is impossible to have freedom in the absence of security." Now, on the surface that sounds right. It sounds humanitarian; it sounds idealistic; it sounds almost religious—that there can be no freedom unless there is security.

Well, I would like to analyze for a minute a little place down in Pennsylvania known as Valley Forge. Security? There was no security. They had nothing to eat. When they were operated on they didn't even have any palliative drugs. They still find bullets down there that were chewed flat by men who put them between their teeth when they were operated on in the name of freedom, and had their legs cut off. They walked bleeding on the snow. They had no clothes. They had left their homes. They hadn't a vestige of security, but I will venture the assertion that as long as the American Republic lasts Valley Forge will be seen to be the purest fire of freedom that ever burned. *Dr. Norman Vincent Peale, minister, Marble Collegiate Church, New York City*

Opportunity

I think the temptation to reminisce is very great when an oldster such as myself gets up in front of a younger generation. I will take advantage of that habit to go back to my boyhood for just a moment, but I assure you I am not going to bore you with long tales of the Kansas prairies.

The feature of that boyhood I'd like to mention is this: I was of a big family of boys, six of us. And we were very poor, but the point is we didn't know we were poor, and that's the point I want to make with you. The mere fact that we didn't do all the things that others in cities may have done made no impression upon us whatsoever because there was constantly held out in front of us by every one around us, and certainly it was embedded in our consciousness, that opportunity was on every side.

In those days we didn't hear so much about the word security, personal security through life from cradle to the grave, some kind of assurance that we were not going to have to go out with a tin cup or sell apples on the streets. But there was constantly around us the right and the opportunity to go out and do better for ourselves than merely to follow the plow down through the field, or to work on the section gang, or anything else that we might do to make the extra few dollars in the summer that we needed.

And I believe that came about because of the character of the country in which we were raised and in which you are raised. I do not mean the character in terms of cities, vast resources, agriculturally and in every other way. I mean because of the system under which we live. It is a free system that gives to each of us of any religion or of any location in that country the right to do something for himself. *From an address by General Dwight D. Eisenhower, president, Columbia University, before the First Columbia College Forum on Democracy, attended by student representatives of sixty-five preparatory and high schools and their headmasters or principals, Columbia University.*

INTERNATIONAL TRADE

Having been a merchant I always think in terms of nations trading with each other, buying goods from each other, and doing business at a profit under our system.

My friends who knew me in the mail order business will remember that one of my slogans was:

> "Count that day lost,
> Whose low descending sun

Finds goods sold for cost,
And business done for fun."

Donald Nelson, business executive, before the Executives' Club of Chicago

PLEASURES OF THE MIND

In old age we have the pleasures of the mind. It is good, in old age, to have made friends with the great minds. From the day you leave college you should begin your education, first by living, second by reading. I grant you that life is better than learning, but even the second-hand experience of reading is valuable and delightful. Just remember that in some mysterious country of the mind, all the great writers, artists, scientists, philosophers that America has thought worthy to remember are still there, waiting for you. All you have to do is open a book, sit before a statue or a painting and there they are. That is perhaps the most precious thing that we have in life, next to the affection of those whom we love. *Dr. Will Durant, Philosopher, in an address before the Executives' Club of Chicago*

THEORISTS

More than ever before technology and production are utterly dependent upon the theorist. Few studies were ever more "abstract," few more "remote from daily life" than the pioneer work in modern physics. Studies on the disintegration of atoms during the thirties were sensational in a limited circle—but unknown or a joke to the "real" world. No one thinks them funny now. It was the "pure," "useless" research spreading from university to university around the world which supplied the foundation for the use of atomic energy. If, as is so often asserted, we live in an atomic age, that age was born in the universities. *From an address by Henry M. Wriston, president of Brown University, delivered before the Chamber of Commerce of the State of New York*

PURE SCIENCE

Do you practical men fully realize that the airplane was only made possible by the development of the internal combustion engine, and that this in its turn was only made possible by the development of the laws governing all heat engines, the laws of thermodynamics, through the use for the hundred preceding years of the steam engine (1780-1880), and that this was only made possible by the preceding 200 years of work in celestial mechanics; that this again was due to the discovery by Galileo and by Newton in the first half of the fifteenth century of the laws of force and motion, which have to be utilized in every one of the subsequent developments? That states the relationship of pure science to industry. The one is the child of the other. You may apply any blood test you wish and you will at once establish the relationship. Science begat modern industry, and the son now owes a great debt to its parent. *From an address by Dr. Robert A. Millikan, professor emeritus of physics, California Institute of Technology, at the 53rd Annual Congress of American Industry, New York*

Is the Machine Age Evil?

The fashion in some circles is to deride the machine age, to call it a sordid age, an age when men's souls are bound to the machine. As though the machine and not the man were master, as though man's spirit was more free before he had the machine to serve him.

The fashion is not new. An hour's ride from here, by grace of this machine age, is a body of gray-green water called Walden Pond. By Walden Pond, a hundred years ago, a young man built a hut, lived in it for two years, and emerged to praise the self-sufficient life and to decry industrialism, the use of the machine. The machine was evil, because it chained man to his work and made him dependent on the work of other men. If Thoreau was right, then our growing use of minerals is not a blessing but a curse.

But was Thoreau right? Did he prove that man should live by his own hand, without aid from the work of other men, or that if he did his spirit would be more free?

Thoreau built his hut with his own hands, but did he find the mine and smelt the iron ore to make the axe and saw to build it? Did he forge and shape and temper them?

He gathered clam shells and burned them and made a handful or two of lime; he showed that he could do it. But he plastered his house with lime that he bought from a store, the product of the work of other men. He hunted and fished for part of his food, but did he make the gun or even the fishhook? He grew a garden, but did he make his spade or his hoe?

Yes, he built his own small house and he won a small part of his own food, and he had time to think long thoughts and to write with a charm few men have equaled. He had time for the freedom of his spirit. But the time to think and the time to write were not the products of his own work; they came from the work of other men, the men who mined and quarried, who smelted and burned, who wrought and fabricated the mineral things he used, the men whose work he bought. Some of them in turn may have bought and read his book.

If he had fed, clothed, and housed himself by his own sole efforts, without things made for him by other men, he would have had little time for abstract thought and no time at all to write, and the world would have been poorer without the beauty of his writing. We owe that beauty, that freedom of spirit so charmingly expressed, not to the self-sufficiency he praised, but to the industrialism he decried.

The industrialism he feared has grown beyond his most fearful thinking. Men of cloistered minds still fear and decry it. Has it justified his fears and theirs? Has the machine ground the color from men's lives, the freedom from their spirits?

When Thoreau lived by Walden Pond, the typical workman walked to his job while night was still dark, worked through the day, quit and walked home when night was dark again. To make a scanty living, he drudged for 70 or 80 or 85 hours a week, every week in the year. Today's typical workman rides to and from his job in his own car. He drudges little. He makes a far more abundant living in about half the time. The rest of the time is his own. He has leisure and unused energy, instead of long hours of exhaustion. A similar change has come to all of us, differing only in degree.

Whether we use our leisure wisely or unwisely is beside the point. The machine has given it to us to use as we will; we have a choice that our forebears did not have. If we fail to think as widely and as wisely as we should, if we fail to court beauty, if our spirits crawl instead of soar, the fault is with us, not with the machine. Industrialism, with its increased output per man, has given us each a golden age, if only we make it so.

Increased output per man, the making by each of more and more goods for other men to use: that is the meaning of industrialism. Each man helps to make goods for other men, instead of making goods solely for himself. The more he makes, the more other men may have. *From an address by Max W. Ball, director, Oil and Gas Divisions, U. S. Department of the Interior, Washington, D. C., delivered at the University of New Hampshire*

Those Who Disagree With Us

A friend of mine once uttered a prayer: "Deliver us from the deadly danger of denying to those who disagree with us the attributes of rightness and reasonableness that we so easily arrogate to ourselves." *Lowell B. Mason, Federal Trade Commission*

Too Late

As Potash said to Perlmutter, "After the milk is spoilt, it don't make any difference who left the ice-box door open."

Carelessness

A Nicaraguan proverb says, "One man in one day with one match can clear a hundred acres."

Self-confidence

A young veteran advertised for a job as a copy writer. His letter said, "Let me remind you that the best copy has not yet been written. I am the fellow who has not yet written it." I think any of us would like to hire a fellow with that much nerve, originality, and ingenuity, who is not afraid to say what is on his mind. *Rilea W. Doe, vice-president, Safeway Stores*

Atomic Energy

One pound of uranium, in a little cube less than the length of my thumb joint, is the equivalent of three million pounds of coal. You start playing with three million pounds of coal, putting it in freight cars and coal cars, and you'll see how much you really have. One tiny pound of uranium is equal to all that.

It is said that the power of one pound of uranium also would light twelve million 100-watt globes for ten hours, or it would be enough to light New England for a night.

The power that holds the atom together can be thought of in this way: If it were represented by a steel cable, you could dangle the entire United States Navy on the end of it. That is the power that is released, of course, when the atom is split.

I do not claim these are accurate, scientific facts. They are told to me as being accurate. *From an address by John A. Hancock, well-known industrialist and investment banker, before the Executives' Club of Chicago*

Middle Age

One of the greatest gifts of middle age, I think, is the quiet coming of a certain understanding, a kind of quiet comprehension that is hard to name. To "comprendre" is to "pardon"—to understand is to forgive. You will notice middle age is more tolerant, it is more moderate in its opinions than either youth or senility. Middle age realizes the truth of the old Greek adage of "meden agan"—nothing too much; nothing in excess—and it serves as a healthy mediator between the radicalism of youth and the timid conservatism of old age, between young imagination and old fear. The people of middle age are the sanity and stability of this society. *Dr. Will Durant, philosopher, in an address before the Executives' Club of Chicago*

Trees

If you wish to be remembered, said the English essayist in *Dreamthorp*, "better plant a tree than build a city or strike a medal—it will outlast both." In England there are oaks whose acorns were forming that June day when King John signed Magna Charta at Runnymede, and a few years ago there still existed in Newland, Gloucester, oak mentioned in the Domesday Book which was compiled in A.D. 1080-1086. It is claimed that sequoias of California have rings going back to 1305 B.C. And in Mexico there is a cypress said to be 3,000 to 5,000 years old. . . .

Studies show that the principal causes of soil erosion are the removal of timber, burning-over of land, breaking up the vegetative soil cover, cultivation of crops on steep slopes, and over-grazing of pasture land. As Zimmerman puts it: First the axe, then the plough, then the rain, then erosion, finally the desert.

When the British tanks stormed into Tunis in 1943 they churned up the dust of Carthage, the great city of a million people built by the Phoenicians in 850 B.C., the wealthiest city of antiquity. The people of Carthage in 393 B.C., when their city had been standing just as long as from Columbus' discovery of America to this present year, would have mocked anyone who told them their buildings would be buried in sand, merely a nuisance to be fought over. *From the Royal Bank of Canada Monthly Letter*

ACCURATE

In a small town there was a jeweler who had the usual big clock hanging up in the window. Everybody in the small town set his watch by it. The jeweler noticed that every morning a big, tall fellow came along and set his watch, and every night he came back past there and set his watch again. This went on for weeks and in a small town you notice those things.

One day the jeweler went out and stopped him and said, "My curiosity is getting the best of me. I want to know why you set your watch every morning and every night by this clock here. I'm glad it's helping you, but why do you have to do it every day?" The other man said, "Well, I'm the fellow who blows the whistle down at the factory to bring the people to work and send them home again in the evening. I want to be sure my watch is right."

The jeweler said, "That's quite significant, because I set my clock by your whistle." *Rilea W Doe, vice-president, Safeway Stores*

Public Service

In the next three decades I urge that every educated person who is qualified to do so, plan definitely to set aside a number of years for the rendering of service in the legislative, or executive branches of his local, state or federal government, and that as nearly as possible this be full-time service.

I am proposing a widespread rotation of the not-too-pleasant duties of the public service. And I do not mean merely part-time or "dollar-a-year" service alone. Nor in my opinion will it meet the situation to put this public service off until you are of retirement age.

I propose that, out of the best and most productive years of your life you should carve out a segment in which you put your private career aside to serve your community and your country, and thereby to serve your children, your neighbours, your fellow men, and the cause of freedom. *David E. Lilienthal, formerly chairman, United States Atomic Energy Commission, in a commencement address at the University of Virginia*

Atomic Conversation

I think I am like the New Mexican Indian who several years ago was sending a few smoke signals. He had his dampened blanket at work and the puffs of smoke were going up as he was communicating with a representative of an adjoining tribe on a distant mesa. The puffs of smoke continued and he had just about gotten through the news events and was going into the sports final. It happened to be the day on which the atom test Number One let loose, and over there in a far, far distant section of the desert this huge mushroom of smoke ascended to the skies and a few minutes later there came the most earth-shaking boom which this or any other mortal had ever heard. The Indian simply folded up his blanket, dampened the fire and trudged disconsolately off into the deepening shadows of the desert muttering to himself, "I wish I could talk like that." Well, so do I. *Hugh D. Scott, Jr. speaking as national Republican chairman before the Executives' Club of Chicago*

Women

When a woman wants an article, you may be sure it is for one of the following seven reasons:

1. Because her husband says she can't have it
2. Because it will make her look thin
3. Because it comes from Paris
4. Because her neighbors can't afford it
5. Because nobody else has it
6. Because everybody else has it
7. Or just "Because"

Paul M. Corbett, vice-president, Youngberg-Carlson Company, Chicago

The Art of Detachment

John Masefield was one of our great poets. Masefield had a secret. He said, "Early in life I began to practice the getting of tranquility." And one of the methods for the practicing of the getting of tranquility, according to Masefield, was to practice the art of detachment; that is, to lift your mind out of a situation in which you find yourself and elevate it to an area of calm. You are in the midst of a disturbing situation, you are working hard at it, but you can put your mind into an attitude of detachment so that you look from a great height upon the tumult that surrounds you. *Dr. Norman Vincent Peale, minister Marble Collegiate Church, New York City*

Faith

Christianity is not primarily a lesson in logic, although there is genuine logic in it. Neither is faith a matter of believing what is not so. Faith does not deny the relevance of reason. It reaches beyond reason on the assumption that a man ought to live by the noblest hypothesis consistent with the facts of human experience. Certainly, as Professor MacIntosh notes, we have a right to "believe as we must to live as we ought." What is more, it is instructive to observe that a considerable proportion of the greatest thinkers of our time are devout Christians. They have gone beyond intellectual arrogance to the intellectual humility of the wise. Fifty years ago Mark Twain put the matter in its proper perspective when somebody tried to sell him a ticket to one of Robert Ingersoll's lectures. Ingersoll, the atheist, intended to give his famous lecture on "The Mistakes of Moses." Mark Twain observed that he would not give a plugged nickel to hear Ingersoll on "The Mistakes of Moses," but he would pay a pretty penny to hear Moses on "The Mistakes of Ingersoll." Fundamentally, the important question is not, "What do you think of God," but rather, "What does God think of you, and your mistakes." *Dr. Harold Blake Walker, minister, The First Presbyterian Church, Evanston Illinois*

ACHIEVEMENT

For those who will take the time to ponder it, here is a thought-provoking piece of advice from Henry Ford: "Make your program so long and so hard that the people who praise you will always seem to you to be talking about something very trivial in comparison with what you are really trying to do." *From the Monthly Letter of the Royal Bank of Canada*

THE RAILROADS

Man has not yet developed any other means of transportation for the mass movement of freight and the mass movement of people even remotely comparable in cost and efficiency to power on wheels applied to cars on rails. One Diesel locomotive pulling a freight train of 5000 tons with a crew of five and using one teaspoonful of fuel oil per ton mile illustrates the observation. It would take 500 trucks, with each truck carrying 10 tons, to duplicate this feat. *Ambrose W. Benkert, president of A. W. Benkert & Co., Inc., New York*

MILITARY COURTESY

There was a colonel, the supply officer, who was a very nice colonel, and I remember running into him on the road into town (as we called Kunming) one Sunday morning. He was coming toward the field, and I was going toward town, and I noticed that he was in full dress. He had on matching trousers and jacket, and a necktie and socks. I didn't think much about it, and I waved at him like this

—"Good morning, Colonel." As I did that, I saw his own hand come up to his forehead as if returning a salute, and I felt very embarrassed for him because I hadn't given him a salute. I had walked about two and a half steps further when I heard the Colonel's voice: "Sergeant Hargrove!" I came back. He said, "You've been in the army a few years, Sergeant, and you know about military courtesy, I presume?" "Yes, sir," I replied. "You don't salute, Sergeant?" (Nobody had been saluting around there.) I said, "I beg the Colonel's pardon; I failed to see him"—which is the proper answer. "Well," he said, "let's have a little more military courtesy around here." So I gave him a frenzied salute and asked him, "All the time, Colonel?" "Well," he said, "when you see a full colonel on the road on Sunday morning, who spent an hour and a half getting dressed up, it's common decency to salute him." That was about the extent of the rigors of military courtesy in that Air Force unit. *From an address by Marian Hargrove, author and humorist, before the Executives' Club of Chicago*

HAD NOT HEARD HIM BEFORE

It is, indeed, a privilege and a pleasure for me to meet with the business leadership of this great city. I never appear before a group to talk but that I am reminded of what happened to me one evening when I was invited to speak to the editors of the McGraw-Hill Publishing Company. There were about thirty or forty of them and as we were having dinner I turned to one of my associates and said to him, "As I look around I see many men I know, and I am just wondering if I have spoken to this group before."

My associate said very seriously, "I am sure that you have not, because if you had you wouldn't be here tonight." *Marriner S. Eccles, formerly chairman, Board of Governors of the Federal Reserve System, acknowledging an introduction as he began an address before the Executives' Club of Chicago*

THE HOUR IS LATE

The other day a preacher friend of mine told the story

of a little boy who awakened from his sleep close to midnight, and as he turned over in his bed he heard the big clock downstairs striking. He counted the strokes—nine, ten, eleven, twelve. It should have stopped then, but it didn't. It went on—thirteen, fourteen, fifteen, sixteen. Leaping from his bed he shouted to his mother: "Wake up, mom, it is later than it's ever been before." *Dr. Harold Blake Walker, minister, The First Presbyterian Church, Evanston, Illinois*

ONE MAN MUST LEAD

Turn back to British history, to the days just before Waterloo. Napoleon was on the march and England had come to the end of her rope. The credit of the nation was in danger, and panic was sweeping the people. Investors were dumping their securities to save themselves. Baron Rothschild believed that unless the panic could be halted, it would destroy England. He sat in a room adjacent to the stock exchange, giving orders to buy all the vital securities that were being dumped. One of his aides came in to report and Rothschild asked: "How long before the exchange closes for the day?" "Two hours," came the reply. "Two hours! I wonder if I can last that long." "Oh, Mr. Rothschild," his loyal aide replied, "you, too, must begin to sell. No one man can stem the tide today. Sell now so you may have something left when it is over. England will need your help tomorrow." Rothschild's shoulders straightened. "What a man can do for England tomorrow I know not. I know what one man can do today—buy." And historians are unanimous in saying that he saved England that day.

One man always has to lead, and one man can stand against the tide and change it if he will. A very small boy put it aptly once when he wanted to wear a gaudy pair of girl's mittens. "The boys aren't wearing mittens like that," his mother said. To which he replied: "They will after I wear them." We do not need to follow the fashion: we can set it. We do not need to be victims of the fearful mind; we can set the fashion with a trustful mind.

No one knows which way America will be led in the days to come. One thing, however, is clear. Doubt and fear, if they possess us, will be our doom; for

> "Our doubts are our traitors
> And make us lose the good we oft might win.
> By fearing to attempt."

If we doubt, we Christians cannot lead; we shall be led by men who do not doubt. We shall be led, for good or ill, by zealous men, possessed by an idea, who passionately believe what they teach. We shall be led by men who believe that the future belongs to their God or gods. We cannot live or lead on our doubts. *Dr. Harold Blake Walker, minister, The First Presbyterian Church, Evanston, Illinois*

The Greatest Freedom of All

We have one freedom left in this country, and it's the greatest freedom of all. To my way of thinking it's far greater than freedom from fear or want, or freedom of speech or assembly or press. It is the freedom to fail—the greatest freedom of all, without which no people are really free.

We are one of the few peoples of the world that still retain that freedom. We are one of the few people who are still free to fail. Nobody is going to guarantee that my business or yours is going to succeed. It's still up to *you*, as an individual. You're free to make mistakes; you're free to grow too fast; you're free to overextend yourself.

That's the way this country was built—on failures. Yes, it was—on failures. The failure of men with maybe a little too much vision, a little too much enthusiasm. If the men who shoved the railroads from Chicago across that vast expanse to the west coast had sat down and figured it out on an economical basis—population and what not —they would never have left home. But they had the guts and the daring to try. Most of those roads went through the wringer once, twice and three times, but because there was that freedom to fail, we opened up a great new country, with great opportunities, to millions of people. Just think what might have happened if there had been some sharp pencil expert in some bureau in Washington to say, "No, you can't try it. It isn't economically sound." *From an address by Arthur H. Motley, president of Parade Publications, Inc.*

THE COMMON MAN

The founders of America's free economic system had a great faith in the fellow called the "common man."

As a new decade of American history begins, this same common man in America finds himself in an uncommon era of social upheaval. The favor of the common man is sought by forces representing not just political parties, but different economic systems.

Those on the left wing say, "What is the world going to do for the common man?"

And those on the right ask, "What is the common man going to do for the world?"

Between these extremes is the middle way of freedom which asks only, "what is the common man going to do for himself?" *From an address by Carrol M. Shanks, president, The Prudential Insurance Company of America*

SECURITY

On a farm, when a man was young, maybe he milked 20 cows a day. When he got old—say, 65—maybe he could milk only 12, and when he got to be 80, if he was still in good health, maybe he just fed the cows, but he still had at least a part-time job.

In a modern plant, with progressive manufacturing and with conveyor assembly lines, a man who can't keep up his part of the work must be taken off that job. He can't do 60 per cent of it as he gets older because he would reduce the whole production down to 60 per cent, and if we did that in consideration for the old men—reducing the production of everybody in the group to their level—the whole country's production would be slowed down. Costs and prices would go up, prosperity would be lost, and all of us, including the old men, would not get along very well.

The feeling of insecurity on the part of the industrial worker in a city which has led to the public approval of pension plans merely points to the desire on the part of all for some similar economic security in old age. Men of good will in all countries, whether they be politicians, labor leaders, industrial executives, professional men or workmen, recognize the same desirable objective, namely, a stable society with a continuing improvement in the welfare of all the people. Everybody is for that, but there is a terrific difference of opinion as to the best means of achieving this desirable objective and how to measure the progress that is or is not being made toward this objective. Apparently these same differences of opinion exist regarding ways to take care of the aged. However, the desire for economic security in old age, in one form or another, is generally looked upon as one of the normal desires of enlightened human beings. *From an address by Charles E. Wilson, president, General Motors Corporation, before the Executives' Club of Chicago*

Why Rome Fell

For a thousand years the builders of the Roman empire labored diligently and effectively to bring light, freedom and justice into a world which had been barren of such things. Their armies and their navy welded into the Roman empire the major part of the known world and brought peace and law and order to its peoples. Commerce reached the highest degree of development ever known and brought to the Romans a standard of living not to be approached for another thousand years, and a generous measure of leisure and culture.

Then the sun began to set on Rome. Slowly but steadily the tide of empire ebbed and the glory and power that once was hers became faded and tarnished. The barbarians stormed her gates and the light which Rome had brought to the world dimmed and died. Not for another thousand years was the world to know anything but chaos and fear and suffering and ignorance. Why did Rome fall? As Franklin Bliss Snyder says "Rome fell because the nation collapsed spiritually; because a hardy race succumbed to the insidious poison of the idea that 'the government will do it' because rulers bought power at home and favor abroad by gifts of treasure and food; because integrity and thrift and industry gave place to corruption and waste and indolence; because the nation bartered its ancient heritage of hard-won-freedom for the specious ease and false security which a corrupt government promised it." *From an address by Paul C. Clovis, president, The Twentieth Century Press, Inc., Chicago*

MAKING UP YOUR MIND

The ability to decide—to make up your mind—to quit straddling—to choose wisely and courageously under any circumstances—is unquestionably one of the earmarks of greatness in men and women. It means the ability to choose between the wise and the foolish, between wasting time and using it wisely, between the safe and unsafe, the sound and the unsound, the good and the bad, the beautiful and the ugly, the virtues and the vulgarities of life. It is in a large measure the only true test of whether a man is educated, regardless of how many years he may have spent in college. What choices does he make of books, of friends, of ways of recreation? It is the only assurance that parents have relative to the conduct of their children when they cannot watch over them personally. Let them be certain that a son or daughter will choose wisely—will make the best decisions—and serenity comes to them in mind and heart.

Every minute and every hour of the day we are confronted by choices. What are you doing now to improve and use your talents? How will you use your time today —tonight—tomorrow and tomorrow night and so through the weeks, months and years? Of course you will make intelligent decisions when it is easy, but, honestly, have you the courage to do the intelligent thing when it is not, popular, or when it is inconvenient or possibly embarrassing? Will you decide to read some great literary work every week? Will you decide to take a constructive part in building up the community where you live? It is easier, you and I know, to let some one else do it and then criticize.

Many times decisions are not easy. For some men they have meant life itself. Livingstone dying in a Negro hut in Central Africa for his ideals; Mark Twain at sixty years of age bankrupt, shouldering his debts and starting out on a heart-breaking lecture tour to earn enough money to be out of debt in four years so he could start life all over again at the age of sixty-four; Abraham Lincoln carrying on his shoulders the terrible burden of a nation engaged in civil war, his methods criticized by his own party and his generals denouncing him—these men could testify to the price men pay for courageous decisions. Small minds, lazy minds, weak minds always take the easiest way—always make the easiest decision. In life, the line of least resistance is always the busiest boulevard.

In the last analysis, life is going to be the sum total of the decisions we have made. Nothing more—nothing less. We can make it a blind experience or a great adventure.

A university president says that one spring time he was in the north of Canada when the frost was breaking up and the roads were almost impassable. He comments that at one crossroad he saw this sign: "Take care which rut you choose; you will be in it for the next fifty miles." One would like to say that to every young man and woman. Take care the kind of life you choose. You will be in it for the next fifty years. Choose to live without vision, without courage, without depth and breadth and height to your life and it will be simply a blind experience. But make those decisions daily that give direction, meaning and character to life and it will be a great adventure. *From an address by Herbert V. Prochnow, vice-president, The First National Bank of Chicago*

A Mistake to Sell America Short

Here is a statement, quoted from a government report during a depression:

"Industry has been enormously developed, cities have been transformed, distances covered, and a new set of economic tools have been given in profusion to rich countries, and in a more reasonable amount to poorer ones. What is strictly necessary has been done oftentimes to superfluity. This full supply of economic tools to meet the wants of nearly all branches of commerce and industry is the most important factor in the present industrial depression. . . . There will be no room for a marked extension, such as has been witnessed during the last fifty years, or afford a remunerative employment of the vast amount of capital which has been created during that period. The day of large profits is probably past. There may be room for further intensive, but not extensive development of industry in the present area of civilization." That statement was made in 1886 by Carroll D. Wright, our first U.S. Commissioner of Labor.

Which merely goes to show that it is human to be mistaken and that you are likely to be mistaken when you sell America short. Let me call the roll of some of the goods we did not even know of, far less produced, back in 1886. Cream separators, diesel engines, pipe lines, electric stoves, washing machines, motion pictures, airplanes, automobiles, farm combines, tractors, fuel oil burners, radios, air conditioning and mechanical refrigeration; we had no rubber industry, no chemical industry to speak of, no plastics and no electronics.

Now think of the new opportunities these new industries provided to men with mechanical skills, for engineers and salesmen, for people with money to invest, and for enterprisers and managers with ability. Yes, there has been some technological unemployment as machines took the places of men, as new industries replaced old ones. But the 75,000 workers who lost their jobs in the carriage, wagon and sleigh industries because of the automobile, found half a million new opportunities in the automobile factories; the 15,000 who lost their jobs in the piano industries found more than 40,000 new openings in the radio and phonograph factories. And those who today predict that we've reached the end of our growth probably are again all wrong. *From an address by Willard Chevalier, executive assistant to the president, McGraw-Hill Publishing Company, New York City*

CRITICISM

Vice-President Barkley, then the majority leader in the Senate, was confronted with criticism because he could not satisfy at once all the demands which several of his colleagues were making. He said that his attitude toward criticism was like that of the farmer's dog who used to go to town with his master. While the farmer was busy, small boys would catch the dog and tie tin cans to its tail. The dog got so used to this that whenever he saw a tin can he backed right up to it. *From an address at Wesleyan University by Dean Acheson, Secretary of State*

FAITH, HOPE, AND CONFIDENCE

Some years ago I came across an article by a rather violent young man, about the age of the older among you of the graduating class, who was described in effusive terms by the editor as the spokesman of a skeptical generation. All doctrines of a personal God and of a life after death he dismissed as "cowardly fictions." Although he denied the natural goodness of man (a view which the last decade amply supports) he believed that somehow man will be able to work out his happiness for himself by his own courage and determination. We have heard a great deal recently about the new philosophy of atheistic existentialism (quite a mouthfilling phrase), and its gospel of despair that tells us that this is man's world alone, that there is no power that can help him extricate himself from its anguish and suffering. Man has only his ego; he must establish his dignity and worth himself. There is no God.

This is a large order which the human race will never be able to fill by its own strength alone. The average man understands better than some philosophers the internal contradiction that vitiates all doctrines of self-worship. In the modern phraseology of an eminent scientist, he knows that "the hypothesis of God gives a more reasonable interpretation of the world than any other." This University was founded in response to our divine thirst for something that will not perish; our craving for fellowship with the eternal which drives us to faith in an unknown permanence which in our innermost souls we know to be real and good. This Chapel stands today as the symbol of that truth and of the University's continued acceptance of it.

I submit that it is wholly natural and reasonable to yield one's destiny to someone, not a force or a tendency, but the Lord God Almighty, a being in personal relationship to each of us, of infinite goodness whose ways are not the ways of man but who will reveal His ways to us if we but listen and heed.

Here is the dynamism that democracy requires. The

ethics of the democratic way of life, which set the pattern by which peace and brotherhood can be achieved, stem straight from the Christian faith. To believe in it is to me so reasonable that I am at a loss to understand why an intelligent person will sometimes go to such extreme lengths to avoid such a simple hope and such a rational conclusion to an otherwise endless riddle.

"God is our refuge and strength (said the Psalmist), a very present help in time of trouble.

"Therefore will not we fear, though the earth be removed and though the mountains be carried into the midst of the sea.

"The Lord of Hosts is with us; the God of Jacob is our refuge."

This song of hope and confidence has come down through the centuries, as bright and gleaming today as when it was first composed. If America will make this psalms its own, if she will resolve to be worthy of the blessing it promises to those who merit it, our deepest anxieties for the future will be put to rest. *From an address by Dr. Harold Willis Dodds, president of Princeton University at a Princeton Baccalureate Service*

A DEFINITION THAT APPLIES TO MANY PERSON

An economist is rather widely defined as: A man who sometimes uses language to express thought, who frequently uses language to conceal thought, and who generally uses language instead of thought. *From an address by Dr. G. Rowland Collins, dean, Graduate School of Business Administration, New York University, New York*

JUST SIMMERING THROUGH LIFE

It was a great prophet, Paul, who said, "This *one* thing I do." In unmistakable terms he stated that his life was to have a singleness of purpose. *One* thing he would do.

"This day we sailed westward," were the simple words Columbus wrote in his book each day. How definite, how determined to do *one* thing. The crew might rebel, storms might come, but he had a single objective. Nothing was to interfere. And with that objective a new world was discovered and the history of mankind changed.

FACTS, FICTION, AND FABLES

Many of us would be great in some field, but we are unwilling to sacrifice everything to that one ambition. We dilly-dally with one thing or another, unwilling to pay the price demanded of giving up all for a single objective. Too many lives are like the man Voltaire described as an oven, always heating but never cooking anything. As Walt Whitman said, "I was simmering, simmering, simmering: Emerson brought me to a boil." Many of us in life may succeed to where we almost reach the boiling point. Nearly, you see, almost, but not quite.

The famous actor, Jefferson, spent a lifetime to become a great Rip Van Winkle; Webster spent thirty-six years on the single job of making a dictionary; Field crossed the ocean fifty times to lay a cable so men could talk across thousands of miles of water; Schumann-Heink's parents were so poor they could not buy her a good piano, but finally they got a dilapidated old instrument. For twenty years she fought off poverty to become one of the world's greatest singers. It is the slavery to a single idea or objective that has given to many a person of seemingly mediocre talent the ability of a genius.

Hand in hand with a determination to achieve greatness in a chosen field is the willingness to struggle through every kind of hardship. When we are confronted with the necessity of paying the price, we turn away.

Beethoven, the great musician, probably surpassed other musicians in his painstaking fidelity and persistent application. There is hardly a bar of his music that was not written and rewritten at least a dozen times. Gibbon wrote his autobiography nine times and was in his study every morning, summer and winter, at six o'clock; and yet young men and women wonder at the genius which could produce *The Decline and Fall of the Roman Empire*, upon which Gibbons worked twenty years. There are many of us who would envy the great master Josef Haydn who produced over 800 musical compositions and at the age of 66 years gave to the world that matchless oratorio *The Creation*. We envy his achievements, but we so often never look back to the days of his hardship. A Michelangelo worked seven long years decorating the Sistine Chapel with his "Creation" and the "Last Judgment." *One* thing they would do.

A leading magazine ridiculed Tennyson's first poems and consigned the young poet to temporary oblivion; Milton worked on *Paradise Lost* in a world he could not see; Balzac toiled in a lonely garret; *Pilgrim's Progress* was written in a Bedford jail; Robert Louis Stevenson wrote his greatest works when he was blind and sick.

No struggles in life, no strength. No fight, no fortitude. No crises, no courage. No suffering, no sympathy. No pain, no patience. *From an address by Herbert V. Prochnow, vice-president, The First National Bank of Chicago*

Shoes

Up in my little summer home in Vermont there are two little shoes hanging on the wall, and the toes of those shoes are kicked out. What would you give me for those shoes? The leather is not worth anything. But you try to buy those two shoes. You could not buy them for any price.

I had a little wiggling wonder one time crawling around my home, getting into everything, asking for scissors and cups and saucers and hot pokers and everything else. He just wore out the toes of those shoes, and there they have been for many years, up in that little room in my summer cottage: Two little pieces of leather.

But there is memory, there is companionship, there are lovely Christmases, and high school and college ambitions, all tucked away in two little shoes with the toes kicked out. *Dr. Allen A. Stockdale, head of the Speakers' Bureau of the National Association of Manufacturers*

The Common Basis of Our Faiths

There can be no doubt that the Hebraic-Christian tradition with its emphasis on the sanctity of each human soul was one of the mainsprings of the development of democracy in this land of pioneers.... The moral basis of our culture rests on the dual postulate of the sacrasanct nature of the individual and the duty of each person to do unto others as he would have others do unto him.

I am well aware that up to a point a satisfactory system of ethics can be derived solely from a consideration of the welfare of the community. Granted certain premises as to the nature of the free society we wish to perpetuate on this continent, definitions of right and wrong can be formulated in terms of the social consequences of an individual's deeds. I am the last one to minimize the importance of emphasizing this broad ethical basis of our culture. But most of us will not be satisfied unless we dig deeper to find a more solid foundation. To be sure, the agnostic and the liberal Protestant, for example, can go hand in hand in stressing the Christian virtues; the one privately justifying the ethical teaching by reference to the growth of a "normal" individual and a smooth-working society, the other by his belief in the significance of his own interpretation of the Christian dogmas. In most situations the ideal behavior of an American citizen will be identically assessed by these two men. But it is not difficult to envisage cases where the divergence in basic philosophies leads to different judgments. May I give an illustration of what I mean.

Let us imagine two or three individuals on a raft or a desert island with death certain in their eyes within a few days or weeks. Under these conditions which by definition are isolated and mortally terminal can an individual's conduct be said to be right or wrong? Where by hypothesis there are no social consequences of action, is there any standard of reference for what occurs? Is betrayal of a friend or even murder under these highly unusual circumstances to be regarded only as a physiological reflex and described as merely pleasing or offensive to one's taste? Is behavior under these conditions to be judged as right or wrong or merely regarded as similar to that of an insane person or an animal?

To my mind these questions probe deeply into a man's outlook upon the world. They throw a revealing light on the common denominator which unites many Americans of otherwise highly divergent views. For I am convinced that all but a very small number of honest and intelligent citizens of this nation of all ages will answer these questions almost instinctively in just one way. They will affirm that the universe is somehow so constructed that a sane individual's acts are subject to moral judgments under all circumstances and under all conditions. The nature of the "somehow" is the door by which one passes into a vast edifice of philosophical and theological discussion—a mansion in which there are many chambers.

The reasons given for a belief in the significance of the actions of even an isolated individual would be many; but whether Protestant, Catholic or Jew, active church member or non-conformist, almost every American believes that human life is sacred. This fact is the answer to those Cassandras who would have us believe that there is no spiritual unity in the United States. When face to face with the question, is the dignity of man determined solely by the fact that man is a social animal, we automatically would say no. In short, our practical democratic creed turns out on analysis to be an affirmation of the common basis of our many faiths. *From a baccalaureate address by James Bryant Conant, president, Harvard University, at Harvard University, Cambridge, Massachusetts*

CREATIVE ENDEAVOR

In his book, *Possession*, written some twenty years ago, Louis Bromfield makes one of his characters, a young man of twenty-one out in the Middle West, say: "My grandfathers set out into this wilderness to conquer and subdue it. It was a land filled with savages and adventure. I too must have my chance. I am of a race of pioneers but I no longer have any frontier." In that statement was voiced the yeasty restlessness of youth following World War I. It was in those days we talked much about "flaming youth" and the "revolt of youth."

Some ten years passed, and in 1936 *Fortune* took a survey of student opinion. We quote from its findings: "The present day college generation is fatalistic . . . the investigator is struck by the dominant and pervasive color of a generation that will not stick its neck out. It keeps its shirt on . . . its chin up and its mouth shut. If we take the mean average to be the truth, it is a cautious, subdued, unadventurous generation, unwilling to storm heaven, afraid to make a fool of itself, unable to dramatize its predicament. It may be likened to a very intelligent turtle. . . . The turtle has security and . . . security is the *summum bonum* of the present college generation. . . . Yearners for security do not set foot on Everest or discover the Mountains of the Moon."

Whether such a generalization was accurate, I do not venture to say. But the suspicion lurks in my mind that the depression of the 1930's did help to transform the frontier-seeking adventuresomeness of the 1920's into a security-consciousness.

And what has been the effect on youth of World War II? Perhaps it is too early to tell, but certainly ours is a security-conscious generation. Nations and individuals are living on the defensive. And a defensive mood never develops very creative or progressive living. We need to break through our present cautious patterns of personal and public policies and do some dynamic adventuring. There is no zest or virtue in goodness unless it exceed the righteousness of the merely respectable. There is no thrill or satisfaction in work until it has a pilgrim pioneering spirit.

To be sure, the "brave new world" dreamed by the youth of the 1920's is now a broken old world. But there is more real achievement in recreating the old than in creating the new. To take an old farm as Mr. Bromfield has done, and make it into a new adventure of living; to take an old community and make it a frontier of new social experience; to take an old broken embittered world and transform it into a place of hope and promise—such are some of the goals which still beckon the pilgrim spirits. The golden spur of creative endeavor is still available.
From a baccalaureate address by Dr. Ralph W. Sockman, minister, Christ Church, New York City, at New York University, New York

Keep America Close to God

My friends, I am a priest of God, but I speak also as a citizen. You, as you graduate tonight, go forth as citizens into the civil community, but without exception you are the children of God and you are responsive to the things of the spirit. I need not ask you to remember the classroom lessons you have learned at Marquette, but I do ask you to retain always the sense acquired here of the true place of religion in education, of piety in patriotism, of spiritual values in social stability. I beg you be vigilant against those who are attempting to drive the spirit of religion out of education. A nation is cradled in its homes, but it is made in its schools. Unless God be present in both the home and the school, college and university, I know not how He can enter the national life. This only thing I know: Reason, revelation, and history all agree that a nation without God is a nation doomed. Blessed is the nation whose Lord is God. Keep close to God yourselves—keep America close to God. Then you shall have faith and freedom—life, liberty, and happiness—all these, and heaven, too. *From a commencement address by the Most Reverend Richard J. Cushing, D.D., archbishop of Boston, Massachusetts, at Marquette University*

THE BRIDEGROOM

As a minister, I had a little custom of putting my hands on their shoulders and saying: "Mr. So-and-so, this is your wife," and then he takes his wedding kiss. He always remembers that if he does not remember another part of the ceremony.

Down in Boston I was marrying a great big fellow who stood six feet three, and he was the most pathetic looking bridegroom you ever saw, eyes going around like a merry-go-round, knees shaking, hands spread out like a fish's tail. There I was getting him married, and when I came to that little touching part when I put my hand on his shoulder and I said: "Mr. So-and-so, this is your wife," he reached out weakly, took her by the hand, and said: "I am very glad to meet you." *From an address by Dr. Allen A. Stockdale*

THE DETERMINATION TO KNOW

Everyone who has read many of the biographical stories of the lives of great men must have asked himself this question many times, "Why do some persons succeed and others fail?"

There are a great many reasons for success and failure. Some persons work; others loaf. Some have minds open for new ideas; others have closed minds. Some are inquisitive, which leads them to invention and discovery; others lack imagination entirely. Some have great courage. A few are lucky.

However, there is one major idea that seems to dominate many great lives. It is the relentless determination to master some one occupation or profession. One would probably not be far wide of the mark if he said that this

FACTS, FICTION, AND FABLES 343

is the single greatest reason for achievement of a high order in the lives of men and women. It means the willpower and the high vision which drive a human being through unbelievable obstacles to achieve a seemingly impossible goal, such as, becoming the greatest authority on cancer, constitutional law, banking, transportation, or chemistry. It is the old story of Edison working nine years on an electric lamp or making 10,000 experiments on the storage battery. Not one person in a thousand would pursue a goal with such determination. Thus there are only a few Edisons. Voltaire once said, "Too many of us are like an old-fashioned oven. We are always heating, but never cooking anything."

Does this idea apply to men and women in every occupation and profession?

I believe it applies without exception. It drove Columbus to discover a new world, despite storms and the mutiny of a crew. It drove Webster to work thirty-six years on a dictionary, and led Cyrus Field to cross the ocean fifty times to lay one cable so men could talk across three thousand miles of water. It took possession of a young man named Disraeli, who was determined to be Prime Minister of England, and helped him to push his way up through the lower classes to the top. Disraeli was ridiculed and hissed down in the House of Commons when he made his first speech, and yet with his fierce determination to reach his goal, he became one of England's most distinguished Prime Ministers.

The Mayos of Rochester, Minnesota, visiting surgeons over the world to learn about new developments in surgery to save human lives, and Billy Mitchell going through the tragedy of a court martial to help the United States to the forefront in aviation are examples of this determination for leadership.

What leads men on to strive for these great objectives?

An old professor once illustrated how this desire to master some field takes possession of a person. He placed a small circle on the blackboard and said, "This small circle represents the knowledge an average man has of his occupation or profession. As he looks out from this little circle of knowledge, he doesn't see much that he doesn't know, because the circumference of his knowledge is too small. As he applies himself, the circle of his knowledge steadily grows larger and larger, and he sees more and more that he doesn't know. Incidentally, he tends to become less conceited.

"Finally, when he becomes distinguished in his field, the circle of his knowledge is very large. Now he looks out from the circumference of that great circle and sees how much he doesn't know. That realization drives him harder and harder to greater and greater achievements, in his effort to master his field. Thus he becomes a great authority and we have a great life." Most men and women of real distinction, like Lincoln, Newton, Pupin, Einstein, Kreisler, and the Mayos tend to become humble as they compare their achievements with the great accomplishments that are still possible. *From an address by Herbert V. Prochnow, vice-president, The First National Bank of Chicago*

Thomas Jefferson

This is the man who as a member of the legislature of Virginia introduced five bills for human liberty—a bill for the freedom of property from the law of primogeniture, which was a hang-over from the English aristocracy where the oldest son got nearly all of the estate; a bill for the freedom of estates from the entailments that tied up property for years and years; a bill for the freedom of the slaves; a bill for the freedom of the mind, for the establishments of public schools; a bill for the freedom of the soul, a bill calling for the separation of church and state.

This is the man who before he was old enough to qualify for the presidency of the United States wrote the Declaration of Independence. This is the man who was a minister to France, Secretary of State in George Washington's cabinet, Vice-President with John Adams, President for eight years. And then having served two terms as President he borrowed enough money to get back to his home in Monticello, and for seventeen more years he dreamed dreams. He dreamed the University of Virginia into being. He designed its architecture and he saw that on the rotunda of the main building these words of Jesus should be placed: "You shall know the truth, and the truth shall make you free."

This was indeed a remarkable man. He was the most versatile man that was ever in the White House. He was an inventor. He invented the "Murphy bed," although he did not call it by that name. He invented a flexible camp stool. He was the greatest bookman of his day, and had the finest private library, costing him nearly $50,000. He was an expert horseman. . . .

When he was an old man Thomas Jefferson prepared some maxims for his grandchildren. Here are a few of them: "Adore God." "Love your neighbor as yourself, and your country more than yourself." "No man regrets having eaten too little."

On July 4th, 1826, just fifty years after the proclamation of the Declaration of Independence, this great old man stirred in his bed at Monticello, and those who bent over him heard him say: "Now lettest thy servant depart in peace." And so he passed away. And about the same time, in Braintree, Massachusetts, John Adams stirred in his death bed and murmured, "Thomas Jefferson still lives." "Thomas Jefferson still lives," is a phrase that we may well repeat. For Thomas Jefferson believed in the people; believed in the right of a majority to decide great issues. But he did not believe in the people unless the people were informed. He believed that you can trust the masses of the people if the people know. Along with this man's dreams of a democracy is his tremendous emphasis upon education.

ABRAHAM LINCOLN

Mr. Lincoln could not have carried on through the Civil War years had it not been for his sense of humor. Every now and then somebody says to me: "What do you consider the most humorous story about Mr. Lincoln?"

I have one answer to that question. There is one that is in a class by itself. It happened during the second year of his Presidency. There was a small reception of the White House. Mr. Lincoln came into the room where the people were gathered and laid his stovepipe hat on a chair. A little later a rather large woman sat down on it. When Mr. Lincoln came back into the room everybody arose, and Mr. Lincoln saw his hat flat as a pancake. He retrieved the hat, looked at it, and then said to the woman: "My dear madam, I could have told you this wouldn't fit you before you tried it on."

Nobody but Abraham Lincoln would ever have been the author of humor like that. It is that kind of humor, whimsical and ever so laughable, that crops out from time to time. He once said that he supposed that if Minnehaha meant "laughing water," then "Minneboohoo" meant "weeping water. . . ."

Once at a reception in Washington an enthusiastic Lincoln follower shook hands with Mr. Lincoln, and said: "I believe in God and believe in Abraham Lincoln." Mr. Lincoln laughed and said: "My friend, you are just about half right. . . ."

I have never seen anything in the way of a tribute to Mr. Lincoln that surpasses . . . a brief speech which was made by a young congressman from Kansas named Homer Hoch, a newspaperman, the son of Former Governor Hoch of Kansas. . . . He said: "There is no new thing to be said of Lincoln. There is no new thing to be said of the mountains, or of the sea, or of the stars. The years go their way, but the same old mountains lift their granite shoulders above the drifting clouds; the same mysterious sea beats upon the shore; and the same silent stars keep holy vigil above a tired world. But to mountains and sea and stars men turn forever in unwearied homage. And thus with Lincoln. For he was mountain in grandeur of soul, he was sea in deep undervoice of mystic loneliness, he was star in steadfast purity of purpose and of service. And he abides." *The two excerpts above are from an address by Dr. Edgar De Witt Jones*

THE PROGRESS OF MAN

If you look ahead you find at the present time more people carefully trained, supplied with better tools than ever before for the search for new knowledge.

The necessary consequence is that the future will find more rapidly growing understanding of the world, and with that presumably more and more new developments. I do not see any escape from it.

Perhaps I can put that graphically if I use the historian's device of compressing the time scale. Let us say that we will compress it by a million-fold. On that basis a million years becomes a year; a century becomes but an hour. And if you take that type of time scale you can look back a year or two ago to the first primitive man picking up an odd-shaped stick or stone and using it as a tool; finding that sounds take on meaning; and language appears.

About a month ago one of these beings has learned to shape their sticks and stones carefully to fit their needs, and by last week you see the cavemen in their caves drawing diagrams of the animals. By day before yesterday these drawings have got to the stage that they make a primitive type of writing; and by yesterday the alphabet has appeared. Speaking as if it were noon today, it would be about yesterday afternoon that the Greeks are developing their notable art and science; the dawn of Christianity is at dinnertime last evening; and then there is the Roman Empire which at midnight last night falls, and darkness shuts the picture off for a few hours; until 8:15 this morning Galileo, at the Tower of Pisa lets drop the cannon balls and they fall at the same speed, and he starts this interesting experiment which we call modern science. That was 8:15 this morning. By half past ten the first steam engine had been developed; by 11:00 the lights of electricity, and magnetism were discovered by Faraday and his collaborators; which by 11:30 brought us the incandescent light and the telegraph and the telephone. By twenty minutes to twelve we had the telephone; and about a quarter of an hour ago the automobile came into use; and about five minutes ago we began to have the air mail carried over the country; and within the last minute we have had radio programs by short wave making the whole world a unit.

Well, now, if you follow that picture as I have been drawing it you can see how a very slow progress has kept on continuously. Never going down, occasional hesitations, but on the whole rapidly increasing in the rate of growth of knowledge and means of doing things. *From an address by Dr. Arthur H. Compton, distinguished scientist*

Chapter XV

IMPROVING CONVERSATION AND SPEECHES BY READING

ADDISON said that "Books are the legacies that genius leaves to mankind, to be delivered down from generation to generation, as presents to those that are yet unborn." If one is to have a mind that is rich in thoughts which are worth expressing, it is necessary to feed the mind with the thinking of the great geniuses of the past. "Reading," said Bacon, "makes a full man."

It is a safe assertion that the distinguished men and women of our time are those who read great literature. By reading they increase their wisdom, add to their understanding of the history of mankind, and develop the judgment and ability to deal more intelligently with the problems of our age.

In this book we have considered many tools by which to make conversation and speeches more effective. Some readers will learn how to use a few of these tools well. Other readers will learn to use many of these tools to their great advantage. But those readers who desire to approach perfection in their daily conversation and in their speeches will not only study the simple tools but will also spend countless hours in reading the best books. In the last analysis, great conversation and great speeches result from great thoughts. And great thoughts are stimulated by constant association with the written work of the geniuses and great minds of all time.

Ten, fifteen, or twenty minutes of good reading on an average daily will help to enrich one's mind. "The treasured wealth of the world," as Thoreau has described books, is yours if you desire it. We repeat—*if you desire it*.

In the pages which follow there are presented first the lists of great books prepared by the Great Books Foundation, which grew out of the University of Chicago's leadership in this field. Then there follows the list of great books prepared by St. John's College in Annapolis. St. John's College has long been known for the particular books upon which its curriculum is based.

There is likewise included a list of *One Hundred of the Best Novels* prepared by the Free Public Library of Newark, New Jersey. The Newark Library says, "this list does not aim to include the one hundred best novels. About forty of the novels are acknowledged classics; the remaining sixty include some of the more noteworthy later novels and others which were added to give variety and to insure that no one consulting the list would fail to find titles of at least a few books that he had read and enjoyed. One may live well and be happy and read no stories; but most are wiser, happier and worth more to their fellows for the novels they have read."

Finally there is included in this chapter a list of the one hundred outstanding books of 1924-44, prepared by Dr. Henry Seidel Canby in collaboration with the Editors of *Life*. This list appeared in the August 14, 1944, issue of *Life*. Dr. Canby is widely known as an author, editor, and critic. He is chairman of the editorial board of *The Saturday Review of Literature* and has for many years been a member of the faculty of Yale University.

LIST OF GREAT BOOKS OF THE GREAT BOOKS FOUNDATION
OF THE UNIVERSITY OF CHICAGO

The First Course

Opening Session: Introduction and Exemplary Reading of the *Declaration of Independence; The Bible*: I Kings, 21: II Samuel, 11, 12

Plato: *Apology, Crito*

Plato: *Republic*, Books I-II

Thucydides: *History*, Book I, Chaps. 1, 2, 3, 5; Book II, Chaps. 6, 7; Book V, Chap. 17

Aristophanes: *Lysistrata, Birds, Clouds*

Aristotle: *Ethics*, Book I

Aristotle: *Politics*, Book I

Plutarch: "Lycurgus," "Numa," and "Comparison": "Alexander" and "Caesar."

St. Augustine: *Confessions*, Books I-VIII

St. Thomas: *Treatise on Law (Summa Theologica,* Books I-II, QQ. 90-97)
Machiavelli: *The Prince*
Montaigne: Selected *Essays*: "That the Taste of Good, etc.," Book I, Chap. 14; "Of Custom," Book I, Chap. 22; "Of Pedantry," Book I, Chap. 24; "Of the Education of Children," Book I, Chap. 25; "It Is Folly, etc.," Book I, Chap. 26; "Of Cannibals," Book I, Chap. 30
Shakespeare: *Hamlet*
Locke: *Of Civil Government* (second essay)
Rousseau: *The Social Contract,* Books I-II
Federalist Papers: Nos. 1-10, 15, 31; 47, 51, 68-71 (along with the Constitution)
Smith: *The Wealth of Nations,* Book I, Chaps. 1-9
Marx: *Communist Manifesto*

The Second Course

Homer: *Odyssey*
Herodotus: *History,* Books I and II
Aeschylus: *House of Atreus* (Agamemnon, Furies, Libation Bearers)
Sophocles: *Oedipus Rex, Antigone*
Aristotle: *Poetics*
Plato: *Meno*
Aristotle: *Ethics,* Books II, III (Chaps. 5-12), VI (Chaps. 9-13)
Lucretius: *De Rerum Natura,* Books I-IV
Aurelius: *Meditations*
Hobbes: *Leviathan,* Part 1
Milton: *Areopagitica*
Swift: *Gulliver's Travels*
Pascal: *Pensees*: Selections
Rousseau: *Discourse on Inequality; Treatise on Political Economy*
Kant: *Metaphysical Elements of Ethics*
Nietzsche: *Beyond Good and Evil*
Mill: *Representative Government,* Chaps. 1-6
Tawney: *Religion and the Rise of Capitalism*

The Third Course

Aeschylus: *Prometheus Bound; Bible,* The Book of Job
Plato: *Symposium*

Aristotle: *Politics*, Books III-V
Euclid: *Elements*, Book I
Aristotle: *De Interpretatione*, Chaps. 1-4
Lucian: *Selections*
St. Thomas: *De Magistro*
Song of the Nibelung and the Volsungs
Calvin: *Institutes*, Book II, Chap. 2, "Man's Present State"; Book IV, Chap. 20, "On Civil Government"
Shakespeare: *Macbeth*
Milton: *Paradise Lost*
Locke: *Essay Concerning Human Understanding*, Chaps. 1-3, 9-11; Book III
Voltaire: *Candide*
Lavoisier: *Elements*, Book I
Gibbon: *The Decline and Fall of the Roman Empire*, Chaps. 15, 16
Mill: *On Liberty*
Thoreau: *Civil Disobedience; A Plea for Captain John Brown*
Freud: *The Origin and Development of Psychoanalysis*

LIST OF GREAT BOOKS OF ST. JOHN'S COLLEGE
(In Chronological Order)

Homer: *Iliad* and *Odyssey*
Aeschylus: *Oresteia*
Herodotus: *History*
Sophocles: *Oedipus Rex, Oedipus at Colonus, Antigone*
Hippocrates: *Ancient Medicine* and *Airs, Waters, and Places*
Euripides: *Medea, Hippolytus, The Trojan Women*
Thucydides: *History of the Peloponnesian War*
Aristophanes: *Frogs, Clouds, Birds*
Aristarchus: *On the Sizes and Distances of the Sun and Moon*
Plato: *Dialogues*
Aristotle: *Organon, Poetics, Physics, Politics, Ethics, Metaphysics, De Anima*
Archimedes: *Selected Works*
Euclid: *Elements*
Apollonius: *Conics*
Cicero: *On Duties*

Lucretius: *On the Nature of Things*
Virgil: *Aeneid*
The Bible
Epictetus: *Moral Discourses*
Nicomachus: *Introduction to Arithmetic*
Plutarch: *Lives*
Tacitus: *The History, The Annals*
Ptolemy: *Mathematical Composition (Almagest)*
Lucian: *True History*
Galen: *On the Natural Faculties*
Plotinus: *Enneads*
Augustine: *Confessions, On Music, Concerning the Teacher*
Justinian: *Institutes*
Song of Roland
Saga of Burnt Njal
Grosseteste: *On Light*
Bonaventure: *On the Reduction of the Arts to Theology*
Aquinas: *On Being and Essence, Treatise on God, Treatise on Man*
Dante: *Divine Comedy*
Chaucer: *Canterbury Tales*
Oresme: *On the Breadths of Forms*
Pico della Mirandola: *On the Dignity of Man*
Leonardo: *Note Books*
Machiavelli: *The Prince*
Erasmus: *In Praise of Folly*
Rabelais: *Gargantua*
Copernicus: *On the Revolutions of the Spheres*
Calvin: *Institutes*
Luther: *The Liberty of a Christian Man*
Montaigne: *Essays*
Gilbert: *On the Loadstone*
Cervantes: *Don Quixote*
Shakespeare: *Plays*
Francis Bacon: *Novum Organum*
Kepler: *Epitome of Astronomy*
Harvey: *On the Motion of the Heart*
Galileo: *Two New Sciences*
Descartes: *Geometry, Discourse on Method, Meditations*

IMPROVING CONVERSATION AND SPEECHES 353

Hobbes: *Leviathan*
Boyle: *Sceptical Chymist*
Moliere: *Tartuffe*
Pascal: *Pensees*
Milton: *Paradise Lost*
Racine: *Phedre*
Grotius: *Law of War and Peace*
Spinoza: *Ethics, Theological-Political Treatise*
Newton *Principia Mathematica*
Locke: *Second Treatise on Civil Government*
Huygens: *Treatise on Light*
Berkeley: *Principles of Human Knowledge*
Leibniz: *Discourse on Metaphysics, Monadology*
Vico: *Scienza Nuova*
Swift: *Gulliver's Travels*
Hume: *Treatise of Human Nature*
Montesquieu: *Spirit of Laws*
Fielding: *Tom Jones*
Voltaire: *Candide, Micromegas*
Rousseau: *Social Contract*
Gibbon: *Decline and Fall of the Roman Empire*
Smith: *Wealth of Nations*
Kant: *Critique of Pure Reason*
Constitution of the United States
Federalist Papers
Bentham: *Principles of Morals and Legislation*
Lavoisier: *Treatise on Chemistry*
Malthus: *Principles of Population*
Dalton: *A New System of Chemical Philosophy*
Hegel: *Philosophy of History*
Fourier: *Analytical Theory of Heat*
Goethe: *Faust*
Lobachevski: *Theory of Parallels*
Faraday: *Experimental Researches in Electricity*
Peacock: *Treatise on Algebra*
Boole: *Laws of Thought*
Virchow: *Cellular Pathology*
Mill: *On Liberty*
Darwin: *Origin of Species*
Bernard: *Introduction to Experimental Medicine*
Mendel: *Experiments in Plant Hybridization*
Riemann: *Hypotheses of Geometry*

Dostoevski: *The Brothers Karamazov, The Possessed*
de Tocqueville: *Democracy in America*
Marx: *Capital*
Tolstoi: *War and Peace*
Dedekind: *Essays on Numbers*
Maxwell: *Electricity and Magnetism*
Kierkegaard: *Philosophical Fragments*
Melville: *Moby Dick*
Flaubert: *Madame Bovary*
Ibsen: *Ghosts, Rosmersholm*
Joule: *Scientific Papers*
James: *Principles of Psychology, Essays in Pragmatism*
Freud: *Studies in Hysteria, The Interpretation of Dreams*
Cantor: *Transfinite Numbers*
Hilbert: *Foundations of Geometry*
Poincare: *Science and Hypothesis*
Russell: *Principles of Mathematics*
Nietzsche: *Beyond Good and Evil*

THE NEWARK, NEW JERSEY, PUBLIC LIBRARY LIST OF ONE HUNDRED OF THE BEST NOVELS

Allen: *Anthony Adverse*
Asch: *The Nazarene*
Austen: *Pride and Prejudice*
Baker: *Young Man with a Horn*
Balzac: *Magic Skin*
Barrie: *Sentimental Tommy*
Bennett: *Old Wives' Tale*
Blackmore: *Lorna Doone*
Boyd: *Roll River*
Bronte: *Jane Eyre*
Buchan: *Adventures of Richard Hannay*
Buck: *Good Earth*
Bulwer-Lytton: *Last Days of Pompeii*
Butler: *Way of All Flesh*
Canfield: *Seasoned Timber*
Cather: *My Antonia*
Chase: *Windswept*
Collins: *Moonstone*
Conrad: *Lord Jim*
Cooper: *Last of the Mohicans*

Cozzens: *Just and the Unjust*
Crane: *Red Badge of Courage*
Dane: *Broome Stages*
Defoe: *Robinson Crusoe*
Delafield: *Diary of a Provincial Lady*
De Morgan: *Alice-for-Short*
Dickens: *David Copperfield*
Dickens: *Tale of Two Cities*
Dostoevcki: *Brothers Karamazov*
Doyle: *Hound of the Baskervilles*
Dumas: *Count of Monte Cristo*
Du Maurier, Daphne: *Rebecca*
Du Maurier, Gerald: *Peter Ibbetson*
Eliot: *Adam Bede*
Ferber: *Cimarron*
Feuchtwanger: *Paris Gazette*
Field: *Time out of Mind*
Forester: *Captain Horatio Hornblower*
Forster: *Passage to India*
Galsworthy: *Forsyte Saga*
Gaskell: *Cranford*
Glasgow: *In This Our Life*
Golding: *Magnolia Street*
Goodrich: *Delilah*
Gulbranssen: *Beyond Sing the Woods*
Hardy: *Tess of the D'Urbervilles*
Hawthorne: *Scarlet Letter*
Hemingway: *For Whom the Bell Tolls*
Hergesheimer: *Java Head*
Hilton: *Lost Horizon*
Hindus: *To Sing with the Angels*
Holme: *Splendid Fairing*
Howells: *Rise of Silas Lapham*
Hudson: *Green Mansions*
Hugo: *Les Miserables*
James: *The American*
Kipling: *Kim*
Knight: *This Above All*
Lewis: *Arrowsmith*
Llewellyn: *How Green Was My Valley*
London: *Call of the Wild*
Mann: *Magic Mountain*

Marquand: *Late George Apley*
Maugham: *Of Human Bondage*
Melville: *Moby Dick*
Meredith: *Richard Feverel*
Mitchell: *Gone with the Wind*
Mulock: *John Halifax, Gentleman*
Nathan: *Portrait of Jennie*
Priestley: *Good Companions*
Rawlings: *Yearling*
Reade: *Cloister and the Hearth*
Rolvaag: *Giants in the Earth*
Sackville-West: *All Passion Spent*
Saint-Exupery: *Night Flight*
Santayana: *Last Puritan*
Sayers: *Nine Tailors*
Scott: *Quentin Durward*
Seghers: *Seventh Cross*
Sharp: *Nutmeg Tree*
Sinclair: *Mary Olivie*
Steinbeck: *Grapes of Wrath*
Stern: *Matriarch Chronicles*
Stevenson: *Treasure Island*
Stockton: *Casting Away of Mrs. Lecks and Mrs. Aleshine*
Tarkington: *Seventeen*
Thackeray: *Vanity Fair*
Tolstoy: *Anna Karenina*
Tolstoy: *War and Peace*
Trollope: *Warden*
Twain: *Tom Sawyer*
Turgenev: *Fathers and Sons*
Undset: *Kristin Lavransdatter*
Walpole: *Rogue Herries*
Wells: *History of Mr. Polly*
Werfel: *Forty Days of Musa Dagh*
Wharton: *Ethan Frome*
Wister: *The Virginian*
Wolfe: *Look Homeward, Angel*
Woolf: *To the Lighthouse*

THE 100 OUTSTANDING BOOKS OF 1924-44

A list prepared by Dr. Henry Seidel Canby in collaboration with the Editors of *Life*. The list appeared in the August 14, 1944, issue of *Life*.

Adams, James T.	*The Epic of America*
Allen, Hervey	*Anthony Adverse*
Anderson, Sherwood	*Dark Laughter*
Asch, Sholem	*The Apostle*
Auden, W. H.	*Poems*
Beard, C. A.	*The Republic*
Beers, Thomas	*The Mauve Decade*
Benet, Stephen	*John Brown's Body*
Boyd, James	*Drums*
Brooks, Van Wyck	*The Flowering of New England, 1815-1865*
Buck, Pearl	*Dragon Seed*
Buck, Pearl	*The Good Earth*
Burnham, James	*The Managerial Revolution*
Caldwell, Erskine	*Tobacco Road*
Cather, Willa	*Death Comes for the Archbishop*
Cather, Willa	*Shadow on the Rock*
Churchill, Winston	*Blood, Sweat and Tears*
Davenport, Marcia	*The Valley of Decision*
Day, Clarence	*Life with Father*
Dewey, John	*Logic*
Dos Passos, John	*U.S.A.*
Dreiser, Theodore	*An American Tragedy*
Eliot, T. S.	*Four Quarters*
Farrell, James T.	*Studs Lonigan*
Faulkner, William	*Sanctuary*
Ferber, Edna	*Show Boat*
Fitzgerald, F. Scott	*The Great Gatsby*
Forster, E. M.	*A Passage to India*
Freeman, Douglas S.	*R. E. Lee*
Frost, Robert	*Poems*
Galsworthy, John	*Swan Song*
Glasgow, Ellen	*Barren Ground*
Gunther, John	*Inside Europe*
Hellman, Lillian	*Plays*

Hemingway, Ernest	*A Farewell to Arms*
Hemingway, Ernest	*For Whom the Bell Tolls*
Hilton, James	*Goodbye, Mr. Chips*
Hitler, Adolph	*Mein Kampf*
Hogben, L. T.	*Mathematics for the Million*
Housman, A. E.	*The Collected Poems*
Joyce, James	*Finnegans Wake*
Jeffers, Robinson	*Roan Stallion*
Koestler, Arthur	*Darkness at Noon*
Lardner, Ring	*Round Up*
Lawrence, D. H.	*The Plumed Serpent*
Lawrence, T. E.	*Seven Pillars of Wisdom*
Lewis, Sinclair	*Dodsworth*
Lewis, Sinclair	*Arrowsmith*
Lindsay, Vachel	*Every Soul Is a Circus*
Llewellyn, Richard	*How Green Was My Valley*
Lippmann, Walter	*A Preface to Morals*
Mann, Thomas	*The Magic Mountain*
Mann, Thomas	*Joseph the Provider*
Marquand, John P.	*H. M. Pulham, Esq.*
Millay, E. St. Vincent	*Wine From These Grapes*
Milne, A. A.	*When We Were Very Young*
Mitchell, Margaret	*Gone With the Wind*
Morison, S. E.	*Admiral of the Ocean Sea*
Nathan, Robert	*One More Spring*
Nordhoff and Hall	*Mutiny on the Bounty*
Odets, Clifford	*Plays*
O'Neill, Eugene	*Strange Interlude*
Porter, Katherine A.	*Flowering Judas*
Priestly, J. B.	*The Good Companions*
Proust, Marcel	*Remembrance of Thing Past*
Rawlings, Marjorie	*The Yearling*
Remarque, Erich	*All Quiet on the Western Front*
Richter, Conrad	*The Sea of Grass*
Roberts, Elizabeth M.	*The Time of Man*
Roberts, Kenneth	*Northwest Passage*
Robinson, E. A.	*Tristram*
Sinclair, Upton	*Dragon's Teeth*
Saint-Exupery	*Wind, Sand and Stars*

Saroyan, William	*The Human Comedy*
Smith, Betty	*A Tree Grows in Brooklyn*
Smith, Lillian	*Strange Fruit*
Steinbeck, John	*Of Mice and Men*
Steinbeck, John	*The Grapes of Wrath*
Santayana, George	*The Last Puritan*
Salten, Felix	*Bambi*
"Saki"	*Short Stories*
Sandburg, Carl	*Abraham Lincoln*
Spender, Stephen	*Poems*
Stuart, Jesse	*Man with a Bull-Tongue Plow*
Tarkington, Booth	*Kate Fennigate*
Tomlinson, H. M.	*Gallion's Reach*
Undset, Sigrid	*Kristin Lavransdatter*
Van Loon, H. W.	*Lives*
Welles, Sumner	*The Time for Decision*
Werfel, Franz	*The Song of Bernadette*
West, Rebecca	*Black Lamb and Gray Falcon*
Westcott, Glenway	*The Grandmothers*
Wharton, Edith	*The Old Maid*
Wilder, Thornton	*The Bridge of San Luis Rey*
Wolfe, Thomas	*Of Time and the River*
Woolf, Virginia	*Mrs. Dalloway*
Wright, Richard	*Native Son*
Wylie, Elinor	*Last Poems*
Young, Stark	*So Red the Rose*
Zweig, Arnold	*The Case of Sergeant Grischa*

JAICO BOOKS
bring to you
world famous classics
—the great works of literature
which you have always wanted
to read—and own.
Of handy size
and handsomely printed, set in
an especially easy-to-read type,
JAICO BOOKS provide
the best in reading values,
at a price within
the reach of all.